Merrill Lynch:
The Cost Could Be Fatal

Merrill Lynch: The Cost Could Be Fatal

My War Against Wall Street's Giant

Keith Schooley

Lakepointe Publishing
ENID, OKLAHOMA

First printing 2002

ISBN 0-9716103-6-3
LCCN 2001099068

ATTENTION CORPORATIONS, UNIVERSITIES, COLLEGES, AND PROFES-SIONAL ORGANIZATIONS: Quantity discounts are available on bulk purchases of this book for educational, gift purposes, or as premiums for increasing magazine subscriptions or renewals. Special books or book excerpts can also be created to fit specific needs. For information, please contact Lakepointe Publishing, P.O. Box 528, Enid, OK 73702; (580) 242-1262; www.LakepointePublishing.com.

*This book is dedicated to my children,
Tyler and Tara, who were safely held in
the hand of God on June 18, 2001,
and to my mother who went home
to the Lord on December 24, 2001.*

*...For the Lord has both purposed
and performed
What He spoke concerning
the inhabitants of Babylon.
O you who dwell by many waters,
Abundant in treasures,
Your end has come...*
(Jeremiah 51:12–13)

A NOTE TO READERS

This book is based on my own experiences. They are supported by the accounts and reports of others as the matter unfolded. In my effort to present a readable narrative, I took minor liberties with grammatical errors, digressions, punctuation, and the like with some of the material quoted. In particular, I quoted only limited, but significant, revealing, and representative portions of several lengthy phone conversations and the extensive transcript of the four-day legal proceeding.

—Keith Schooley

CONTENTS

FOREWORD

Keith Schooley is both a friend and a client. For a period of time, as he outlines in this book, I served as his lawyer in advising him with respect to his conflict with Merrill Lynch. Ultimately, for the reasons that Keith outlines, I could no longer represent him because I was not comfortable in the arbitration setting where his case would be tried. I believed then and now, that in a court of law in front of a jury, Keith would have prevailed.

It was a surprise to me, as I suspect it will be to many people, to know that conflicts with your brokerage house have to be resolved, except in very few instances, through arbitration. While many arbitrators are fair, impartial, and objective, they are not a jury. They are not a representative cross sample of the community from which a jury is selected and their experience and knowledge are often that of a "professional" trier of fact, often with intimate knowledge or personal experiences in the very industry whose activities are under review. Indeed, arbitration often is the exact opposite of the impartial jury drawn from the community at large where most members, if indeed not all of them, have no personal knowledge or experience with the parties, the issue, or the industry. I have frequently stated that the best argument for the jury system in this country is the alternative, and the alternatives are usually a trial to the judge or a trial to arbitrators.

Keith's experiences set forth dramatically everything that is wrong, unwise, and indeed unhealthy and unfair, about the arbitration proceedings.

There is another aspect here, and that is the story of David versus Goliath. The events complained of took place largely in a small town, Enid, Oklahoma. They involved a local businessman, young and ambitious, a hard worker, a family man, and one active in his community. His opponent was one of the very largest, wealthiest, most successful and prominent brokerage houses in the country. Merrill Lynch is "every man's broker." Its reputation has for the most part been favorable, and it is the broker of Main Street, not Wall Street.

Keith's story, however, sheds an entirely different light on what occurred and may offer an entirely different explanation for Merrill Lynch's success.

Keith's story is unusual for yet a third reason. He lost. He admits it. The arbitrators turned him down, his efforts to obtain a jury trial were unsuccessful, and the United States Court of Appeals turned him down on his demand for a jury trial. Keith was not able to persuade any judge or any arbitrator of the correctness of his position. So, like others who have been in that position whose names are far better known—Alfred Dreyfus, Alger Hiss, and indeed Richard Nixon—he has taken his case into the court of public opinion where every reader is a juror. Keith has been fair in presenting the other side's viewpoint. So, in the final analysis, the reader of his book is one of the jurors he never had, and I leave it to you after careful review to determine whether Keith got a fair shake.

But the story is greater than Keith's. The real issue here is whether the American stock-buying public is prepared to continue to tolerate indefinitely having claims adjudged by arbitrators rather than jurors. You wouldn't want your lawsuit against your doctor to be heard by a panel of arbitrators, which might consist of fellow doc-

tors, pharmaceutical salesmen, pharmaceutical company employees, nurses, and people associated with a hospital. You wouldn't
want a lawsuit against a lawyer for malpractice to be heard only by
people who were professional judges or who might have an association with the legal profession. Yet, that is basically what happened
to Keith. No matter how fair and impartial the arbitrators may
have thought they were, the process was unfair and it is the process
that more often than not determines the results.

—Stephen Jones
Enid, Oklahoma

All That Glitters

Don't worry about product knowledge.
Just sell.

—QE

"If a problem comes to our attention, we must act on it—no matter who the individual is that is involved. A problem handled at an early stage may be a little difficult to swallow but—cover up a problem—well, when it surfaces it becomes indigestible. Perhaps we cannot calculate a 'return on integrity'—but let integrity slip and take second place to revenue—then it will cost us more than dollars. *The cost could be fatal.*"

This statement was made by Merrill Lynch's distinguished general counsel and vice chairman of the board of directors, Stephen Hammerman (renowned for having created the finest legal and compliance departments on Wall Street) in the May/June 1992 issue of Merrill Lynch's *We The People*. Right about the time this statement was published, a rookie financial consultant employed by Merrill Lynch was preparing to act on what he had discovered firsthand. That discovery was that at least some of the highest level of senior management of the largest securities firm on Wall Street had little regard for the very principles on which Charlie Merrill founded the firm. Despite outwardly claiming to still uphold these principles, that rookie financial consultant came to believe Merrill Lynch's de facto corporate philosophy had evolved into "might makes right," "win at all costs," and "let's just cover up."

Merrill Lynch had a potentially huge problem on its hands. But Merrill Lynch also had no peer on Wall Street when it came to managing potential problems. After all, the firm had the best legal minds money could buy. Merrill Lynch made one miscalculation, though—it had never been up against someone like that rookie financial consultant.

Those members of Merrill Lynch's senior management are lucky Charlie Merrill is not alive today because if he were, they would be out on the street—any one but Wall Street. If somehow Charlie Merrill were to know what this rookie financial consultant knew, I believe he would be turning madly in his grave. I am that rookie financial consultant. My name is Keith Schooley.

In the Beginning

After four months of intensive training and studying, I was at last a licensed stockbroker. I had scored very high on the licensing exam and was eager to proceed full steam ahead in my exciting new career with Merrill Lynch.

I was not overly anxious but certainly had the usual first-day-on-the-job jitters. I had done well in the training period but I knew there was still a lot to learn. I was a little apprehensive about approaching prospective clients, afraid I would not be able to answer their questions. Yet despite my concerns, I thought if so many others had done it before me, I could too.

In fact, I knew some seasoned brokers in town. They had been in the business for a while and I knew they were making $250,000 a year or more. I did not see anything they had that I didn't, so I saw no reason to doubt I could achieve that level of success.

This was especially important to me, not for the material benefits themselves, but because my past career in the oil and gas business had caused great ups and downs in my family's financial situation. Things had actually been quite rough for a few years by then and we were long past due some peace of mind. Our financial circumstances were causing tension in my marriage and I wanted to do everything in my power to better the situation.

I was confident the opportunity with Merrill Lynch would be an excellent solution to our problems. I had its easily recognizable, well-respected name to take with me out into Enid, Oklahoma, a community very welcoming to both my family and me. My wife grew up in a town just 15 miles away and her father was the state senator for the area. Her mother was also active in the community. I knew I would be able to make many valuable contacts through their network of friends and colleagues.

I had always been fascinated by Wall Street and stockbrokers. I saw them as charismatic figures in an exciting world. I was also drawn to the independent aspect of the job. Even though I would be working within Merrill Lynch, there was still an entrepreneurial aspect. My income would be directly related to my efforts; therefore, I had a great deal of control over what I would earn.

This excited me as I had always had a strong work ethic. As a youngster I was very involved in sports, which I believe helped me become both an ambitious and competitive person. I tapped into these strengths when I needed to motivate myself to achieve a goal.

I learned by my parent's example how to be a decent and moral person. We attended church regularly and were always reminded to treat others as you would want them to treat you.

My value system was, in fact, one of the reasons I was so delighted to be working at Merrill Lynch. When I joined the firm, I had the impression it was managed with impeccable integrity and the highest regard for ethics. That was definitely the kind of company I could fit into.

The declarations of Merrill Lynch's honor were evident in all its corporate publicity. For example, in 1992, the year most of my employment took place, Merrill Lynch's annual report spoke about the firm's values. The glossy document stated, "Merrill Lynch's corporate culture embraces a number of basic principles—client focus, respect for the individual, teamwork, responsible citizenship and integrity. Employees frequently are reminded no one's personal bottom line is more important than the reputation of the firm. The corporation's policy for ethical business practices, *Guidelines for Business Conduct*, is part of every employee's orientation and is reissued periodically. All employees are expected to comply with these policies and as part of a management assessment process, managers are evaluated on how well they embody the corporation's values."

The annual report also said, "Because of Charlie Merrill's insistence on integrity and on placing clients' interests first, he became known as the man who brought Wall Street to Main Street." Charlie Merrill, the patriarch and founder of Merrill Lynch, provided the moral compass which was to guide the behavior of all the firm's employees.

I too believed in those basic principles and was reassured I had found an employer that shared them. Yet it was also pleasing this was no mom-and-pop operation. This was Merrill Lynch, the financial powerhouse.

In 1992, Merrill Lynch reported it had experienced a second straight year of record profits. The net earnings to common shareholders and shareholders' equity were the highest ever achieved by a U.S. public securities firm. Before income taxes and accounting changes, Merrill Lynch earned more than $1.6 billion. Assets entrusted to it by clients increased nearly 10 percent to $476 billion worldwide—far more than any competitor's. As of the 2000 annual report, released in April 2001, shareholders' equity was $18.3 billion, pre-tax income was $5.5 billion, and client assets were $1.7 trillion.

Edwin J. Perkins' 1999 book *Wall Street to Main Street* stated, "Merrill Lynch has emerged as the single most recognizable name in the financial services sector; and it may be the most recognizable name around the globe. Today, Merrill Lynch has offices in forty-five countries, including representatives on every continent except Antarctica. Merrill Lynch has more than eight million retail customers."

I was definitely on the championship team but I was still a rookie fresh off the bench. As a financial consultant, it was my responsibility to help my clients achieve their financial goals. Whether they wanted to save for retirement, their children's education, or generate investment income, I would show them how to achieve their objective. In addition, I would do this within the ethical guidelines instilled in me not only naturally, but also through the policies of the firm.

I had a lot to learn and to achieve, and I was ready to get started. However, like a baby just learning to walk, it was not long after I took my first steps I started to stumble. It turned out it was not my job duties that were tripping me up, but the environment in which I was trying to do them that caused me trouble.

Even before I had reached my one-year anniversary of employment with Merrill Lynch, it had become apparent to me its claims that it upheld the highest ethical standards were empty declarations and complete falsehoods. In a short amount of time I had witnessed numerous incidents of wrongdoing management both participated in and sponsored, and had become painfully aware of the culture and mindset that permeated my work environment.

A particular example stands out in my memory. On one occasion I approached my manager, Brent Barton, regarding how he had been representing certain securities to his clients. Soon thereafter his boss, Quinton Ellis, Jr., confronted me. He pulled a chair up to my desk, put his face within inches of mine, and reprimanded me, saying, "Don't worry about product knowledge. Just sell."

I was shocked, then crushed. This was not an attitude I thought would exist in a financial services firm that boasted to uphold impeccable ethical standards. I was confused and disappointed that someone who felt this way could not only be working at Merrill Lynch, but hold a management position to boot.

I wanted to think everyone in the firm was there because they wanted to make their living with a well-established, respectable company that reflected the values they held for themselves. However, I was not completely naïve. I knew in such a large organization there were bound to be some bad apples and people would cut corners here and there. Yet Ellis' statement still threw me for a loop, especially since I wondered if perhaps one of those bad apples was my direct superior.

I had bought the image Merrill Lynch had sold me and millions of others. I fell for it hook, line, and sinker. I have a story you need to hear. If right now you buy into Merrill Lynch's public campaign about the importance it puts on integrity and that the client comes first, well, you are sorely mistaken. I know this from my own experience. However, do not just take my word for it. The record can speak for itself. This is the record I put before you here. You be the judge.

CHAPTER 1

Keith Schooley

I never had trouble knowing the
difference between right and wrong.

—KS

I was born and reared in Oklahoma City and had a typical, middle-class upbringing, not unlike most people living in the heartland of the United States. I was taught to believe in the values of common decency, patriotism, and a God who would someday judge everyone.

My father has a law degree, although he has never practiced. He taught school for a while, was in the oil business for a short period, and spent most of his working career as a systems analyst for the Federal Aviation Administration. He has served as a councilman for The Village, a suburb of Oklahoma City, for 40 years, including several terms as mayor. Dad is conservative, frugal, well-read, and disciplined. If he told you he was going to do something, it was done.

My late mother, who met Dad while in college at Southwest Missouri State, was a mother, homemaker, and volunteer. She, as well as Dad, grew up on a dairy farm near Springfield, Missouri. Mom had a heart of gold. I have yet to meet anyone as loving and compassionate as she. Mom, over the years, had empathy for the plight of African Americans as they struggled to achieve a level playing field with white Americans. Consequently, she served as an associate member of a Christian Methodist Episcopal church in Oklahoma City for 30 years while also participating as a full-time member of the church our family regularly attended.

Mom and Dad both emphasized the importance of moral virtue. I never had trouble knowing the difference between right and wrong.

I am the second oldest of four children. My older sister is Anne. Brent and Jill are my younger siblings. We were a normal, happy family that lived a comfortable and modest lifestyle. We participated in Cub Scouts, Brownies, church choir, Little League baseball, basketball, and football. We had picnics, took trips to the lake and fun family vacations every summer. We visited relatives in Missouri once or twice a year, always at Christmas, and usually once in the summer. All four of us graduated from college, with three of us earning masters degrees.

I have always been a motivated and competitive person. If something was important to me and I really wanted it, I would spare no effort in trying to reach my goal.

Growing up, I loved sports. I could never get enough of watching or participating in baseball, football, and basketball. I spent hours in the front yard working on my football skills in passing, kicking, and punting. Hour after hour, day after day I would pass, kick, punt, chase after the crazy-bouncing football, and do it again. When I was 10 years old, my practicing paid off when I won the state championship in the Ford–sponsored Punt, Pass and Kick competition for my age group. I learned early on that hard work could provide results.

In the sixth grade my parents made me start taking violin lessons. I protested; I was an athlete. They overruled my objection. While I am glad to say I have no emotional scars, I can still remember the embarrassment of having to carry my violin case to school through the ninth grade. I do suppose this situation built character in me since I had to do something I did not care for, including lots of uninspired practicing over a four-year period. Thank goodness my violin-playing days were over by the time I started high school.

I got my first job in junior high school as a door-to-door salesman. I sold greeting cards and flower seeds. While a young teenager at Eisenhower Junior High School, I delivered morning papers for *The Oklahoma Journal.* This required I get up every morning at 4:00. At one point, the newspaper sponsored a contest for all its paperboys where the top 20 in new subscriptions would win a three-day trip to Chicago. The trip sounded really exciting to me. I told my dad I was going to be one of the 20 winners. He told me not to get my hopes up too high since *The Oklahoma Journal* had a lot of paperboys and I was one of the youngest. I made the trip to Chicago.

My parents emphasized a strong work ethic since they had lived through the Great Depression era as children. In addition to my paper route, I had a part-time job in high school working at Humpty Dumpty, one of the local supermarkets. In the summers I also did a lot of yard work, in our own yard for free, of course, and in our neighbors' yards for profit.

Both my parents, but especially my dad in view of his many years in local politics, always encouraged my siblings and me to participate in high school activities. I was not very active in extracurricular activities since my interest continued to be in sports. However, I did serve a term as president of Key Club, a civic organization, and as president of the local chapter of the Fellowship of Christian Athletes.

Throughout junior high school and high school, I was always practicing my sports—baseball in the spring and summer, basketball in the fall and winter, and track, once I started competing in it, year-round. As it turned out, my main sport became track.

I got involved in running my sophomore year in high school. I decided to participate in cross-country for conditioning purposes. Cross-country is the sport of distance running. The daily team workout would usually exceed 5 miles. I soon realized how tough cross-country really was. It is truly a sport where you must push yourself to the limit to achieve the best performance possible. There are no time-outs or substitutions in cross-country.

By the end of my first season I had become John Marshall's best distance runner. I was surprised because distance running had never been a sport I had been interested in or involved in before.

While cross-country took place in the fall, track was in the spring. In track I also competed in distance running and my success continued. In my senior year, 1971, I won second place in the 2-mile at the state track championship. That same year I was also honored when I was selected by the coaches at my high school as Outstanding Senior Athlete. The honor was especially significant considering John Marshall was one of the state's largest high schools and it had its most talented senior class of athletes ever in 1971, with at least 10 receiving athletic scholarships—including four to the University of Oklahoma, two to Tulsa University, and one to Oklahoma State University.

Although I felt others may have deserved the award more than I did, I believed I received it not only because of my accomplishments on the track but also because the coaches knew no one trained harder than I did. I was known to do three workouts a day. I was a competitor and wanted to win. The discipline, dedication, endurance, and mental toughness I developed in high school would, 20 years later, be valuable qualities when I took on Merrill Lynch.

After graduating from high school, I hoped to receive a track scholarship from the University of Oklahoma (OU). However, the available spots for distance runners were awarded to two prep All-Americans. So I decided to accept a scholarship from Central State University. But when the spring semester rolled around, I decided I needed a break from track and soon from college as well.

My parents were concerned I would not go back to school, but I knew I would. I worked full-time at Humpty Dumpty in Oklahoma City, earning enough money to support myself. Also during that time, my weight ballooned and I gained more than 30 pounds. I kept thinking about not getting to run track at OU. The more I thought about it, the more convinced I became I could successfully compete at that level. A fire started burning in my overweight belly and by the summer of 1973 I decided I would walk onto the OU track team and see what I could do.

After having to sit out from competition for a year due to my ineligibility resulting from the transfer, I soon earned my track scholarship and eventually ran a 9:06 in the indoor 2-mile. This was one second faster than what had been the school record at OU when I graduated from high school. Once again I had learned believing in myself and working hard pays off in the end.

I graduated from OU in the spring of 1977, earning a B.B.A. in Petroleum Land Management. During my last year at OU, I actually started making a lot of A's as it finally dawned on me my sports career would soon be ending and I had better start getting serious about my future. In fact, I became serious enough to enroll in and finish Oklahoma State University's M.B.A. program, one of the best in the southwest United States.

Growing up I truly believed if you worked hard, did the right things, were a good, decent, and honorable person, everything would work out just fine. At that point in time, though, I had not yet had a taste of the real world. My eyes would eventually be opened.

I decided to put my Petroleum Land Management degree to work and began my professional career in the oil and gas business just as the oil boom was beginning in 1979. I found myself in what appeared to be the right place at the right time. Within about a year I had interests in 125 oil and gas wells, which gave me, at the age of 27, a net worth of $1.3 million. I was feeling pretty good, driving a new Cadillac and wearing a $10,000 gold Rolex.

In 1981, I married Donna, who was from a prominent family in north central Oklahoma. We met on a blind date set up by my sister Jill, who had been a sorority sister of Donna's at Oklahoma State. We had a wonderful 10-day honeymoon in Europe. Everything was first class all the way including flying on the Concorde both ways and staying at the Ritz in Paris. Upon our return, we settled into our Oklahoma City home, which backed onto the 17th tee box of The Greens Country Club. Within a few years we would be blessed with two delightful children, Tyler in 1984 and Tara in 1988.

Everything could not have been going any better but soon I would learn how quickly things could change. My prosperous life as an oilman would end almost as quickly as it had begun.

As oil prices escalated to stratospheric levels, with an ultimate high of $42 per barrel, I leveraged what I thought to be a relatively conservative percentage of my net worth with several energy-lending banks. Little did I realize the oil boom was on the verge of collapsing in 1982.

Difficult times in the oil and gas business followed, putting our family through financial strain and creating tension in my marriage. However, in 1984 I landed a position managing and eventually serving as vice chairman of a small oil and gas exploration and production company. This appeared to be a promising opportunity for me until the oil industry became even more distressed in 1986. The continuing decrease in oil prices eventually led to the curtailment of any significant exploration and development by my employer. This soon resulted in my departure.

After fighting personal financial difficulties for several years as a result of the oil bust, I filed for Chapter 7 bankruptcy in 1985, a truly disappointing moment in my life. But there is always some positive that can be gleaned from a difficult circumstance, and I soon realized life goes on and bad memories fade in time. I also realized the truth in the saying "That which does not kill me makes me stronger."

During the next several years I put together and promoted a number of wildcat oil and gas prospects in Oklahoma and Kansas, which achieved only marginal success. The luck factor, an important one in the oil industry, was not in my favor. Consequently, I decided in 1990, at the age of 37, to consider other professional opportunities outside the oil industry so I could better support my wife and our two young children, then ages five and two.

I learned through my mother-in-law that Merrill Lynch was opening an office in Enid, Oklahoma, which is 80 miles northwest of Oklahoma City and just 15 miles from my wife's hometown. The idea of moving closer to home was appealing to Donna, and I thought being a stockbroker for Merrill Lynch might be the right opportunity for me. I had an M.B.A. and in addition to that, I also had a long-time interest in Wall Street. I read *The Wall Street Journal* and was captivated by the finance culture. I thought a career as a stockbroker had an exciting, glamorous quality.

Enid, a town of about 45,000, was the largest town in northwest Oklahoma. It served as the area's center for retail trade, agriculture, energy, health care, and cultural activities. Enid was also home to Vance Air Force Base and a small, private university.

Being a stockbroker in Enid was also a unique opportunity since the town was known to have a lot of wealth. Even more importantly, I knew a lot of doors could be opened for me through my in-laws. Donna's father was the state senator from the Enid area, a successful businessman, and former regent of higher education. Her mother was a successful fundraiser for the local university. After a disappointing ending to what was earlier a successful career in the oil industry, I thought the opportunity with Merrill Lynch in Enid might be just the right move to turn the corner.

On July 1, 1991, I became a financial consultant trainee with Merrill Lynch in its Enid, Oklahoma, office. Little did I realize this career change would lead to adverse consequences not only in my professional life, but in my personal life as well. It would soon prove to be the beginning of what has turned out to be a more than nine-year war against the firm with the most sterling reputation on Wall Street.

CHAPTER 2

The Fast Track.
The Downward Spiral.

I was beginning to see trouble at the
Oklahoma City Complex that was my
work environment, and soon it became
treacherous.

—KS

In 1991, the Merrill Lynch Enid office was small. It was about a thousand square feet and had five employees. It was known as a "special market office," since it was located outside of a large metropolitan area where most Merrill Lynch offices were located. The expansion of special market offices was an important part of Merrill Lynch's growth strategy.

The resident manager was Brent Barton, who grew up in Enid but was now commuting each day from Oklahoma City. His father was president of a successful national trucking concern headquartered in Enid. Barton walked with a swagger and had a strong personality. He could be loose with his lips and would sometimes shoot from the hip. The Enid office was Barton's first management position with Merrill Lynch after having been a financial consultant (FC) in the Oklahoma City office for four years. I would constantly hear Barton on the phone letting whomever he was speaking to know he was Brent Barton, *resident manager* of the Enid office.

It was during an interview with Barton, prior to my employment, I first encountered Barton's superior, Quinton Ellis, Jr., the senior resident vice president of the Oklahoma City Complex of which Enid would soon become an associate office. He came to speak to Barton for only a minute or two but it was enough time for him to leave a distinctive first impression on me.

Ellis was a good-sized man, about 6 feet 2 inches tall and 220 pounds. He was fit, walked confidently, and had a commanding physical presence. Although his complexion was quite rough and pockmarked, he was meticulous about his appearance. He dressed for success in expensive suits and silk ties. He wore his hair slicked back. Later, one of the other FCs would tell me he had once seen Ellis returning from the restroom carrying a brush, hairspray, and toothbrush.

It seemed to me appearing powerful and successful was important to Ellis. In that first brief meeting, he hardly acknowledged me. It did not seem to matter to him I had been a successful businessman in the past. To Ellis I was just some unknown, potential rookie FC. Never mind I might soon be joining one of the offices under his management and therefore contributing to his bonuses. I sensed Ellis had no time for the little people.

During my first month of employment with Merrill Lynch, Barton would tell me Ellis was very materialistic and not popular in the Oklahoma City office. I was surprised at my own resident manager's candor about his superior. Barton also told me Ellis was nationally known within Merrill Lynch for his antics in starting big contests as he did in previous years when he motivated his FCs by appearing at kick-off sales meetings in a costume. I believe Barton even said one year Ellis wore a peacock outfit.

In addition to myself, the Enid office had two other FCs—Barry Clark and Joe Bazzelle. Barton and Ellis had recruited them both from Prudential Securities in Wichita. Clark and Bazzelle were true gentlemen with whom I enjoyed working very much. Their values were the same as mine. They were thoughtful and considerate and had their clients' best interests at heart. The administrative assistant of the Enid office was Kim Feightner, who had previously worked for several other securities firms in Oklahoma.

Merrill Lynch offered a standard salary of $2,000 a month for the first four months, which was a training period. I was concerned as this was not nearly enough to support my wife and two children. I negotiated with Ellis, citing not only my family's needs but also the excellent position I was in to succeed in light of my in-laws' contacts. Ellis agreed my situation had great potential and so raised my compensation to $3,500 a month.

I immediately showed my desire not just to succeed as a stockbroker but to excel. As a member of Class 377 of the Professional Development Program (PDP), the four-month training program, I ranked in the top three overall in my class of 32 FC trainees. Part of PDP Class 377 included preparing for and passing the notoriously difficult Series 7 examination, which is required to become a registered representative in the securities industry.

I scored 93.2 percent on the Series 7 exam. Barton told me Ellis had said that was the highest score he had ever heard of in his 20 years with Merrill Lynch. I was proud my hard work had paid off but that feeling did not last long. In the same breath he told me mine was the highest score Ellis had ever heard of, Barton quickly pointed out there was usually an inverse correlation between high exam scores and success as a stockbroker. Barton felt anyone academically oriented, or basically anyone who could study and do well on an exam, would never make it in a sales environment. I thought it was both strange and disappointing this was how my superior reacted to one of his employees doing well in something. I would think he would want to use my success as a vehicle to motivate me, not discourage me.

Upon graduation from PDP Class 377 on October 29, 1991, I received my production number from Merrill Lynch, making me a full-fledged stockbroker with the credentials to prospect for and service my own clients. I aggressively went about developing relationships with business owners, lawyers, accountants, doctors, and other professionals in my new hometown of Enid. I was building a base of contacts for what I was hoping would prove to be a successful career. My approach was not really sales oriented right away. I thought it would be more beneficial to set up a solid network at the beginning so it could pay off down the road and well into the future. I became active in the community by joining the locally prominent Rotary Club, serving as a director of a local charitable agency, and making numerous public speaking appearances on securities investing.

I was soon in the top 10 in sales production out of about 400 rookie FC peers in the Western Sales Division of Merrill Lynch. It seemed the financial stability my family and I needed so badly was finally within reach. I was on the fast track. My new career with the most highly respected securities firm on Wall Street was looking extraordinarily promising—except for one problem. For every positive development I made in my own independent efforts, something seemed to happen on the corporate side to counteract my enthusiasm. I was beginning to see trouble at the Oklahoma City Complex that was my work environment, and soon it became treacherous.

When I joined Merrill Lynch in July 1991, I had the impression the firm was managed with impeccable integrity and the highest regard for ethics. As a condition of employment I was required to sign a document that stated I had read the firm's *Guidelines for Business Conduct* and accepted the obligation to follow the guidelines set forth, including: "Merrill Lynch asks and requires that every employee make a personal commitment to the observations of the highest ethical standards and exercise of proper judgment in all aspects of his or her business dealings."

It was this reputation for integrity Merrill Lynch had so masterfully burnished that was a major factor in my decision to become a stockbroker with the firm.

One of the first incidents that made me pause concerned one of my fellow FCs, Bazzelle. Right around the time I received my license, Bazzelle had been orally advising some of his former Prudential Securities clients in regard to a real estate partnership, VMS Mortgage Investors Fund. This partnership had guaranteed its investors high income for three years, then a return of the original investment. Instead, it simply collapsed, losing most of the investors' principal. Bazzelle was now suggesting these clients contact an attorney who could possibly enhance the value of their investment in the VMS debacle. He also contacted these clients in writing. The letters, which were not on Merrill Lynch letterhead, were sent in several boxes to the Enid office by the attorney involved. These boxes lay conspicuously for one to two days beside the administrative assistant's desk, which was just outside Barton's office. Bazzelle spent most of an afternoon and the next morning in his office signing and stuffing about 100 letters. It was clear to me Barton knew, at a minimum, Bazzelle was orally directing his clients to consult an attorney. Also, I had little doubt Barton could see Bazzelle was contacting his clients in writing too.

When Prudential Securities learned what its former FC was doing, it complained to Merrill Lynch. Merrill Lynch promptly asserted Bazzelle violated firm policy in some way, perhaps by making his suggestions to these clients in writing without management approval. Even though the letters were not on Merrill Lynch letterhead, as a result of this situation, Bazzelle was fired.

I was confused by management's position on Bazzelle's situation but put it aside for the moment. I had a new career that was going well, and I wanted to put my energy there. However, November 1991 and the following few months would prove to be such an eye-opening time in which so many disturbing incidents would occur, it would become difficult not to doubt the ethics around me.

On November 15, 1991, I had a phone conversation with Sarah Graham, an insurance administrator with Merrill Lynch Life Agency in Dallas, Texas. I had been told to contact her for instructions on how to take a correspondence examination to meet the requirements of Oklahoma's continuing education law to maintain a life insurance license. She revealed to me what would later become the most serious incident of wrongdoing I would encounter at Merrill Lynch.

During the conversation Graham said, "Well, let me send you a cheat sheet so you can pass that. What we have been doing is using cheat sheets so the FCs can get the test behind them and study the materials at their convenience." The manner in which Graham said this indicated to me this was an ongoing common practice. She was so casual in how she said it—like it was no big deal. I was caught so off guard by Graham's comments, I had no response. All I knew was a cheat sheet was on its way.

I received what she called a cheat sheet around November 19. The use of a cheat sheet with the exam would have been in direct violation with the affidavit everyone who takes the exam must sign. The affidavit stated the exam was taken without any outside help.

In the same month, I again saw problems beyond the Oklahoma City district. One day Bob Sherman was in town. Sherman was Ellis' superior and the district director of Merrill Lynch's Texoma District, a superdistrict that included most of Texas and all of Oklahoma. Sherman and Ellis were in Enid for the annual Grand National Quail Hunt, an event that attracted business leaders and celebrities from across the nation. At one point Sherman, Ellis, and Barton were all in my office. Barton told Ellis and Sherman how he had received a phone call from the manager of the Oakwood Country Club. The manager was upset since he suspected Barton of misusing a proprietary list of the country club members for mass mailing purposes. Barton said he denied to the manager he had improperly used the list. (The list had been previously provided to Barton for a one-time limited use basis.) Barton then proceeded to brag about how, in reality, he had been mass mailing the hell out of the list.

"That's great; keep on doing it," Ellis said. Sherman was silent.

I was in total disbelief. Here was Barton, a resident manager, bragging about his improper action in the presence of a senior resident vice president, Ellis, and a district director, Sherman—a man who was perceived to be in line to become one of the top four senior executives of Merrill Lynch, Pierce, Fenner & Smith (Merrill Lynch's retail division which I was employed by). Equally alarming was Ellis' laudatory comment about such conduct in the presence of a district director. Perhaps the most disturbing was the gross lack of judgment shown by all three men in the presence of a rookie FC who, at the time, was in his first month of production and who had been reading and hearing about the *requirement* all Merrill Lynch employees must adhere to the highest ethical standards. This incident made an indelible impression in my mind and my concern was a harbinger of things to come.

In early November while visiting with Barton, I realized he had been incorrectly representing a bond fund called MuniYield. He was selling it as pre-refunded, yet according to the information I had reviewed this was incorrect. This was important because a security with a pre-refunded status is given the highest quality rating of AAA. However, the MuniYield prospectus represented that the fund could include a significant amount of junk bonds in its portfolio; therefore, the AAA rating would be misleading. I spoke to Barton about the situation, but he disagreed with my assessment of the product.

It was this issue that a couple of weeks later caused Ellis to put his face inches from mine and tell me, "Don't worry about product knowledge. Just sell."

Ellis' admonishment spoke volumes to me, and I did not like what I had heard. It would be one thing to hint at such an attitude but to come right out and say it—I was shocked. I could not understand how someone with that mindset could take pride in how he does business and makes recommendations to his clients. It seemed to me Ellis' position showed dreadful disregard for the clients. His objective was just to get them to sign on the dotted line. Not needing to know what you were selling implied the customers did not need to know what they were buying. I did not like the way Ellis did business.

In further conversations I had with Barton about MuniYield, he told me if I paid that much attention to details I would never be a success in this business. So it seemed Barton's approach was right in line with Ellis'. Soon after I would receive a wire from Merrill Lynch marketing saying the MuniYield fund should not be sold as a pre-refunded product. I had received confirmation of my initial research on the product, but in the process, I had also seen a picture of Merrill Lynch I did not like.

By the end of November I was disturbed by these events and a number of others I had witnessed in a short time at Merrill Lynch. I decided to consult Stephen Jones, the attorney who would later become known for representing Timothy McVeigh in the Oklahoma City bombing case. I felt this was the right thing to do because I now found myself in an environment where I was beginning to wonder if unethical and possibly illegal business practices were not only condoned, but also encouraged and expected. Furthermore, I did not want to be inadvertently implicated by remaining silent. I compiled a confidential memo to Jones outlining the disturbing incidents I had witnessed at Merrill Lynch. Little did I know how many more incidents there would be to come.

In early December, Feightner told me Barton was having her falsify eight seminar lists of about 20 attendees for each of the seminars that was represented to have been held at the Oakwood Country Club. She said Barton instructed her to obtain names from the phone book randomly for the fictitious seminars. As a result, Merrill Lynch reimbursed Barton for the phantom expenses by making payment directly to his personal account at the country club.

Shortly thereafter, I took the continuing education life insurance exam for which I had received what I thought was a cheat sheet. I did not use it in the exam. Afterward I told Barton, "Brent, the insurance exam was certainly a lot more difficult than I thought it would be. I had to study pretty hard for that."

Barton started to laugh. "Well, what I did with five or six other FCs is we got together on a Saturday morning and we had Bill Hall, who's the resident insurance specialist out of Dallas, walk us through that 25-hour continuing education exam." Barton also said this was all with Ellis' approval.

I sensed by the way Barton described their actions he believed what they did was wrong; however, he minimized it by saying, "Well, we don't really sell life insurance, we simply need our life insurance license to get commissions." I was not surprised. I was getting the impression rules, regulations, and laws were for others to obey. It appeared the only thing that mattered to Ellis, Barton, and others at Merrill Lynch was to "get commissions."

Each year Merrill Lynch ran contests to motivate its employees to achieve certain objectives. In 1992, the first big event was to be the Tour de France Cash Management Account (CMA) contest. The CMA was a fee-based account for clients that would provide the firm with a steady base of revenue regardless of market fluctuations, which affect commission-driven revenue. The goal of senior management was to increase the number of CMA accounts. Consequently, Merrill Lynch placed a tremendous amount of importance on how each resident vice president's (RVP's) Complex did in the contest. This was a big factor in the RVP's annual bonus that could easily be $100,000 to $150,000 per year *more* if the RVP received an evaluation of "far exceed" rather than "met."

Shortly before the Tour de France CMA contest started in January 1992, Ellis held a kick-off sales meeting in the Oklahoma City office. The FCs from the associate offices in Enid and Lawton were required to attend. Ellis would know the largest part of his annual bonus would depend on how his Complex performed in the contest. There was also incentive for Ellis to play every card he had so he could win kudos from his superiors and continue climbing the intensely competitive Merrill Lynch corporate ladder.

The kick-off sales meeting was about to begin. The FCs and others wondered what theatrics Ellis would perform this year. Sixty FCs and another 25 staff personnel from the Complex offices were seated in the large conference room at Merrill Lynch's office on the 18th floor of the prestigious One Leadership Square in downtown Oklahoma City.

Suddenly, there was a loud roar at the back of the room. Coming through the door was none other than Quinton Ellis, Jr., riding his own Harley-Davidson motorcycle. He was wearing a black leather jacket and black gloves, and had his hair greased back. He slowly rode his bike up the center aisle as many of the FCs and staff started to cough because of the exhaust. The sound was deafening. Ellis seemed to burst with pride.

Ellis then gave his Tour de France pep talk, telling his FCs about all the prizes they could win, courtesy of his Oklahoma City Complex. He pointed toward the back of the room where many of the prizes were stacked up 6 feet high and about 10 feet wide along the wall. There were a variety of prizes such as crystal, televisions, stereos, bottles of expensive wine, wine glasses, a home entertainment system, and gift certificates. Ellis also told his FCs the prizes were in addition to other promotions and incentives Merrill Lynch would offer including an international trip to Paris and a domestic trip to Lake Tahoe. Ellis explained the way they could win the prizes in Oklahoma City would be by accumulating "Quint Bucks," which they could use at the auction the Complex would have after the contest ended four months later in April.

A Quint Buck was play money with a picture of Ellis in the center dressed as Elvis. Ellis' FCs would earn Quint Bucks in accordance with the number of fee-based CMA accounts they opened during the contest. Ellis was in a league of his own. Elvis could only have dreamed of being as flamboyant as Quinton Ellis, Jr.

To make sure his FCs performed during the contest, Ellis would have his administrative manager issue "parking violation" tickets to any FC who did not open point-producing CMA accounts for the previous week. She would put on a police helmet and leather jacket and walk around the office issuing tickets to the offending FCs. A senior FC in the Oklahoma City office, robed in black and displaying other accoutrements befitting a judge, would then conduct court each week in a sales meeting of all FCs and staff personnel. Every FC who received a ticket would have to explain to the court and spectators why he or she produced no contest points the previous week. The judge would fine each offender the appropriate amount in Quint Bucks. Ellis was a master in the art of intimidation, dressed up as fun and games.

To further motivate the Enid FCs, Barton told us Ellis promised to allocate $20 million in client assets to the Enid FCs, based on their contest performance. These assets would come from those Oklahoma City FCs who had clients in northwest Oklahoma—clients that could be better served by the Enid office.

Several weeks before the Tour de France CMA contest was to begin, Barton, as instructed by Ellis, announced to the Enid office in the interest of making the office look better, they would be managing the headcount. This meant they would temporarily take away some of the FCs' production numbers, including mine. I would no longer be in Merrill Lynch's system as a producing FC even though I really was one. As a result, all point-producing new accounts were divided between a fewer number of FCs who still had their production numbers. This would improve the average FC output for the office, therefore improving its performance in the contest. In other words, Ellis and Barton did not want to play on a level playing field in their competition with other Merrill Lynch managers. A larger annual bonus and other rewards would be the result of a superior contest performance.

I objected adamantly to this move, and even though I no longer had a production number, I continued to sign my name to all my new account forms, against management's instruction. I was concerned about the restrictions my assisting management in cheating could put on my accessibility to my clients' accounts. As I understood the system, I could not access an account on my computer unless it was in my production number. This also meant I would not be informed by the computer system when my clients' bonds were being called or maturing. I would not be notified when the research department downgraded its ratings on my clients' holdings or changed its recommendation from buy to sell. Despite my objections, management went ahead anyway.

Barton became so caught up in the Tour de France excitement he purchased as many Quint Bucks as he could from the other FCs. When the auction of prizes was held in the Oklahoma City office after the contest ended, Barton would leave the competition in the dust by carting off more prizes than anyone else, by far. Barton seemed proud of himself, perhaps knowing within months Ellis, his mentor, would name him the sales manager of the Oklahoma City Complex.

Ellis was doing pretty well himself. He was on his way toward personally winning the coveted trip to Paris since his Complex was in the top 20 out of 174 Complex offices nationwide. Ellis knew how to motivate his troops and he knew how to win. At least he thought he did.

I knew managing the headcount was cheating, so I decided in March to call the hotline Merrill Lynch had just for the purpose of reporting wrongdoing I had seen. The hotline was advertised as confidential. Anyone who used it was assured his or her identity would be protected. Through the hotline I spoke to Patrick Murphy, director of worldwide security. I spoke mainly of the Tour de France CMA contest. I was to have several more conversations with Murphy through the hotline to help him figure out how the contest cheating worked. It was soon determined by New York cheating had, in fact, occurred. Murphy told me New York would inform Ellis it had discovered the cheating by happenstance.

When Merrill Lynch adjusted Ellis' contest points, he was knocked out of the top 20 RVPs and denied the trip to Paris. Instead, both Ellis and Barton ended up being awarded the trip to Lake Tahoe. Later, and upon further investigation and confirmation of their actions, Ellis and Barton had to pay the cost of their Tahoe trips back to the company.

During the four months the Tour de France CMA contest ran, on top of the headcount cheating, additional troublesome incidents continued to occur.

I learned FCs were allowed to open out-of-state accounts without being registered in that state. The account could simply be opened in the name of an FC who was registered in that state. I soon became concerned this was illegal.

At the end of January I wrote a letter to Barton to request a certain pay arrangement for the future. In it, I explained I was out of production for a number of days for various reasons. One of these reasons I told him was I spent three days studying for the continuing education life insurance exam, despite having been provided a cheat sheet from Merrill Lynch Life in Dallas. The cheat sheet comment elicited no response from Barton or Ellis, who would have had to see the memo to grant the new pay arrangement. While they may have overlooked that part of my letter, I took this to imply they knew about the cheating but were either unconcerned, chose to ignore it, or hoped by not addressing the issue, it would not become a problem.

Also at the end of January, Barton left the Enid office for a near-term promotion as sales manager in the Oklahoma City Complex. He was replaced by Jack Thomas. Thomas was a likeable guy. He was well-mannered and thoughtful. I hoped with the departure of Barton, my concerns about the Enid office would come to an end. My hope was in vain.

Only days after Thomas' arrival, the computer system made an inadvertent miscalculation on one of my client's commission. As a result, the client was overcharged $15. When I learned of the mistake I issued the client a personal check for $15 since he was upset and wanted immediate satisfaction.

When Thomas found out about the refund, he reprimanded me harshly and made me sign an acknowledgment that stated rebating commissions is forbidden by regulatory agencies and if I were to make another "rebate" I would be immediately terminated. I did not feel I had done anything wrong, but even if I had, this was a minor infraction at best. In light of all the improper actions by management I had witnessed in the last few months, none of which had resulted in anyone being terminated or as far as I knew even threatened with termination, I was perplexed this situation harbored such an extreme response. I suspected Thomas' reaction was perhaps fueled by Ellis' anger at me for not cooperating in the Tour de France scheme.

It did not take long for me to learn the confidentiality of the hotline was a farce. On April 9, Thomas walked down the hall and into Michael Deline's office. Deline, recently recruited to the Enid office, was another rookie FC whose office was right next to mine. I heard Thomas say, "Michael, have you called anyone back east or called Princeton or called somebody complaining of being a mistreated PDP?" (PDP not only referred to the Merrill Lynch training program but also was often used to refer to anyone in the program.)

Deline said he had not called anyone so Thomas proceeded into my office and asked me the same thing. I denied it. I was not about to tell him the truth. At this point, I was stunned.

I quickly called Murphy and had two hotline calls with him that same day discussing what happened. Murphy told me he had shared the whole story with Bob Dineen, the national sales manager of the Western Sales Division. Murphy also told me Dineen had shared part of the story with Sherman who spoke to Ellis about it, who then spoke to Thomas. I believed Ellis knew who cost him the trip to Paris and the embarrassment that went with it. As time went on, I saw he was not about to forget it.

At least some of my superiors probably knew I was upset about much more than just the contest cheating. If I had confronted someone regarding the contest, perhaps they were worried I would start bringing up the other issues as well. Perhaps New York was also concerned about the rookie FC in Enid, Oklahoma.

This is what I thought when in mid-June I came across a wire sent to the Enid office. It was from Merrill Lynch's registration department and was directed to Ellis. It requested names of personal references to verify my period of self-employment for July 1987 through June 1991. It said, "Please respond via wire ASAP."

This wire led me to believe perhaps Merrill Lynch was trying to find some flaw or misrepresentation in my employment application that it could use to terminate me. I could not think of why else an employer would check references almost a year after hiring someone.

The incident that was the last straw for me occurred a few days after I learned Ellis had been asked to investigate my background. Thomas walked into my office and in a belligerent manner confronted me about how I had opened a new account.

I explained to him I had recently sent out an Oklahoma Turnpike bond mailer to a number of people. This included this new client's husband. She saw the mailer then proceeded to call me. She said she wanted to invest in the bonds. She also had a Merrill Lynch account in Oklahoma City that she wanted transferred to Enid.

The client came in and we completed the transaction. I had her sign a letter of authorization to transfer the Oklahoma City account to me at the Enid office, and it was done.

"Well, that's not what I heard," Thomas said.

"Well, what did you hear?" I asked him.

"You know, evidently there's some duplicity involved in how you got the account," Thomas said. He then told me he had talked to the two brokers in Oklahoma City who lost the account. They claimed they had a note on their holding book saying they had been had on it.

"That's not true," I said. "It happened just exactly as I told you."

"Well, I'm going to have to call the client," he said.

I was hot. I could not believe he was taking the high and mighty route with me. However, I remained cool on the outside. I did not want Thomas to know just how much he had gotten to me. So I said, "That's fine. We'll just call her right now."

I whipped around in my chair to my phone directory and opened it to the client's phone number. As I started dialing, Thomas began walking around the desk.

"I'm not trying to..." he stuttered, attempting to back up. "I'm not trying to call you a liar or anything like that."

"That's fine," I said. "Just go ahead and call her anyway."

So Thomas spoke to her and determined things happened exactly as I had said.

I was beginning to feel there was not a whole lot I could do without being confronted by management. I was so offended by this last confrontation. In and of itself it was not a huge deal; however, on top of everything else, it just pushed things over the edge.

I felt like I was at the point where I needed to do something that resulted in some explanations. I had seen too many things that made me uncomfortable.

I understood people cut corners and do things they should not, but I became truly bothered when I felt there was a double standard. I was hearing things from management like my $15 "rebate" was really serious and if it ever happened again I would be immediately terminated. Bazzelle was fired for trying to help clients in the VMS debacle. Clark told me he was promised assets by Ellis as an inducement to move from Prudential Securities to Merrill Lynch as an FC and that promise was not fulfilled.

During that first year of employment with Merrill Lynch, I would often tell my wife I could not believe what I had seen or learned that day. I was amazed, shocked, and disgusted to find myself in an environment that was absolutely in opposition to my own standard of ethics as well as the published standard of ethics Merrill Lynch espoused and *required*. Furthermore, I found the way Ellis was willing to exploit his subordinates to be lacking in decency. I was growing increasingly disturbed and restless.

However, we had moved to Enid in hopes of regaining financial stability with the Merrill Lynch opportunity. My wife would always urge me not to rock the boat and encourage me surely the situation would get better. I agreed to be patient and hoped she was right.

Unfortunately, the situation did not get better, but continued. I decided it was time to do what I knew I had to, regardless of the consequences. Knowing what I was planning to do was an aggressive move with unpredictable results, I did so without informing Donna. I wanted to do everything my instincts told me to do without interference, and I did not want her to have to deal with the anxiety that would surely follow.

In light of my sense of the place, you would think I would have been quite skeptical regarding the chance things would be put right within the office. However, I truly believed New York senior management would address and satisfy my concerns about all the incidents I had seen over the past several months. That would be a grave miscalculation.

CHAPTER 3

Schooley
Declares War

I had to act.

—KS

If it had not been for the environment I found myself working in, my career at Merrill Lynch would have been going well. I had scored well on the Series 7 exam, built an impressive network of clients and contacts, and was in the top 10 in sales production among the rookie FCs in the Western Sales Division. In January 1992, I was responsible for bringing 70 of 95 attendees to a professional money manager program hosted by the Enid office at the Oakwood Country Club. That evening, the Oklahoma City office hosted the same program. All of its FCs had attracted only 92 attendees. After the event, Ellis wired the Enid office saying its turnout was the best he had ever heard of for four FCs.

My most important reason for wanting to succeed at Merrill Lynch—long-term financial stability for my family—was within reach.

I had much to lose—a fact that might have caused me to remain silent. I could have ignored the problems, as I largely already had for about eight months. I could have continued to try to stay quiet and just make a living at a company in which I no longer believed. I certainly had much more to gain from going along with the situation.

It just was not in me. I could not let things I had seen just slide under the rug. I had to act.

Merrill Lynch's *Guidelines for Business Conduct* stated, "Protecting the Firm's reputation is a collective effort. Employees should be diligent in questioning situations they believe violate Merrill Lynch's high ethical standards. Improprieties should be reported to whatever level of Management necessary to properly address the situation." In compliance with these guidelines, I created what Merrill Lynch would later represent in a legal pleading as "Schooley Declares War": my June 29, 1992, four-page memorandum to my manager, Thomas, documenting the events I had witnessed.

I thought the management of the Oklahoma City Complex should be removed. I felt the need to appeal to someone, despite the fact my confidence was beginning to waver in the belief New York senior management would do anything. I had my doubts for three reasons.

First, I had earlier called Merrill Lynch's confidential hotline to report Ellis' cheating in the Tour de France CMA contest. That confidentiality had been violated and leaked back to Oklahoma City management.

The second reason I doubted support from senior management was because of the background check I discovered Merrill Lynch had ordered Ellis to conduct. I was concerned Merrill Lynch was looking for an inaccuracy in my application for employment so it could terminate the rookie FC in Enid, Oklahoma, who was causing trouble.

Third, in one of my calls to the confidential hotline, I mentioned to Murphy I was concerned Ellis would suspect me of calling the hotline since I had tended to rock the boat, for example, by previously flagging the use of cheat sheets in the continuing education life insurance examination in a letter to Barton, which Ellis read. Not only did the Oklahoma City Complex management not bother to ask me about the cheat sheet comment but neither did Murphy. Only later would I conclude the reason neither Oklahoma City management nor New York senior management reacted to my comment concerning cheat sheets was because they knew about it already and I suspected, wanted it kept quiet.

I had my reasons for questioning senior management's willingness to act. However, only later would I realize just how well-founded my concerns were. Nevertheless, I decided to submit the memorandum and I advised my colleagues in the Enid office to buckle up.

With my memo, I was far from blowing the whistle in the conventional way. I took the matter *directly* to Thomas, who was himself involved in some of the events. There would be no question my action was a frontal assault.

My memo to Thomas stated that the many incidents I had observed in the Oklahoma City Complex did not conform to the high professional and ethical standards espoused by Merrill Lynch. I outlined 10 incidents and suggested to Thomas perhaps he could explain and justify them.

The concerns I reported were:
- The Tour de France CMA contest cheating by management;
- The apparent use in the Texoma District of what appeared to be cheat sheets or other improper means used in taking the self-administered life insurance examinations;
- The unauthorized use of a proprietary country club membership list by management;
- The falsification of expense reports by management;
- The misrepresentation of MuniYield as pre-refunded by management;
- The improper opening of out-of-state accounts by management;
- The failure of management to deliver a promised $5 to 10 million in "assets under management" to Clark;
- The failure of management to deliver a promised $20 million in "assets under management" to the FCs in the Enid office;
- The unfair termination of Bazzelle; and
- The overreaction to my $15 "rebate," including the threat I would be terminated if it happened again.

I concluded the memorandum, saying, "I find it incredible I found myself in the position where I would feel compelled to write a memorandum like this. I always expected all levels of management within a highly respected firm, which strongly values its reputation such as Merrill Lynch, would serve as exemplary role models in light of their leadership position. I have not found this to be the case with the management of the Oklahoma City Complex."

As great as my disappointment was in management of the Oklahoma City Complex, I was soon to be even more disappointed to find out how New York senior management would respond to the reported wrongdoing.

CHAPTER 4

The First Response

What if the right solutions aren't
arrived at? What does Keith Schooley
do then?

—HM

The bomb that was my memo had started to make waves, and the ripples were spreading throughout Merrill Lynch. By the end of the day on June 29, 1992, my memorandum had been faxed to Ellis in Oklahoma City and to Leo Roepke, the district director of the Arkoma District (which had replaced part of the Texoma District as the result of a recent reorganization). Sherman had been promoted to New York and was now in charge of the Eastern Sales Division. Roepke was Ellis' new superior and was considered by many to be an institution within Merrill Lynch, given his 32 years with the firm. In addition, my memo had also been faxed to the compliance department in Merrill Lynch's New York headquarters where, I would soon learn, senior management was quickly putting things in motion to control the situation.

Among the immediate measures taken by Merrill Lynch was the direct involvement of Helmuth Meditz, manager of internal reviews. Meditz was a more than 20-year veteran of compliance matters in the securities industry and was in charge of internal investigations for the firm. He called me on July 1 and informed me the matter was serious and he would like to meet with me on July 7 in Enid.

I agreed the matter was serious but did not realize how unusual it was for Meditz himself to visit a branch office when doing an investigation. Meditz later testified he interviewed more than a hundred people a year, mostly in New York, and only on occasion would he go out to a branch. Furthermore, he also later testified he was surprised and disturbed by my memorandum, enough to be in Enid within days of receiving it in order to make every effort to immediately jump on the situation and try to resolve it.

I knew that virtually everything reported in my memo, although showing a distinct pattern of bad judgment by the management of the Oklahoma City Complex, could be easily dealt with by New York senior management. Everything, that is, except for one matter: the allegation of the widespread use of cheat sheets or other improper means used in taking the self-administered life insurance examinations in the Texoma District. Although I believed the insurance cheating was widespread, I had no idea the extent of it.

On July 7, Meditz and Rich Cordell, a vice president of the Western Sales Division from Los Angeles, both came to Enid to meet with me. Cordell was present to provide a business perspective as a complement to Meditz' compliance expertise, so they could completely understand the report I had made.

Meditz and Cordell decided it would be best to meet with me away from the Enid office so we met at the local Best Western. Meditz, who I found to be intense but likable, was in charge of the meeting. He said New York wanted an independent review of the situation pursuant to the memorandum; and Cordell said Chairman and CEO Dan Tully and Vice Chairman and General Counsel Stephen Hammerman both meant what I had quoted them as saying in my memorandum about the importance of integrity.

The meeting began with each of us providing some background information. During the next several hours, Meditz and Cordell listened attentively as I provided the details of the events I had reported. They seemed especially interested in the Tour de France CMA contest cheating. They seemed shocked to learn that, against Oklahoma City management's wishes, I had signed about 30 of my clients' new CMA account forms as the FC of record even after my production number had been taken away because of the contest cheating. My signing of the new account forms had led Ellis to instruct the Enid manager, initially Barton, then Thomas, to have my name replaced with another FC's signature who still had his production number. I told Meditz and Cordell that honest managers with Merrill Lynch would be irate at Ellis' scheme because his superior annual evaluation was deceptive.

I was surprised at how little Meditz and Cordell seemed to be concentrating on my allegation of widespread cheating in taking the insurance exam. Their interest was not even piqued after I told them I knew Hall had walked a number of Merrill Lynch FCs through the insurance exam on a question-by-question basis, with the knowledge of Ellis. I also informed them I had received from Graham what she called a cheat sheet, and she said the FCs were using it to get the exam behind them so they could study the course at their convenience.

Notwithstanding my providing this information, I did not perceive the serious concern by Meditz and Cordell I had expected, even after I suggested there could be national scandal implications. Later, I came to believe their seeming lack of interest was intended to downplay what Merrill Lynch would soon be hiding.

After five hours, Meditz and Cordell went to the Enid office and met with Thomas behind closed doors for an hour. They then came back to my office to visit with me again. They tried to convince me the cheat sheet I had received was most likely for a practice exam and not the real exam. I said I did not think so and that was certainly not the impression Graham had made in our phone conversation. Meditz then suggested, since the title on the cheat sheet Graham sent me was *Estate Planning Training Course*, it likely was a course for financial planning rather than life insurance. I pulled a file out of my desk drawer and showed them a voluminous document that listed the various life insurance correspondence courses that had been approved for continuing education requirements. One of the courses listed was, in fact, the *Estate Planning Training Course*. At this point it seemed to me Meditz and Cordell were up against a wall.

Meditz said he understood my feelings. He paused for several seconds, then asked, "What is it Keith Schooley wants to come out of all this?"

"The right answers," I replied.

"And what are the right answers?" Meditz asked.

"Quinton Ellis and Brent Barton need to go, and based on your assessment of Jack Thomas' involvement, maybe he needs to go too," I said. "At a minimum he needs to be reassigned to Oklahoma City. All I have ever wanted was a proper environment to do business in."

"You know, I don't know Ellis that well but he has been with the firm for more than 20 years—" Meditz said.

"Ellis and Barton are not Merrill Lynch's kind of people," I interrupted. "They need to go."

"What if the right solutions aren't arrived at? What does Keith Schooley do then?" Meditz asked.

"I don't know," I answered. Our eyes locked on each other's for several seconds, and I said again, "I really *don't* know."

The next sequence of comments and questions by Meditz spoke volumes to me and led me to believe Merrill Lynch feared a possible widespread scandal concerning the insurance cheating. Meditz said the matter was "really serious" and when I did not respond he asked me, "Why did you do it—why the memorandum to Jack? You had to know it would have to go all the way to senior management. You had to know."

I responded that the thought had crossed my mind. However, I always knew the memo would go to New York senior management. I knew this because if the memo had not made it to New York on its own, I would have sent it myself. I felt the people running the company should know what was going on here. At one point Meditz had even commented that based on the way the memo was written, it was clear I had intended outsiders' eyes to see the document. Indeed, I had compiled the memo in such a way that someone unfamiliar with the players or their backgrounds would be able to understand the context.

"If you hadn't written that memorandum maybe things could have been resolved," Meditz said. "You know, it's like you are out on the middle of a bridge and you're not sure what will happen. The bridge could hold or it could collapse. What does Keith Schooley do after the movie?" I now felt Meditz knew where I thought this could lead, to a scandal that could hurt the firm.

"A movie was never my intention," I said.

Meditz and Cordell politely thanked me for my time. I told them to let me know if I could be of further help. As they left the office, I sat in my chair for several minutes, drained and introspective. I believed Merrill Lynch had a major problem on its hands with insurance cheating that appeared to be widespread and I could only imagine the possible course of events that would play out. But never could I have imagined what the future would really hold.

On July 16, Meditz called me and we had a 20-minute conversation. He let me know they were working on the various issues. Meditz said senior management was involved with an ongoing review and had not reached any conclusions, and the people doing the investigation were slow and methodical. Meditz conceded some of the wrongdoing I reported had occurred but many of my concerns were not checking out. I told Meditz I had given considerable thought before writing the memorandum and would not have stated such serious concerns if I were not confident they were true.

I felt Meditz was downplaying the situation and did not want to find the right answers, so I said to Meditz, "It sounds like maybe you feel management is okay." Meditz assured me the investigation was ongoing. I told him I knew what the right answers were and would refuse to accept FCs being held to a higher standard than management.

After reflecting on that conversation with Meditz, I was concerned he was not coming to the conclusions I had hoped he would, so I decided to write him. On July 18, I sent him a certified letter saying first I appreciated his call on the 16th, updating me on the investigation. I went on to say I felt every one of my concerns would check out and if he could not find the right answers, I would help him do so. The letter also expressed my concern a cover-up was already in progress.

In a hope to motivate Meditz into doing the right thing, I reminded him of what Vice Chairman Hammerman said in an issue of Merrill Lynch's *We The People*. "If a problem comes to our attention, we must act on it—no matter who the individual is who is involved. A problem handled at an early stage may be a little difficult to swallow but—cover up a problem—well, when it surfaces it becomes indigestible. Perhaps we cannot calculate a 'return on integrity'—but let integrity slip and take second place to revenue—then it will cost us more than dollars. *The cost could be fatal."*

I wanted this letter to send a signal that could not be mistaken. I was in Merrill Lynch's face and intended to stay there until I saw results.

A short time later, an announcement, which I thought to be unbelievable, was made. Barton had been promoted to sales manager of the Oklahoma City Complex. Barton, who along with Ellis was one of the two primary targets in what I was told was an ongoing investigation, was now second in command of the Oklahoma City Complex. Now I had absolutely no doubt New York senior management had decided not to do the right thing.

On August 10, Meditz called me to set up a meeting on August 13 at Oklahoma City's plush Waterford Hotel. Meditz said Roepke would also be present. Meditz did not tell me the purpose of the meeting, which made me think they wanted further insight and clarification into the matters I had reported.

I would guess Meditz and Roepke expected the meeting at the Waterford Hotel to take about 20 minutes. Instead, it lasted three hours. As it turned out, Meditz and Roepke had flown to Oklahoma City to tell me the investigation was concluded, and more importantly, to persuade me to accept senior management's decisions and move forward with my career at Merrill Lynch. I would have none of it.

The meeting started out with a few minutes of small talk. Meditz then told me Merrill Lynch had looked at the matter and wanted me to know I did the right thing by bringing these situations to its attention and wanted to thank me for doing so. Furthermore, Meditz said I was right in most of the situations I had reported in my June 29 memorandum but Merrill Lynch's perspective of the severity of the incidents was not the same as mine.

Roepke told me he was asked by senior management to join the meeting and hopefully get things resolved so everything could be put behind us. I was listening attentively and waiting with bated breath to hear if anything they had to say could achieve that goal for me.

Meditz assured me everything had been looked at in detail—thousands of dollars had been spent. Roepke reinforced, "Thousands!" Meditz said decisions have been made but he did not believe I needed to know how every situation was being handled.

Meditz said that three days earlier Roepke and Ellis had met with senior management in New York to discuss the situation. He mentioned how unusual it was for a district director and resident vice president to be called to New York to be questioned. Roepke told me in his 32 years with Merrill Lynch, he had never been to New York for such a visit.

Meditz also informed me he had briefed 10 to 12 senior executives in a three-hour meeting that included both the former and the current director of compliance. Also in attendance were the heads of law, litigation, regulations and state regulations, another senior compliance executive, the senior vice president of the Western Sales Division, and others. Meditz also said the general counsel was involved but had been out of town and he expected to be briefing him on the situation soon. I now concluded management saw how serious the matter was and assumed it could only be because of one allegation of wrongdoing I had reported—the insurance cheating.

Meditz then said one particular area where there was a difference in the perception of severity was regarding the $15 rebate situation. I did not think this was a big deal, but Meditz insisted it was a serious New York Stock Exchange (NYSE) violation. I believe Meditz was trying to intimidate me, suggesting I had implicated myself in something serious. Instinctively, I knew the direction the meeting was headed. Later, Meditz again mentioned how serious my rebate situation was.

Even as Meditz was partially conceding some of what I had reported had occurred, it was clear to me he was putting a spin on it in Merrill Lynch's favor to make it seem less grave than I saw it. For example, Meditz said the senior executives felt nothing wrong had happened at the Saturday morning meeting when Hall led the FCs through the insurance exam on a question-by-question basis. However, just to be safe, the FCs were going to retake the exam. Meditz was far from finding the right answers for me and I knew it.

I asked Meditz what Ellis, Barton, and Thomas had said concerning the comment in my January 20 letter to local management about being provided a cheat sheet for the insurance exam. Meditz said they claimed they did not focus on that part of the letter. I told Meditz of course that was what they would say. I believed if it had been a surprise to them they would have reported it to Sherman or to the compliance department.

As various issues were discussed during the three-hour meeting, I noticed both Meditz and Roepke frequently took deep breaths, and their body language signaled discomfort. I assumed they were under a lot of pressure to bring an end to the matter, and it was clear to me they did not like the way things were going.

At one point, Meditz excused himself to use the restroom and while he was gone, Roepke told me Ellis and Barton were not going to be fired. What they had done, Roepke said, was use poor judgment, and they were being dealt with. I was in shock. I said I had a real problem with a double standard where an FC gets fired but not management.

Soon after, Meditz asked me, "So where is Keith Schooley?"

"You have not come up with the right answers," I replied bluntly. "They are all the wrong answers. Quinton Ellis and Brent Barton need to go." Meditz and Roepke were not happy.

As the meeting continued, Meditz lost his cool and said, "You knew that memo would have to go to senior management."

"No," I answered. "I didn't know for sure but would have bet it probably would." The tension was building.

Later, when I questioned Roepke's assertion an audit was done and everything was okay concerning the allegation of falsified seminar expenses, Roepke became furious. In a loud voice he said, "You're calling me a liar. You don't believe me when I have told you an audit was done. I can't believe a rookie FC is saying this, and you are saying the right answers have not been found. I can't believe it!" Roepke lost his composure several other times during the meeting. He was annoyed; maybe he was feeling the pressure to put the matter to bed and sensed he was not achieving that result.

"So where is Keith Schooley?" Meditz asked again.

I responded that I was unhappy with senior management's decisions. I told them I had gone out on a huge limb doing what was right and what was actually my obligation to do, but felt the right answers were still not found. I did not like the fact that Ellis and Barton would remain my superiors given what had happened. Also, I feared they would be looking for anything they could use to get back at me. Roepke emphatically insisted they had been told retribution would not be tolerated. I replied, "I hope you can empathize with my feelings because this is the real world."

Meditz went on to tell me I did not have the expertise to know what qualified for termination. Meditz said he had been in the compliance business for more than 20 years and dealt with many serious issues every year and my concerns did not qualify as such. As Meditz spoke I wondered to myself if his assertions were true then why did the senior executives, all the "big names" according to Roepke, get involved if *everything* was so minor?

Roepke told me again Ellis and Barton were being dealt with and tried to placate me by saying, "Let's get this behind us so you can become the superstar producer you and I both know you can be." I had no response. My main concern at the time was not becoming a superstar in a company I did not respect. What I really wanted was to see the firm live up to its reputation.

Meditz angrily told me he was *really* disappointed I was not accepting top management's decisions, nor was I trusting them to do the right thing. After Meditz said this, Roepke, who was standing up and shaking his head at this point, emphatically said he was really disappointed too. I could see Meditz was displeased and knew he would have to go back to New York with bad news. Meditz' and Roepke's mission had failed. I was not going to keep quiet.

After three hours of almost constant tension between Meditz, Roepke, and me, and my complete refusal to accept senior management's decisions, Roepke angrily said, "I'm finished. I'm going downstairs. I'll leave you guys to finish up." Meditz said he had nothing more so everyone got up to leave the room.

As we were walking down the hallway to the elevator, Roepke, in what I guess was a last ditch effort to change my mind, switched gears and started going on about how he wanted to build Enid into a successful office and how he wanted me to do really well. I felt Roepke's true concern was not about my success as an FC, so I did not respond. His job was to protect Merrill Lynch.

As we went down the elevator, Roepke continued talking, commenting the situation must be affecting my home life. I responded to this saying, "Yeah, sure."

Roepke then said, "You must talk to your wife about it all the time." I did not respond to this either, nor did I tell him my wife knew nothing about the memorandum and the subsequent events. The three of us shook hands and parted company. Meditz and Roepke had no idea what I would do next. Neither did I.

I felt I had done the right thing in reporting my complaints against the Oklahoma City Complex management but Ellis, Barton, and Thomas would continue to be my superiors. I felt vulnerable.

As I drove back to Enid I was stunned the matter had concluded with senior management's conspicuous failure to find what to me were the right answers. I was disappointed to realize there was nothing more I could do because everything had already gone to the top of Merrill Lynch. I really had counted on senior management to act aggressively on what I had reported.

As I continued on my way to Enid, a new thought struck me— what about the board of directors? Sure, the top legal and compliance executives had reviewed my memorandum but they had not come up with the right answers. As I reflected on my new thought, the more I liked the idea that the board of directors, as representatives of the firm's shareholders, might have the resolve and willingness to find the right answers.

Had Ellis, Barton, and Thomas been harshly dealt with by senior management, everything would have been over. I then would have moved forward with my career as an FC with the firm. Instead, it was now clear I would have to take the conflict to the next level if there was any hope the right answers would be found. It was also clear my conflict was no longer just with the management of the Oklahoma City Complex. It was now with New York as well.

Both Merrill Lynch and I continued working on our plans—mine to expose and its to silence me.

I knew the situation with my immediate superiors was going to be uncomfortable because of my assertive actions. Any thoughts I might have had there would be no retribution, as represented by Roepke, would be quickly dismissed.

The day after my meeting with Meditz and Roepke, my office environment was already changing. Ellis phoned me and we had a conversation that lasted 30 seconds. In what I perceived as a threatening undertone, Ellis said, "It's unfortunate you haven't taken the opportunity to visit with me in the past. I have an open-door policy."

"I've talked to the people I believed to be appropriate, being my managers in Enid, who I knew would then visit with you," I replied. "I'll keep your offer and suggestion in mind for the future." Ellis then reminded me we had one week left for TGIF and asked if I was going to do my best. I said I had proposals out and would be talking to people; then the conversation was over.

When he mentioned TGIF, Ellis was referring to another major contest Merrill Lynch was having that had begun July 1 and that would significantly affect management's annual bonus. TGIF stood for Think Global and International Funds, which was a group of Merrill Lynch mutual funds in the international market. There had already been conflict for me surrounding this contest, and although it had been resolved, there was still more to come.

My office doubled as the conference room for the Enid office; therefore, Thomas had placed a chart up on the wall in my office, showing the rankings of all the Enid FCs in the TGIF contest. I had asked Thomas early in the contest to remove the chart because I would feel uncomfortable encouraging my clients to invest in the TGIF funds while they could see the chart. They might wonder if I thought the funds were truly in their best interest or if I was just trying to win the contest. Thomas refused to remove the chart, saying Roepke had directed it be posted to encourage sales in the Enid office. Consequently, I decided I would not participate in the TGIF contest.

It is important to understand contests are huge with Merrill Lynch and are to a large extent how it motivates its sales force and management to promote certain kinds of accounts and mutual funds. District directors' (DDs') and RVPs' annual bonuses are significantly impacted by the results of their offices' performance. Consequently, the pressure from senior management to the DDs and RVPs is tremendous, and likewise from the DDs and RVPs to the FCs.

Thomas was receiving enormous pressure from Ellis and Roepke to have 100 percent participation in TGIF. On July 29, when he learned I was not participating in the contest because of the chart in my office, Thomas seemed angry.

The next day, Thomas met with me and grudgingly agreed to take down the chart. With only three weeks left in the contest, I agreed to try to place some of my clients in the TGIF funds. However, I found it difficult to make a serious effort because of the distraction of Meditz' ongoing investigation and upon its conclusion, the renewal of my own investigation. I also began working on my plan to make my case to the board of directors, which took about 100 hours of my time over a four-week period. As it turned out, I sold my first TGIF fund three days after the contest ended.

Upon the conclusion of the TGIF contest, Ellis sent a letter to Thomas saying he was particularly disturbed by the fact the Enid office did not achieve 100 percent participation. He pointed out the only FC in the entire Complex who did not write a ticket on TGIF was in Thomas' office and the only reason he could envision for such poor performance was incompetence or insubordination. He asked Thomas to investigate and reply.

Ellis' letter was brought to my attention initially by Clark and Deline. Since I was well-liked in the Enid office, except by management, my colleagues wanted me to be aware of what Ellis was having Thomas do. Ellis now had TGIF, on top of all the other reasons, to get rid of the trouble-making rookie FC.

While working on my appeal to the board of directors in late August, I received a substantial package that contained valuable information. It was documentation I had been waiting for since soon after my August 13 meeting with Meditz and Roepke. It was from Don Fischer, executive vice president of Pictorial, Inc., the provider of the insurance examination for the *Estate Planning Training Course* that was the subject of my insurance cheating allegations. Meditz had told me I could call Pictorial when I had expressed my dissatisfaction with his investigation into the insurance issue.

I had contacted Fischer and told him I was helping Meditz with an investigation into the possible improper use of cheat sheets by Merrill Lynch FCs. Fischer was helpful and agreed to provide me with a list of Merrill Lynch employees who had taken the exam.

Fischer's package was a 77-page computer printout that listed all the Merrill Lynch employees who had received credit for the 25-hour continuing education examination from 1990 to 1992. The printout showed 281 FCs in the Texoma District had received credit for the exam, and 14 members of management had as well. The computer printout showed the resident insurance specialist who took over Oklahoma and part of Texas after Hall had been terminated for an unrelated matter scored 79 on the examination. Curiously, it showed 160 FCs and members of management did significantly better than the specialist, scoring 90 or above, including 15 FCs who scored in the 95 to 98 range. Altogether, 265 of the 295 Texoma FCs and members of management who took the exam scored *higher* than the specialist. This bolstered my conviction there was widespread cheating.

On September 2, 1992, Barton visited the Enid office. I was not in the office at the time; however, the other FCs told me about his visit. They said he was wearing what he called a "gangster tie." He showed it off to everyone saying it was his symbol he had survived my memo. My colleagues told me Barton seemed disappointed I was not there to witness his declaration of triumph. However, his good cheer was premature.

That same day I had a 30-minute conversation with Fischer. He had also reviewed the listing of Merrill Lynch employees who had taken the exam. Fischer told me the scores seemed unusually similar for those Merrill Lynch employees who took the exam at about the same time and such an occurrence was not typical.

For example, of the 111 Merrill Lynch employees from the Dallas area who took the *Estate Planning Training Course* exam in 1991 and 1992, 80 scored 89, plus or minus one. Fischer believed the scores were abnormally clustered. It was easy to see why he felt this way, when you consider almost three out of every four of these employees had about the same score.

Fischer had said in his accompanying letter he hoped this information helped me with my investigation. He had no idea just how helpful it would be. With this list, I could now truly see something was wrong. I had what I thought to be clear evidence something suspicious had happened, and I thought this would strengthen my appeal to the board of directors.

CHAPTER 5

Round II–
Battle of the Board

The issue is real basic—
right versus wrong.

—KS

Two significant things happened on September 17, 1992, in Enid, Oklahoma. First, President George Bush was in town on the campaign trail. Convention Hall was packed with the Republican faithful, including my seven-year old son and me. The event was exciting and patriotic, and extremely hot in the non–air-conditioned facility. It was also unusual for Enid to be the host of such a distinguished personage. The president's speech and visit were certainly the talk of the town.

Something else, also extremely hot and unusual, happened in Enid on September 17. That was the day I finished my letter to each of Merrill Lynch's 13 members of the board of directors.

It was a detailed, 31-page tome that hit hard. It not only told the board the details of all I had discussed in my first memo, but also informed them how Meditz had addressed many of the situations in ways I felt destroyed the credibility of his investigation. The 13 envelopes, one for each director, were sent by overnight service Friday, September 18, 1992. They were received in New York at 11:00 A.M. EST on Monday, September 21.

43

I began my letter by quoting Merrill Lynch's *Guidelines for Business Conduct* which, in the section titled *Your Obligation to Report Misconduct*, stated, "Employees should be diligent in questioning situations they believe violate Merrill Lynch's high ethical standards. Improprieties should be reported to *whatever level of Management necessary* [emphasis added] to properly address the situation."

I then told the directors I had witnessed such violations of Merrill Lynch's high ethical standards and had addressed these concerns with all levels of management. I told them I believed the recently concluded investigation, which was apparently approved by senior management, was exceedingly incomplete and unsatisfactory. My obligation as an employee of the firm, again according to Merrill Lynch's *Guidelines for Business Conduct*, was to "report to whatever level of Management necessary to properly address the situation." The letter was my way of appealing to the board, which I told them I saw as the ultimate watchdog of the firm's management.

My letter went on to say when I joined Merrill Lynch I had the impression the firm was managed with unimpeachable integrity and the highest regard for ethics. I was required to sign a document that stated I had read the firm's *Guidelines for Business Conduct* and accepted the obligation to follow the guidelines set forth. Again I quoted the publication, highlighting where it stated, "Merrill Lynch asks and *requires* [emphasis added] every employee make a personal commitment to the observations of the highest ethical standards and exercise of proper judgment in all aspects of his or her business dealings."

I also quoted Hammerman's remarks in the May/June 1992 issue of Merrill Lynch's *We The People* when he said, "How our clients, fellow employees, shareholders, and regulators view us depends on two things: First, did we create a working environment that told people and taught people at Merrill Lynch we do not tolerate violative behavior! Because if we create an environment where we say the right words but permit the wrong actions, we have a problem." I told the directors, "I believe Merrill Lynch has a problem."

I expressed my regret in having to take the issues to the board. I also displayed the confidence I had in all that the letter revealed by saying I was willing to submit to a lie detector test regarding any one of my claims.

I told the directors that after doing further research, following my meeting with Meditz and Roepke on August 13, I believed the seriousness of the wrongdoing was even more so than I had originally thought. I apologized for the length of the letter and proceeded to outline details of the incidents I had witnessed.

I started with the most serious issue, the insurance cheating. I explained about receiving what was referred to as a cheat sheet and the inaccurate statement Graham had made to Meditz during his investigation that she never sent such a document. I suggested Graham be questioned again, more thoroughly, and offered that the document could be fingerprinted. I told the directors that Ellis, Barton, and Thomas not focusing on the cheat sheet comment I made in the January letter was unbelievable to me. I said I wondered if this was so because the cheating was commonplace.

I relayed the story of the Saturday morning exam Barton and others were walked through and the justification he gave for their actions. I also included what Meditz had told me about that situation. He claimed the overview was given before, not during the exam, which I later was told was untrue. I suggested any affidavits signed by those attending that meeting, which claimed they received no outside assistance on the exam, might have perjury implications. I told the directors that later, Meditz conceded to me the meeting was "inappropriate." I suggested not only was it inappropriate but according to my sources, that I believed to be reliable, it was also a violation of law.

I shared the information I obtained through the 77-page computer printout from Pictorial. I also said, given the possible magnitude of the wrongdoing, I imagined all 50 states could have been affected by virtue of sales from FCs in the Texoma District.

I ended this section with a list of questions I still had and that I thought should be of interest to the directors as well. The questions were as follows:

Given the openness of these actions, it appears cheating on these examinations was commonplace in the Texoma District possibly involving district directors, resident vice presidents, resident managers, sales managers, and financial consultants. Which other managers and FCs were aware of, or participated in, these improper methods of taking these examinations?

After listing the 14 managers in the Texoma District who received credit for the *Estate Planning Training Course* during 1991 and 1992, I asked, "What was their knowledge? Were they participants, too?"

I would find it highly improbable Bob Sherman (Texoma District Director during most of this time) was not aware of this wrongdoing. Has Mr. Sherman been questioned?

Was a genuine effort made to question Bill Hall, who was the resident insurance specialist during most of this time?

Have other Merrill Lynch Life personnel in Dallas, both former employees and current ones, been questioned?

In light of the fact continuing education laws were passed to protect consumers, how can Merrill Lynch tolerate such behavior and still assert it requires the highest ethical standards and clients' interests must come first?

The next issue I addressed was the misuse of the country club list. I stated I had been told by management such behavior would result in immediate dismissal (as was the case with an Oklahoma City FC about a year before that time) but Meditz claimed there was no wrongdoing concerning Barton's actions.

I talked about the falsification of seminar expenses and said I could only imagine what would happen to an FC who did something similar. I mentioned Meditz had told me at our August 13 meeting although Barton had falsified seminar expense statements, an audit by Merrill Lynch concluded he had not misappropriated any funds since he did not submit claims for other expenses he did incur. This was notwithstanding that these funds were paid to Barton's personal account at the country club.

I explained to the directors the events that had occurred regarding the inaccurate description of the MuniYield fund, including one occasion when Barton said it did not matter if it was rated AAA or A, as long as the yield was 7 percent. I shared Barton's opinion that someone who paid that much attention to details would never be a success in the business.

My letter continued with the incident involving the improper opening of out-of-state accounts. I suggested this practice was commonplace in the Oklahoma City office and I would not be surprised if the activity was also common practice at other Merrill Lynch offices.

I divulged the details of the cheating on the Tour de France CMA contest. I told the directors about the headcount manipulation and how my ability to serve my clients' interests had been compromised. I expressed my chagrin over what Meditz had later said about this situation. He claimed even without manipulating the numbers, Barton and Ellis had enough points to win the trip to Lake Tahoe. This indicated to me the rules clearly stating anyone caught doing anything improper would be disqualified from receiving any benefits did not apply to management anyway.

I criticized Ellis' unfulfilled oral promises of assets to both Clark and the Enid office, and I outlined the unfair treatment of Bazzelle.

I wanted to clearly distinguish for the directors between what I felt Bazzelle did and what the Oklahoma City Complex management had done.

I wrote to the board that while Bazzelle was "innocently placing his clients' interests first," others have participated in unethical behavior at the expense of clients and employees, and in cases, they have participated in the violation of laws and regulations at the expense of the public in general. "Why does Merrill Lynch tolerate this kind of behavior?"

My $15 commission "rebate" was the next subject addressed in my letter. I told the directors I reviewed both the National Association of Securities Dealers (NASD) Manual and Merrill Lynch's Branch Office Policy Manual. I did not find in either manual any rule or regulation this action violated. I wondered if I had done nothing wrong, why was I forced to sign an agreement stating I would be immediately terminated if such a thing were to happen again, and why did Meditz twice emphatically tell me how seriously wrong this was?

At this point in the letter I shared new information with the board I had gathered after writing my June 29 memo. This pertained to a sales meeting Ellis called on July 8 of all the Oklahoma City FCs. At this meeting, Ellis discussed my memo and called me, among other things, a do-gooder and a troublemaker.

I then told the directors what they had just learned was by no means the extent of the problems I had either observed, or been made aware of, during my short career with Merrill Lynch. I went on to briefly describe six additional troublesome incidents.

I wrote about the attitude and culture of what I had seen of the firm's management, which seems to be "do whatever it takes to increase commissions" even if it is at the expense of our clients, the public, and in violation of laws.

I also asked the directors to think about the hypocrisy in FCs being fired or threatened with termination while management's indiscretions barely even generated warnings.

I suggested that to obtain a legitimate independent review of the allegations, an outside person with impeccable credentials and unimpeachable integrity who understands the securities industry, its laws, and regulations, be named as a special investigator. I recommended someone like Rudolph Giuliani who, prior to his tenure as mayor of New York City and his short-lived bid for a seat in the U.S. Senate, was a feared U.S. attorney. In the 1980s he aggressively and successfully prosecuted Wall Street figures for white-collar crime.

I then quoted Hammerman's statement from *We The People* when he said the cost of letting integrity slip and take second place to revenue "could be fatal."

Finally, I said I understood Merrill Lynch's bottom line was profitability. "But," I asked, "at what cost and whose expense? Where is Merrill Lynch's social conscience?" With this, I brought the letter to a close.

Figuratively speaking, a huge bomb exploded in Merrill Lynch's corporate headquarters at the World Financial Center the day my 31-page missive arrived. Meditz would say in a future legal proceeding the document "caused quite a stir."

On that very same day, Merrill Lynch would send someone from its Princeton corporate campus, headquarters for the firm's retail division, to Enid so he could immediately meet with Ellis and Thomas. It would be years later before I would discover who that person really was. Hammerman was wasting no time in trying to protect Merrill Lynch's sterling reputation by dealing quickly with my charges.

It seemed to me the downside was enormous and Hammerman must have known it. Now that the board of directors was involved, Vice Chairman and General Counsel Hammerman had to persuade the directors he was properly handling the situation.

While senior management in New York was handling my letter to the directors, I wrote another letter, this one to Ellis. In it I thanked Ellis for his call several weeks earlier when he told me about his open-door policy and it was unfortunate I had not talked to him in the past concerning matters that had been recently scrutinized. I then shared in detail with him how I had handled each incident which, in most cases if not all, had been timely and appropriately brought to his attention. I concluded by saying, "I am disappointed that our perceptions are so different."

The day after my letter to the board arrived in New York, Deline and I were scheduled to fly out to a training program at Merrill Lynch's Princeton campus. When Deline picked me up 30 minutes late on Tuesday morning to go to the airport, he told me he had been delayed because Thomas wanted him to drop by the office for a headcount. A man from Princeton who supposedly checked out associate offices was to be there. I, unlike Deline, was not asked by Thomas to drop by the office before leaving town.

At this point, I still had not told my wife anything about what had been going on. I was hoping to get the right answers without her having to worry about all that was happening. Ironically, after Deline picked me up to go to the airport, my wife, Donna, decided to visit the Enid office. She heard Ellis was there, and she was curious to see what he looked like since she had heard so much about him. When I returned from New York, she would share with me that during that visit Thomas introduced her to Ellis. Also, Feightner, the administrative assistant whose desk happened to be just outside Thomas' personal office where on that day Ellis, Thomas, and the man from Princeton were meeting, overheard some of what was being said in that meeting. She whispered to Donna about it, saying, "Keith will not like what's being said."

Deline and I arrived in Newark at 8:00 P.M. and were going to stay in New York that night so we could do some sightseeing the next day before going to Princeton for the training program. I was anxious to hear some reaction from the board but figured it would take a few days. I was hopeful they would come to the right conclusions and the whole thing would be over soon.

To my surprise, at 10:30 the next morning I received a call from George Schieren, assistant general counsel of Merrill Lynch. Schieren said, at Hammerman's request, they wanted to meet with me. I suggested we meet the next afternoon, Thursday. I wanted to first see New York, as planned. Schieren said that would be fine and asked me to call Barry Mandel first thing the next morning to set a specific time.

After calling Mandel Thursday morning, I also called Clark, who had recently transferred to the Merrill Lynch Wichita office. I shared with him that Schieren had called on Wednesday. Clark told me Feightner had called him from the Enid office on Wednesday too, and told him things had broken loose and she was faxing documents to New York. Clark said Barton also called him on Wednesday saying he knew about my 31-page letter as of Tuesday afternoon, the day the man from Princeton met with Ellis and Thomas. Apparently, according to Clark, Barton had retained counsel and told Clark, "You know I have made some mistakes, Barry. So what if I made some mistakes, you know? Is it anything that I should get fired over?" Clark told me he wanted to say, "Could you let me get Joe Bazzelle on the line?"

I told Clark, "Merrill Lynch has been playing by its rules. Now we're playing by Schooley's rules. The issue is real basic—right versus wrong."

The meeting in New York was to begin at 1:30 in a conference room on the top floor of the North Tower of the World Financial Center. I took the firm's commuter van from Merrill Lynch's campus in Princeton, where I was now staying, to its Wall Street world headquarters. I spent some of my travel time imagining the possible scenarios that might play out, how I would react, and what my position would be for each one. For the most part, however, I was simply curious to see what Merrill Lynch had to say.

I arrived a few minutes late and as I walked into the conference room I saw the senior executives representing Merrill Lynch standing, waiting for me. Introductions were promptly made. The representatives of Merrill Lynch were Mandel, assistant general counsel, Orestes Mihaly, assistant general counsel, and Dineen. Dineen was the national sales manager of the Western Sales Division with whom Murphy had shared the details of my hotline calls.

We sat at the conference table with me on one side, Dineen to my left, Mihaly across from me, and Mandel to my right, at the head of the table. As I looked past Mihaly out the 34th floor window, I could see the Statue of Liberty in all of her splendor. This was a long way from Enid, Oklahoma. I was playing in the big leagues now and there was no turning back. However, I would not let that intimidate me. I had no doubt I was correct in all my allegations, including the one that the firm's senior management had covered up the insurance cheating. It was going to be interesting to see what Merrill Lynch would do next now that its board of directors was involved.

I was surprised Hammerman was not present since Schieren had told me the day before that the meeting was arranged at his request. I wondered if his absence might have been a ploy to downplay the importance of the meeting because if the top guns were there it would reinforce my belief the situation was serious. Also, I thought if the new investigation flopped, Hammerman could claim the investigators misled him.

Mandel took control and said as evidenced by the meeting, the investigation had been renewed as a result of my letter to the board. He then asked everyone to give some background information about themselves. In a few minutes, the real meeting began and the three Merrill Lynch senior executives were all business.

I was quickly asked who else had seen my 31-page letter. I said no one. I was then asked who typed it. I said I did.

The two attorneys asked me if I had changed my opinion on anything in the letter. I said no.

Mandel said he would like to go through the letter to clarify certain things. He explained it was their mission to determine the facts.

I told Mandel, Mihaly, and Dineen my motivation for everything I had done was simple and basic—right versus wrong, fairness versus unfairness, decency versus indecency, and no double standards. Dineen said my situation was not the first of its kind that Merrill Lynch had had to deal with, and with 45,000 employees not everyone was perfect. I thought Dineen was trying to imply my letter was just another routine situation. I knew there was nothing routine about my letter.

It seemed to me Mandel, Mihaly, and Dineen shared my view that without question, the most serious allegation was that of the widespread insurance cheating. The two attorneys brought up the Pictorial computer printout I had received. They appeared dismayed and disturbed I had obtained it because of the information it contained. Mihaly was visibly upset that Pictorial, as a vendor, had provided me with the information. I informed Mihaly and the others that Fischer told me before he provided me with the list, he would make sure Pictorial's user agreement with Merrill Lynch did not prevent him from doing so.

I shared with the three executives that Fischer told me the exam results looked suspicious with so many FCs scoring right around 89.

Mihaly then said to me, "Didn't you, too, score about 90?" The implication was my score was also suspicious or it was a normal score.

"Yes," I responded. "But I studied hard for two and a half days and I'm a good exam taker as evidenced by my 93 percent on the Series 7. It is highly unlikely 80 out of 111 Dallas FCs would have done equally well. I can add two plus two and it equals four."

The meeting went on for four hours. We discussed most of the allegations and issues mentioned in my letter to the board. While each one of the allegations had varying degrees of seriousness, it was clear to me they all paled in comparison to my charge of widespread insurance cheating. Not only did this situation appear to involve a multitude of FCs and members of management in a superdistrict, but this superdistrict happened to be supervised by Sherman, now a high-level senior executive in Merrill Lynch's headquarters. Mandel, Mihaly, and Dineen probably assumed all the other wrongdoing could be easily managed. They had to be concerned about the insurance cheating.

Dineen and Mihaly told me they were proud of what I had done in reporting the wrongdoing and appreciated it. Dineen said Merrill Lynch was a great company, sincere in its concern over this matter, otherwise they would not be meeting with me. They said we were there for my well-being. I was incredulous. I had to believe their only concern was for Merrill Lynch's well-being. Dineen said one or two people would not keep Merrill Lynch from doing what was right and it would never cover up a problem because its reputation was too important.

While the meeting was mostly cordial and professional, at one point I sensed scorn when I made the comment I had followed the obligation of "reporting unethical situations and to do so diligently."

At that Mihaly said in a deep resonant voice laced with sarcasm, "You have certainly done *that!*" Mihaly's comment spoke volumes to me as to how much he really "appreciated" my reporting.

Dineen asked me what triggered my June 29 memorandum. I said it was progressive but the final straw was when Thomas accused me of using unscrupulous tactics to obtain an account.

As the meeting continued, I told the others that in my first interview with Ellis, he told me 80 percent of his brokers made $100,000 a year or more within their first three to five years. I soon learned this was a gross exaggeration. I said I did not appreciate someone like Ellis being misleading when the information he was giving was being used to make both a career and family relocation decision. I said in my opinion if Merrill Lynch was half of what it promoted itself to be, it would not want Ellis and Barton as employees.

I also expressed a concern about my future with Merrill Lynch. Even though I knew it was the right thing to do, I still worried about how bringing these issues out into the open would affect my career potential. Dineen assured me my concern was unnecessary; however, he doubted there was anybody at Merrill Lynch, including Tully, the firm's CEO, who could make me believe I would have the same opportunities to succeed everyone else had. I agreed.

I shared with the executives an article I had read about Merrill Lynch, which said, "Young Turks are ostracized and are not included in those promoted from within the firm." I continued saying I felt by doing right, the door to opportunity had slammed shut. Dineen tried to reassure me even though I would not believe him now, in 10 years when I was senior vice president of marketing I would. Little did I know at the moment I would not even see another 10 days at Merrill Lynch, never mind 10 years.

Toward the end of the marathon meeting, Dineen told me he wanted to give me two scenarios to see what my reaction would be to each. He said, "Scenario A is Joe A and Joe B are fired. What else does Keith Schooley want?"

"I would want Joe Bazzelle made whole, Barry Clark made whole, the $20 million in assets delivered to the Enid office," I answered.

"What do you think Bazzelle should get?" Mandel asked.

I said I did not know and that would have to be worked out with him.

"What else?" Dineen then asked.

Again I said I did not know. "That's too big of a question to answer without a lot of thought." Dineen asked me to give it some serious thought and I said I would.

"Scenario B is no one is fired and Keith Schooley doesn't get the answers he wants," Dineen said. "What then?"

"I don't know but I will be unhappy," I answered.

"You've *had* to think about the possibilities of what you do next in light of all the time and thought given to your 31-page letter to the board," Dineen said emphatically.

"I could do nothing, and then just have to deal with Quinton Ellis and Brent Barton for the next 20 to 30 years," I said. "My family's security and stability are important to me, which could cause me to do nothing. I really don't know."

Dineen, getting even more excited, insisted, "You've *had* to have thoughts, you've *had* to."

"Yeah sure, thoughts have gone through my mind, how could they not?" I replied. "You can't help but have a thought about a book or a movie, but I certainly have made no such decisions. I really don't know. On July 7 when Meditz asked me what was next if I didn't get the right answers, I told him I didn't know. The thought of writing to the board of directors had never entered my mind at that time. I really don't know what is next if the right answers aren't found again."

"Would you really give this a lot of thought and let me know?" Dineen then asked me. I agreed to do just that.

After the meeting, Dineen invited me back the next day for a tour of the Direct Broadcast Satellite facility where Merrill Lynch broadcasted messages and programs, via satellite, to all of its offices worldwide. Dineen said it was a fascinating facility. I found it interesting Dineen would take time out of his busy schedule to give me, a rookie FC, a personal tour. I said I would play it by ear.

I sensed Merrill Lynch was scared and it was desperately trying to determine what my next move would be if its second internal investigation did not come up with what I deemed the right answers. Ellis, Barton, Thomas, Meditz, Roepke, and now Mandel, Mihaly, and Dineen knew I was a fighter and wanted the right answers. Merrill Lynch just did not realize how much of a fighter I really was.

While the Merrill Lynch senior executives were thanking me for reporting the wrongdoing and declaring how proud they were of me for what I had done, my superiors in the Oklahoma City Complex must have been outraged and certainly not thankful or proud of what their rookie FC had done. My actions were possibly jeopardizing their careers with Merrill Lynch. The hostility level had escalated upon the heels of the meeting in Enid between Ellis, Thomas, and the man from Princeton.

The next day, Friday, I decided, rather than accepting Dineen's invitation to tour the DBS facility, I would do some more sightseeing in New York. While at Penn Station, I called Clark, who told me when he was visiting the Enid office the day before, Thomas had told him I was a cancer and he was not going to have me in the office infecting Deline and Greg Stong, the other FCs. Clark also said Barton told him he hoped a special investigator was not named for a new examination of the allegations.

When I checked into the Princeton Marriott Friday evening after spending the previous two nights at the Merrill Lynch campus, Deline was already in the room. He had heard about my letter to the board and was furious. He angrily shouted everything had been resolved by senior management after my first memo and because of me, he feared the Enid office could be closed. I stood my ground as the argument continued for about 20 minutes. Finally, Deline, a nervous rookie just two years out of college, calmed down.

Upon returning to Enid Saturday evening, I had barely walked in the door when my wife confronted me. Unbeknownst to me at the time, Lisa Brainard, who was a former employee of Barton's when he was the resident manager of the Enid office, had called my wife on Thursday. Brainard reported Barton had told her I was the world's biggest liar and had a twisted mind. My wife, who still knew nothing of my memorandum almost three months earlier, nor of any of the consequential events, was shocked to hear what Brainard had to say. She knew something big was going on yet she was understandably clueless as to the details.

Arrangements had already been made for our two children to spend the night with my in-laws. After hardly more than a hello, Donna pointedly said, "I want some answers."

We talked for the next five hours until 2:30 A.M. I told her everything that had gone on, beginning with the memorandum. During our long discussion, she told me about Brainard's call and what Feightner had whispered to her when she had visited the office four days earlier.

Donna was concerned I had put our family's financial stability, so important to us at the time, at risk. She was also disappointed and hurt I had kept such significant events a secret. I insisted I had kept quiet to keep her from worrying. By the end of our discussion, Donna was feeling better and pledged her support.

On Sunday, I called Brainard and confirmed what she had told my wife a few days earlier concerning the words Barton had said about me.

I knew things would be awkward and stressful in the Enid office Monday morning, my first day back to work after everything had broken loose. I had my guard up; however, I had not realized just how tense the situation would actually be. First thing that morning, I had to provide Thomas with a weekly performance chart. When I walked into Thomas' office to deliver the chart I said, "Good morning, Jack." I was making an effort to be civil at least.

Thomas had his head down, reviewing some documents on his desk. He did not look up as he muttered in an ice-cold voice, "Good morning."

Later that morning another rookie FC in the office told me a person by the name of Paul from Princeton, who assesses rural Merrill Lynch offices, had spent the previous Monday night in the Enid Ramada Inn prior to meeting with Ellis and Thomas on Tuesday. This would turn out to be valuable information.

Also on that Monday morning, Dineen called from New York and discussed my making up the training program I had missed because of the meeting I had with him, Mandel, and Mihaly. However, I suspected the real reason he called was because he wanted to know if I had given any thought to Scenario A and B which he had proposed in New York four days earlier. When Dineen asked about the two scenarios, I told him I had not given them any thought because I had been trying to block all that out of my mind for a few days. Dineen said he understood. I said I would give the scenarios some thought soon.

I assumed Dineen and the others were nervous and wanted to know what my next move would be, sooner rather than later. However, before I had the chance to plan, never mind make, another move, something happened that was a complete surprise, at least to me.

CHAPTER 6

Preparing for More War

*...The whole time I was just
looking at the floor 'cause I was
like, "Wow!"*

—MD

Monday, September 28, 1992, had been a normal business day, at least as normal as it could be under the circumstances. However, that afternoon at 3:55 Thomas walked into my office and asked me to meet with him. I said I would finish what I was doing and be right there.

When I walked into Thomas' office I was surprised to see Deline there, already seated. Thomas told me to have a seat because he had something he wanted to read to me. Thomas went to his desk, sat down, and picked up a sheet of Merrill Lynch stationery. He read:

"I wanted Michael to be present so the content of what I have to say to you could not be misconstrued, misinterpreted, or altered in any way by any future correspondence of yours."

He then proceeded to deny any improper activity on his part in connection with the alleged insurance wrongdoing. He finished with:

"If I don't receive a written retraction and apology by this time tomorrow addressed to me and copying every single one of the board of directors of Merrill Lynch, Helmuth Meditz, Tom Muller, Bob Dineen,

Leo Roepke, Quinton Ellis and anyone else who might have received your letter, I will advise my attorney (with whom I have already spoken) to proceed with a suit against you and yours for liable [sic] and defamation of character.

"That is all I have to say on the matter.

"Michael, you are welcome to stay in my office as long as you like for whatever reason. Keith—you are not—please leave."

Thomas read his statement to me in a manner I found threatening, belligerent, and intimidating, frequently looking up to make eye contact with me. The whole time I kept my gaze directly focused on him. When Thomas finished his statement he said to me I could have a copy of it and Deline could sign it.

I said to Thomas without hesitation, "Make a copy."

I then looked at Deline and said, "Sign it."

A few days later, Deline told me, "When Jack was reading his statement, the whole time I was just looking at the floor 'cause I was like, 'Wow!'"

Those were my sentiments exactly. My boss had just said he would sue me and mine, meaning he had not only threatened me but my family as well. Short of having a gun held to my head, the hostility directed at me by Thomas could not have been greater.

I was truly shocked at what had just happened. I could not believe with New York's involvement, Thomas himself had just threatened litigation against me. It made no sense at all—that is, until I later learned who Paul was.

After the two-minute meeting, I took my copy of Thomas' statement back to my office and sat down to read it carefully. I wanted to be sure I fully understood what Thomas had just said to me. It was then I noticed the statement was not dated. Since Thomas threatened to sue me if an apology was not received by "this time tomorrow," I went back to Thomas' office and asked him to date and sign it so there would be no confusion about the deadline. I also wanted there to be no confusion as to whose action this was. Thomas signed it and then asked me to sign it as well, which I did.

I again went back to my office to reflect on what just happened. I could not believe the level of hostility and tension. My immediate thoughts were of my family, and the disappointment my career with Merrill Lynch, which held so much promise in the beginning, had unraveled so disastrously. I also started thinking about the lawsuit Thomas assured me he was going to file if I did not make a retraction within 24 hours. I had no intention of making a retraction or giving him an apology since I genuinely believed all my accusations were true and valid. I needed to figure out how to prepare for the lawsuit I assumed was forthcoming.

While Thomas did not come right out and say I was terminated, this incident was added to what I had been told just a few days earlier—that Thomas had told Clark I was a cancer and he was not going to have me in the office infecting Deline and Stong. I also had heard Barton had told Brainard, and perhaps others, I was the world's biggest liar and had a twisted mind. Furthermore, I knew Feightner had told my wife, "Keith will not like what's being said," in regard to what she overheard of the meeting six days earlier between Ellis, Thomas, and someone else, at the moment still known only to me as a man by the name of Paul from Princeton who evaluates rural offices.

As a result of my memorandum and then my 31-page letter to the board of directors, I figured Ellis, Thomas, and Barton, my superiors in the Oklahoma City Complex, were on the defensive and in fear of losing their jobs. As a matter of fact, I assumed they hated my guts. Sherman, district director of the Texoma District when the insurance cheating occurred and now one of the top four senior executives in Merrill Lynch's retail division, was clearly in a position of supervisory accountability and could not be pleased with the rookie FC in Enid.

Meditz, manager of internal reviews, presumably was under fire because I had essentially accused him of a cover-up in my letter to the board. For that matter, Hammerman, as well as Merrill Lynch's senior law and compliance executives may have *approved* Meditz' efforts in investigating my memorandum and could have been concerned they, too, were exposed. And now, Mandel, Mihaly, and Dineen were testing the waters to see how I would react to another do-nothing investigation. As tense as things were in Enid, I assumed they were even more so in New York.

The next day, I returned to the office to collect documents I believed might prove helpful if Thomas did in fact file a lawsuit. I was anxious about returning, fearing the possibility that when I entered the office, Thomas might explode with anger and demand to know what I was doing there since I had been fired. There was little doubt in my mind Thomas intended to terminate me the day before, but I wanted to do all I could to protect myself and my family in case of litigation. Fortunately, Thomas was not there when I arrived and when he did come in, he never came back to my office. I collected my papers for a good part of the day before leaving to go see my attorney, Stephen Jones.

Jones was well known in Oklahoma. He had a reputation for being aggressive and had a penchant for high-profile cases that attracted media attention. Jones was a strong Republican having served as a personal aide in 1964 to Richard Nixon before he became president, and also having made an unsuccessful bid for the U. S. Senate. Jones was recognized as having a brilliant legal mind that, in the view of some, was surpassed only by his ego. For these reasons, among others, I thought Jones would be the one to go to war with against Merrill Lynch.

I met with Jones that Tuesday afternoon, because time was short before Thomas would be filing his lawsuit against me. Jones first read Thomas' prepared statement and saw he threatened to sue me, and then he instructed me to leave his office.

Jones looked at me and asked, "Why did Thomas fire you?"

I handed Jones the 31-page letter I had just days earlier sent to Merrill Lynch's board of directors and said, "Because of this."

Jones reviewed my letter, as well as some other documents, and was satisfied I had grounds for my allegations. Jones then called the Enid office and informed Thomas I had nothing to retract therefore I would not do what he had demanded. Thomas said okay. Jones told Thomas normally he contacts someone's attorney; but since he did not know who Thomas' attorney was, he had no choice but to call Thomas. Thomas said he would have his attorney contact Jones; however, the attorney who would contact Jones was Merrill Lynch's assistant general counsel, Mandel.

Jones had partially addressed my immediate legal concern, the lawsuit. However, now I needed legal advice on how to remedy the difficult position I found myself in after having complied with Merrill Lynch's policy to report improper behavior by employees of the firm.

Jones advised me if I pursued my legal rights I would likely be in for a lengthy and hard-fought battle, especially considering the sensitivity of my letter accusing Merrill Lynch of serious and widespread wrongdoing, as well as effectively accusing senior management of covering up. Jones asked me if I was ready for that. I said I was.

At this point, I had no interest in winning my job back at Merrill Lynch. Even if the appropriate figures were removed from the Oklahoma City Complex, I no longer believed in the company as a whole. I did not want to be a part of an organization I saw as infected with hypocrisy, right up to the highest levels. All I wanted to do now was make Merrill Lynch live up to all it claimed to be and see those who did not live up to the image removed from the company.

Jones told me it was important I document whatever I could because evidence would be critical in a forthcoming trial, and since witnesses' memories fade or, if they are still employees of Merrill Lynch, they may be afraid to tell the truth in court. Jones advised me if I really wanted to go up against Merrill Lynch, I needed to record conversations with those parties who were knowledgeable of certain facts. This included Thomas' comment about my being a cancer, Barton's comment about my being the world's biggest liar and having a twisted mind, as well as any others that could establish important evidence. I agreed to document everything from that point forward. Jones felt my case would go to trial within months, unless a settlement could be reached.

Mandel, now in charge of Merrill Lynch's second internal investigation, learned Jones was representing me. On October 1, three days after Thomas read his prepared statement to me, Mandel called Jones and informed him there had been a misunderstanding between Thomas and me, and Merrill Lynch wanted me back in the office as an FC. Jones told Mandel he read Thomas' statement and he saw it as, if not a blatant discharge, certainly as a constructive discharge. Mandel reiterated I had not been terminated.

Jones replied, "I think it was a brutal, undiplomatic, tactless threat and I don't think it was Jack Thomas' isolated act...the fact that Mr.

Thomas is in the office and has made a threat I personally have to tell you as a lawyer in this community, treat very seriously."

Later that day, Mandel faxed a letter to Jones, which again reiterated Merrill Lynch's position there was a misunderstanding between Thomas and me, and I was not terminated. Jones immediately fired back his own fax to first confirm receipt of Mandel's letter. He then outlined the situation in such a way that would make it obvious Thomas did, in fact, have every intention of firing me, even though he probably regretted his actions now, hence Mandel's retraction of my termination. Jones closed in saying he would be pleased to discuss the matter further after he reviewed the rest of the documents I had brought to his attention.

Just a few days later, Mandel again spoke to Jones to say Merrill Lynch did not terminate me. Jones, after having time to review more of my documents, told Mandel, "I am convinced any reasonable person knowing what I now know would conclude Mr. Schooley was in fact terminated from Merrill Lynch employment. I want to tell you that…it was not spur of the moment, out of anger, that in fact he told other people before this confrontation or meeting with Mr. Schooley, and by other people I mean other employees of Merrill Lynch…he made no secret about it that he was very angry at Keith and he said he was going to get rid of him. He even went so far as to tell one of these people Keith Schooley was a cancer that had to be removed…. So when he made the statement this was just for him to leave his private office, the interpretation Mr. Thomas now places on it is totally inconsistent with comments he had made before…. This was not some isolated incident that arose and just represents some misunderstanding."

Later in the conversation, Jones told Mandel my allegations were so devastating to Merrill Lynch's image that Thomas and others likely made the decision to get rid of me, or try to scare me into silence. Jones said he was certainly going to advise me to pursue litigation because in his 27 years of experience in the field he could candidly and truthfully say my case was one of the most shocking violations he had ever seen.

Two days later, Mandel and Tom Smith, Merrill Lynch's head lawyer for human resources, were both on the line talking to Jones. Smith asked if my failure to come back to work meant I had resigned. Jones told Smith and Mandel my position was I had been terminated.

Within days I would receive a copy of my U-5 form, a document filed with the securities regulatory agencies stating the cause for termination of one's employment with a securities firm. My U-5 stated I was discharged for "job abandonment." In Merrill Lynch's *Supervisor's Manual,* job abandonment was defined in a section titled *Serious Misconduct* as being "absences for three consecutive days without notification."

According to this definition, I was not guilty of job abandonment. I had indeed been absent from work; however, all parties had been notified as to my whereabouts and understanding of the situation. In the three days following Thomas telling me to leave his Enid office, Mandel and Jones talked and sent faxes to each other. Merrill Lynch was clearly on notice I believed I had been terminated. I did not just disappear. Nevertheless, Merrill Lynch, in filing the U-5, said to the regulators, other securities firms, and the general public I was nothing more than a derelict who quit showing up for work and consequently, was deemed to have abandoned my job. Merrill Lynch was playing hardball and seemed determined to destroy a dangerous enemy—a former rookie FC from Enid, Oklahoma.

However, I was equally determined to make Merrill Lynch accountable for its actions and see it apply the same standards to management as it did to its FCs.

I learned Ellis announced to his Oklahoma City office of 50 FCs and another 25 staff personnel, I had quit showing up for work so I was fired. Ellis did not bother to say a word about my 31-page letter to the board of directors, Thomas' threat to sue me, Thomas kicking me out of his Enid office, or of Mandel's communications with Jones. According to Ellis' remarks, I just simply quit showing up for work.

I was now officially terminated for *my* "serious misconduct" while Ellis, Barton, Thomas, and others continued generating commissions for the firm notwithstanding what I had reported, which had been my obligation to do according to Merrill Lynch policy. The wrongdoing I had reported did not seem to concern Merrill Lynch; however, my not showing up at the office for three days, all while the firm knew exactly where I was and why, was serious enough for termination. Although Merrill Lynch could have more reasonably taken the position I had resigned, it chose not to. Instead, the firm chose to "terminate" me even though it was known I already considered myself terminated.

So I, who had done what was required by company policy, had been fired; and everyone else seemed to have gotten off practically scot-free. It would be about one month later Ellis and Barton were admonished in letters they both received from Tom Muller III, senior vice president of the Western Sales Division.

Ellis' letter was mild in its criticism of his action. Muller referenced the Tour de France CMA contest cheating saying, "After careful review of the findings, the Firm believes the manner in which you changed Keith Schooley's job classification was not in keeping with the spirit and tradition of the Firm. This caused considerable embarrassment to Mr. Schooley and may have upset client relationships." Muller continued by admonishing Ellis for failing to properly supervise the management of the Enid office.

However, Ellis' letter ended with Muller saying Ellis had a long and unblemished record at Merrill Lynch and had made a valued contribution to the firm. He called Ellis "a real asset" and trusted and hoped he had learned a valuable lesson. Muller said he was confident Ellis had taken the necessary steps to assure similar events did not occur in the future. He closed by saying he trusted Ellis to conduct himself so as to reflect credit both on himself and the firm and to continue being a "loyal and valuable member" of the Merrill Lynch team.

Barton's letter was more serious. It said several matters had come to the firm's attention, which indicated, "a lack of adherence to Firm policies and procedures." Muller said there were a number of indications that should have given Barton cause to "seriously question" certain activities.

Muller then wrote, "As a result of this, we have delayed your management advancement by delaying your Assessment Center eligibility until 1994. In addition, we have asked you to step down from your present position as Sales Manager of the Oklahoma City office." He proceeded to advise Barton this letter was an admonishment and a caution.

Not to be completely critical, Muller concluded the letter by saying besides the matter in question, Barton had otherwise performed well and the firm hoped the future would reflect this.

Soon after these letters, Clark told me Barton had said he had to write a check to Merrill Lynch to reimburse the firm for the trip to Lake Tahoe he unfairly won in the Tour de France CMA contest. Clark also told me Barton said Chairman and CEO Tully blew up about the whole situation and now knew Barton by name.

I was intrigued Merrill Lynch was finally beginning to move in the right direction concerning the wrongdoing I had reported. However, a mild slap on the wrist for Ellis and a demotion for Barton were not enough to satisfy me. In my opinion, Merrill Lynch was still far from finding the right answers.

I fully expected the firm to take other actions, and I was eager to see just what they would be. I was especially interested to see if the second internal investigation would be successful in exposing the insurance cheating scandal, which the first internal investigation had completely failed to do.

Strongly suspecting the Merrill Lynch legal and compliance executives might have difficulty in uncovering the scope of the insurance cheating, I decided maybe I could help. On November 20, I called Hall, the former resident insurance specialist for Merrill Lynch in Dallas. I had met Hall briefly on two occasions when he had visited the Enid office prior to his termination from Merrill Lynch in June 1992.

Hall told me that at the Saturday morning meeting set up for the purpose of allowing FCs to earn credit for 25 hours of life insurance continuing education, he had indeed given an overview on a question-by-question basis. Within that overview was the answer to each exam question. Hall said he thought there was nothing wrong with that, even though each FC had to sign an affidavit affirming he had read the voluminous estate-planning book and had taken the exam without any outside assistance.

Furthermore, Hall told me he was aware of cheat sheets floating around the Merrill Lynch Complex offices in Oklahoma City and Tulsa. Hall indicated the cheat sheets were not used under his regime, he would not allow it, but they had occurred under the supervision of another resident insurance specialist in Dallas. Hall also said he had told two RVPs about the cheat sheets. According to Hall, when he had told both superiors he would not be a party to the use of cheat sheets, they agreed.

Hall also shared with me Merrill Lynch had terminated him for how he had prepared his expense statements, which he said was done similarly by other resident insurance specialists. Hall could not understand why he had been terminated for such a minor infraction, especially considering he was one of Merrill Lynch's top-producing insurance specialists in the nation.

I had my reasons for why Hall was terminated. In my view, Hall simply knew too much about the widespread insurance cheating and had complained about it to his superiors. He had to go.

Jones told me I had a strong wrongful termination case against Merrill Lynch. At this point I not only wanted to see Merrill Lynch own up to its actions, but also I felt I needed to do something to salvage my career. Not in the sense I would get my job back, but I wanted to reap something from this whole experience other than just stress and disappointment.

We set to work preparing to take my case to court. As things progressed, it became apparent to Jones it was unlikely I would receive a jury trial, but rather I would be forced into binding arbitration. Jones had discovered whenever one becomes employed as an FC with a securities firm, he must sign a U-4 registration form. Buried in the small print of this document is the requirement that the FC will arbitrate disputes with his employer through one of the self-regulatory organizations (SROs) with which he is registered, such as the NASD or the NYSE. It appeared, according to these rules, I was required to arbitrate.

I was disappointed with this discovery. My instincts told me arbitration, which would provide for three arbitrators selected by the SRO conducting the proceeding, had the potential of being biased in favor of Merrill Lynch. After all, despite some government regulation and supervision, both the NASD and NYSE are *self-regulatory* organizations, *controlled* by the *securities firms*.

Furthermore, each side in securities arbitration has one peremptory strike. That is one automatic, no questions asked, right to remove any one of the three proposed arbitrators. I knew arbitrators were arbitrators because they wanted to be, unlike jurors who are selected to fulfill their civic obligation. Intuitively, I believed the arbitrators were aware if they should make a wrong decision against a securities firm in a sensitive case, that firm would likely use its peremptory strike against them in any future case. In addition, other securities firms belonging to the clubby fraternity known as Wall Street might also strike against them. In other words, to the extent conducting arbitrations was important to them, they would have committed professional suicide. The arbitrators would have no such concern for me because they would never see me again.

I knew there was not a more influential securities firm than Merrill Lynch on Wall Street. I knew by now Merrill Lynch played hardball. I believed the firm had already covered up widespread insurance cheating, and I suspected the second internal investigation would simply hide the first cover-up. I was not happy with the prospect of arbitration. I feared Merrill Lynch would pull whatever strings it could to defeat me in an arbitration proceeding. I also knew these strings were well-connected and tied very tightly.

The idea of arbitration, and its inherent unfairness in this situation, was so repugnant to me I decided to try another tactic first. Jones advised me it was a long shot; however, I could not pass on even the slightest chance. I was going to try to come up with the funds to pay Jones to file the wrongful termination lawsuit in state court and make the best legal arguments possible to avoid arbitration. This would involve significant legal research and would not be inexpensive. Consequently, my immediate plans to have my day in court were stalled while I was hoping to find a way to come up with the necessary funds. I was going to soon be back drilling wildcat oil and gas wells and hoping to hit pay dirt to finance my legal fight against Merrill Lynch.

In January, I came across two interesting pieces of information. The first was a videotape of an ethics seminar, which had been held at a local private university in the Oklahoma City area in 1989. Ellis was one of the presenters. He made the following comments, among others, in his presentation.

"Ethics is not something we just pay lip service to or should we," Ellis said. "It's vital."

He claimed, "Whether people think you are right or wrong isn't quite so important in their view of you from an ethical standpoint as whether they thought you tried to be fair."

He then asked, "Can your decision in this thorny ethical matter stand the light of scrutiny? Would you be opposed to having your decision on the front pages of the newspaper? Or would you be more inclined to just cover this up? If you're going to cover it up, it's probably not the right thing to do."

I was amazed to see the ease with which this man could insist others have such strong ethics.

My second discovery was a book published in 1988 on securities regulation. Ironically, Chapter 117 of the book was co-authored by Hammerman himself. The chapter was titled *Self-Regulatory Proceedings*. It dealt with how a securities firm should handle an investigation by an industry regulator concerning alleged wrongdoing. I saw Hammerman's advice was exactly in line with how Merrill Lynch had handled its first internal investigation into the wrongdoing I reported.

Two of Hammerman's comments particularly stood out to me. First, he said, "Unnecessary admissions should be avoided." He also said, "The approach would be to insist this is a case that does not call for any penalties but even assuming there were a determination the violative conduct has occurred, given the facts of the case, the conduct at issue is not such as to require a severe sanction."

I could not help but remember Meditz telling me during the first internal investigation that a number of my concerns were not checking out and those that did were not serious. It appeared to me Hammerman's overriding advice and modus operandi was to control the situation.

What I found especially odd was Hammerman, *as chairman of the board of governors of the NASD* in 1988 was, in effect, advising other securities firms to be less than forthright in how they conducted themselves in any NASD investigation of wrongdoing. I had just had a preview of the culture that would control the soon-to-begin investigations of Merrill Lynch by the regulators.

CHAPTER 7

Regulators

The war was escalating and
there were no white flags in sight.
—KS

In the event my case would have to go to arbitration, Jones and I wanted to take every additional measure possible to ensure Merrill Lynch would be forced to atone for its actions. We took stock of all the regulatory agencies that might have an interest in Merrill Lynch's activities and shared my discoveries with them.

Jones first sent a letter to William McLucas, director of the enforcement division of the Securities and Exchange Commission (SEC). This document was also sent to all the SROs I was registered with, including the NYSE and the NASD. The letter told the agencies the representations contained in my U-5 form were false and their falsity was known, or at a minimum, could easily have been ascertained, by senior management at Merrill Lynch. He explained I was discharged because "pursuant to Merrill Lynch's internal policies, Mr. Schooley reported to senior management serious violations of state and federal securities laws and Oklahoma insurance law," and because I "exposed serious and systemic wrongdoing within Merrill Lynch."

Jones told the regulators how Thomas threatened my family and me with a lawsuit. He also included, with each letter, a copy of my U-5 form, my letter to the board of directors, and Thomas' termination statement.

Jones closed saying, "Anyone who carefully reads the three enclosures will find the filing of the U-5 form, containing the misrepresentations Merrill Lynch included in it, particularly galling."

As a result of this document, flurries of letters were exchanged between the various securities regulators and Jones. It appeared the NYSE and particularly the NASD would be the securities regulators investigating the Merrill Lynch matter. The other regulators—including the American Stock Exchange, the Pacific Stock Exchange, and various state regulators—for the most part, deferred the matter to either the NYSE or the NASD.

Jones, soon thereafter, sent essentially the same letter to the Oklahoma Department of Insurance and the Texas Department of Insurance. The Oklahoma insurance regulator decided to investigate. Curiously, the Texas insurance regulator elected not to investigate, eventually saying, "The allegations were reviewed and as the events which you described took place in Merrill Lynch's Oklahoma office, it was determined the matters concerned should be handled by the Oklahoma Department of Insurance."

The Texas Department of Insurance either did not know how to read, or it did not want anything to do with the matter. It had been provided with a copy of my affidavit to the Oklahoma Department of Insurance as well as the pertinent part of my letter to the board, both of which went into considerable detail regarding the apparent involvement in insurance cheating by a large number of Merrill Lynch employees in the Dallas offices and other Texas offices.

My eyes were about to be opened wide concerning how incompetent or disinterested the regulators were, or perhaps, I thought, more likely how they were influenced by the powerful and mighty Merrill Lynch. I would eventually realize if the right answers were going to be found, I would have to be the one to find them.

The more I thought about how Merrill Lynch's senior management had abused its responsibility and obligation in dealing with my allegations that directly impacted the public, the more I thought those with oversight of the securities industry in Congress should be made aware of the situation. Consequently, in March I sent a letter to Congressman John Dingell, chairman of the Committee on Energy and Commerce.

I told Chairman Dingell once he knew the facts, he would "find the related and ensuing internal investigation by senior management was not only dismally unsatisfactory but also a textbook case study of failure to supervise and an unconscionable lack of management's integrity."

I quoted part of Dingell's own introductory remarks he had given at a hearing in the matter of SEC and Citicorp when he said, "One of the more distressing aspects of the Citicorp case is the attitude it appears to reveal of one of our largest financial institutions when confronted with evidence of massive abuses. According to the SEC investigators who looked into the matter, the response was to cover up. There was an effort to make some cosmetic changes but to continue the practices unimpaired. When a Citicorp officer had the courage over a period of two years to complain to his superiors, the response was not a forthright effort to deal with his complaints. Instead, management appears to have tried to keep him quiet or to ease him out."

I told Dingell I, too, had reported wrongdoing to my superiors and was terminated for it. I also told him the description of Citicorp's behavior was virtually identical to Merrill Lynch's attitude and actions. I attached to the letter a copy of my letter to the board and Jones' letter to the SEC.

I also quoted an article from the *Los Angeles Times* from July 1992 that said, "The NYSE rarely imposes severe penalties on managers or high-level executives of established firms."

I told the chairman if appropriate action is not taken against management when they are found culpable of wrongdoing, the system is seriously flawed. I closed by encouraging the chairman and his committee to conduct an investigation into the matter.

Upon receiving my letter, Dingell immediately sent a letter of his own to Richard Breeden, chairman of the SEC, and included the enclosures I had provided Dingell. He asked that the SEC look into the matter and advise his committee of the findings by Friday, April 9, 1993.

When I saw this letter, and upon further consideration of Merrill Lynch's manner in how it had handled my reported wrongdoing, I felt the need to follow up further with Dingell.

I wrote to him, saying, based on my experience with Merrill Lynch, I doubted the firm would be forthright in dealing with the SEC investigation he had requested. To counteract this, I suggested I be given the opportunity to respond to the "answers" Merrill Lynch provides to the SEC so as to offer my knowledge and perspective of the various wrongdoings.

Dingell forwarded this letter to Breeden. The SEC never invited me to offer my perspective. Instead, Director McLucas wrote back to Dingell saying the information already provided by me would receive *careful consideration* in accordance with the SEC's overall enforcement responsibilities under the federal securities laws.

Furthermore, McLucas told Dingell he could not provide any further information regarding the matter so as to protect the privacy of the individuals and entities whose activities were under investigation. The SEC was now involved in the Merrill Lynch matter, which pleased me.

Jones also appealed to Susan Loving, Oklahoma's attorney general. His letter to her outlined the opinion of experienced securities lawyers that Merrill Lynch had committed crimes involving:

- Perjury (affidavits wrongfully signed by brokers who cheated on insurance examinations);

- Conspiracies (insurance cheating and numerous other illegal activities);

- Embezzlement (falsified seminar expenses);

- Falsification of records (effacing and replacing my name on new account forms with another broker's name);

- Insurance law violations (maintaining life insurance licenses under false pretenses per cheating and the selling of life insurance products by brokers not licensed to sell such products);

- Illegal sale of securities by brokers not registered to sell them;

- Misrepresentation of securities (MuniYield bond fund); and

- Misappropriation of property (illicit use of the country club list).

As I continued to think about it, I was convinced Merrill Lynch would have undue influence over the SEC's investigation. I had reviewed the issue of "failure to supervise" in several other cases where the SEC had imposed sanctions. I believed the actions, and particularly the inactions, by Merrill Lynch's senior management and its board of directors had a higher degree of culpability than those involved in these other incidents. With this information, I wrote to Dingell a third time, to again encourage him to investigate independently of the SEC.

I suggested public hearings be conducted on the matter since "the United States' largest and best-known securities firm abused the privilege and responsibility of self-regulation."

I also compared the Merrill Lynch situation to a recent SEC matter regarding Salomon Brothers, Inc. The outcome of the case included members of Salomon's senior management being barred, suspended, or fined for failing to properly deal with wrongdoing in the firm. In the Salomon case, there appeared to be only one loose cannon involved in the wrongdoing, whereas the wrongdoing I reported at Merrill Lynch was committed by what appeared to be a number of management members and FCs. I then listed all the Merrill Lynch parties I felt should be deemed "supervisors" and therefore should suffer consequences similar to, if not greater than, those incurred by the parties in the Salomon case.

My list was long—from the board to the CEO, the lawyers, and management supervisors.

Lastly, I told Dingell public hearings would, "be a singular opportunity to let senior management, subordinate management, and directors of 'Wall Street' firms know Congress takes seriously the securities industry's responsibilities in 'self-regulation' and it also takes seriously Congress' oversight thereof."

With this move I was definitely turning up the heat. I did not want Merrill Lynch to have anywhere to run and hide from its actions. The war was escalating and there were no white flags in sight.

Jones and I felt we were doing an excellent job of covering all the bases. We had appealed to all relevant regulators and were confident we were doing the right thing. However, we would soon be disappointed to learn that only two of the regulators, the NASD and the Oklahoma Department of Insurance, would feel it necessary to contact me as part of their investigations. The NYSE and the SEC, and perhaps others, contacted only Merrill Lynch. I thought in view of my first-hand knowledge of Merrill Lynch's wrongdoing it was odd the NYSE and SEC, even after Congressman Dingell had referred my complaints to the SEC, would not be interested in my version of events.

In June 1995, I would see Merrill Lynch's final report dated April 16, 1993, to the SEC and copied to the NYSE and NASD. Only when I saw its presentation of the situation, which had "Confidential Treatment Requested" stamped across the first page, would I fully realize how misguided the SEC and NYSE were in relying on Merrill Lynch's self-serving responses. Merrill Lynch appeared to have no shame and seemed comfortable dismissing my charges. After all, the firm knew how to play the game. There was none better on Wall Street.

Jerry Paine, chief investigator of the Oklahoma Department of Insurance, contacted Jones in late March 1993, requesting that I provide the department with all relevant documents in my possession and an affidavit discussing the insurance allegations. On April 20, I provided a 14-page affidavit to the department, which outlined in detail what I believed to be substantial evidence of a widespread insurance cheating scandal involving many Merrill Lynch employees, and its cover-up. About a week later, I met with Paine, who told me in his 17 years of investigative experience he had never seen any wrongdoing to the magnitude of what I reported.

The same day I met with Paine, Jim Dicus, an investigator with the NASD in its District No. 5 office in New Orleans, called me. He informed me the NASD was going to investigate the alleged wrongdoing that was discussed in my 31-page letter to Merrill Lynch's board of directors, which the NASD had received as a result of its enclosure with Jones' letter to the agency discussing my U-5 form. Dicus followed up this call with a letter, formally requesting the information that supported my allegations. I provided the NASD with a statement, which contained a description of Merrill Lynch's wrongdoing and supporting documentation.

About three weeks after his call, Dicus, who had nine years of experience with the NASD, traveled from New Orleans to Enid to meet with me. Dicus informed me he was going to be in Oklahoma all week working on the case, and would spend a lot of time in the Merrill Lynch Oklahoma City office. Dicus told me the NASD was taking the matter seriously as evidenced by the time he was spending in Oklahoma.

Since being terminated from Merrill Lynch in September 1992, I had been supporting my family through oil and gas activities. However, because of the risk involved, I was not certain I wanted to continue with it. In June 1993 I decided to inquire about opportunities with other securities firms in Oklahoma City, my hometown.

I sent a letter to PaineWebber, Prudential Securities, Dean Witter, and Shearson Lehman. In my letter I said I had been trained by Merrill Lynch and was a producing FC for one year until I was terminated for reporting wrongdoing. I knew because the U-5 form falsely represented that I had abandoned my job, I would have to offer some explanation of the circumstances surrounding my departure from Merrill Lynch, and so I did that in this letter.

Notwithstanding my excellent track record in production with Merrill Lynch, I quickly received rejection letters from all the prospective employers except for PaineWebber. The manager of the PaineWebber Oklahoma City office, Jock Joseph, invited me for an interview, which I accepted. In our meeting, Joseph told me he had been with Merrill Lynch until just a few years earlier when he accepted his current position with PaineWebber. After hearing more about my situation with Merrill Lynch, Joseph told me he believed it would be difficult for me to be hired by any securities firm because they would be frightened by what had happened at Merrill Lynch. PaineWebber never offered me a position, and I was forced to continue in the risky world of oil and gas exploration.

The next month I received a call from Kelli Metz, a former Merrill Lynch FC in the Oklahoma City office. We had spoken several times before. She had called me after she learned of my situation with the firm. At that time, Metz shared with me her own experience with Merrill Lynch. She told me she had become pregnant and as a result, Ellis terminated her. Consequently, she filed a civil rights pregnancy discrimination action, as well as other causes of action, against Merrill Lynch in federal court. Metz prevailed in her civil rights claim. The noncivil rights causes of action were removed to arbitration and were pending. Metz also told me she had gone to high school and was best friends with Debbie Barton, Brent Barton's wife.

In this last call, Metz told me I would not believe what had recently happened to her.

"I go to my 15-year reunion and Brent Barton, you know of course, we're all together," she told me. "He decides to just lay me out and just cusses and screams at me and uses the most foul language for talking to you and is going, 'I can't believe you're talking to Keith Schooley,' and just, I mean, out of his mind about it. This is at Quail Creek Country Club."

I asked Metz if this had happened in front of other people and she replied, "Oh, lots of people. And the 'f' word every other word to me, just screaming and saying filthy nasty things. It's like every day somebody else calls. Do you know the attorney general's office called wanting him to come in? I mean massive people could hear him he was so loud."

It did not surprise me Barton was not taking things very well. He had a volatile personality. Even though it was disappointing to know so many people had heard Barton speak so badly of me, I could not help but take a little pleasure in knowing that Barton was feeling some of the pressure I had been experiencing for months.

The investigations being conducted by the NASD and Oklahoma Department of Insurance continued. Dicus told me in December that he believed the NASD would take action in the matter and that failure to supervise was a big part of its investigation. I was encouraged.

The insurance regulator requested Merrill Lynch respond to its inquiry regarding the alleged insurance wrongdoing by the firm. Mihaly, Merrill Lynch's assistant general counsel, wrote to Paine in January 1994, telling him that a thorough investigation into the allegations I had made was conducted in the fall of 1992 and did not uncover any evidence of the widespread use of cheat sheets. Mihaly said allegations of a cover-up by management were therefore without merit and that the board was made aware of these conclusions.

Mihaly not only claimed there was no evidence of the use of cheat sheets, but also made light of Hall's actions in taking a group of FCs through the insurance exam on a question-by-question basis.

"It also is not clear that taking the test under such circumstances was inappropriate or illegal," Mihaly wrote. "But to avoid even the appearance of impropriety, the eight individuals who did take the examination under those circumstances were asked to retake the examination under close supervision and all of them have done so."

The letter went on to say the process for state continuing education examinations that was used by the firm at the time in question was no longer in place as of January 1992.

In conclusion, Mihaly accused me of putting words in Hall's mouth during the conversation I had with him regarding the use of cheat sheets. Mihaly insisted a careful reading of the transcript of that conversation would indicate Hall did not support my allegations, but negated them.

When I received a copy of Mihaly's letter nine months later, I was amazed how he and Merrill Lynch could so blatantly twist the facts. First, Mihaly told the insurance department that the take-home examination could only be passed "without assistance from *any* outside source." However, in the same breath he said Hall spending several hours lecturing FCs *as* they answered the questions was not clearly inappropriate or illegal.

Mihaly was also wrong about Merrill Lynch changing its system for the certification of life insurance continuing education. He claimed the firm stopped using Pictorial's *Estate Planning Training Course* in January 1992. However, I had solid evidence 157 Merrill Lynch FCs received credit for Pictorial's exam between January and August 1992. Mihaly's statement that Merrill Lynch changed its system six months before my first letter was false. The system was still being used even *after* my June 29 memorandum.

I also knew the transcript of my conversation with Hall clearly showed he had said, without prompting from me, "The part about the cheat sheet. Those things were floating around the Complex offices." While Hall denied any personal wrongdoing, he represented to me that he was aware insurance wrongdoing had occurred. As a former resident insurance specialist for Merrill Lynch in Dallas, he was in a position to know.

In a legal proceeding in September 1995, Hall and I would blow Mihaly's self-serving representations out of the water. Furthermore, I would show how Mihaly's claim that the legal and compliance department had conducted a *thorough* investigation of my allegations and did not find any evidence of the widespread use of cheat sheets, was a misrepresentation.

I again recalled Hammerman's advice in the book he co-authored that said, "unnecessary admissions should be avoided," and "insist this is a case that does not call for any penalties but even assuming there were a determination the violative conduct has occurred, given the facts of the case, the conduct at issue is not such as to require a severe sanction." Mihaly had been taught well by Wall Street's legal guru.

I never ceased to be amazed by Merrill Lynch. In the same month Mihaly sent his letter to the Oklahoma Department of Insurance, there was a development concerning Barton, who was still under investigation by the NASD and other regulators. After being removed as sales manager of the Oklahoma City Complex for his indiscretions, Merrill Lynch turned around and promoted Barton to resident manager of the Merrill Lynch Lawton, Oklahoma, office. This location, like Enid, was an associate office to the Oklahoma City Complex. Barton probably thought he was on his way back with Merrill Lynch and everything was going to be okay after all. However, with a sudden and strange turn of events, about two weeks after the promotion, Barton was unexpectedly terminated. He must have been stunned and angry and felt betrayed.

Barton's U-5 form indicated he was terminated for signing a client's name on a document even though he had his client's approval to do so both orally and by fax. It seemed odd Barton was able to survive my memorandum but not this relatively innocuous incident. Or could Barton's U-5 be believed? Barton believed his U-5 was nothing more than a charade. He believed he was fired because of what happened in Enid, and so did I.

Barton was not without a job for long. Within days he was working for Thomas who had resigned as the resident manager of the Merrill

Lynch Enid office in July and accepted a management position with another securities firm in Oklahoma City.

Thomas and Barton, former resident managers of the Merrill Lynch Enid office would have a lot to reminisce about—Keith Schooley. They would also have a lot to be concerned about in the future—Keith Schooley. In January 1994, they must have been wondering if the Schooley matter would ever go away.

CHAPTER 8

Pre-litigation

*This was a war against the
most powerful securities firm on Wall
Street and it was clear neither side was
interested in taking prisoners.*

—KS

Since all the securities firms I had contacted several months earlier
had rejected me, I was now back in the oil business full-time. By February 1994, I had promoted three oil and gas wells since my termination
from Merrill Lynch. The first well had a nice-looking pay zone but had
low permeability, which resulted in marginal production. It was soon
plugged. The other two wells looked excellent based on their early production, and it appeared my net interest in each well would have a
value of about $250,000. With a possible net worth of a half million
dollars, I thought I had finally turned the corner financially. I also thought
I would soon have the funds to pay Jones to file my case in state court in
an effort to avoid arbitration.

By April, however, the oil production from one of the two good
wells unexpectedly dropped off the table and was producing only enough
to break even. It was eventually plugged. Production from the other
good well declined to a significantly lesser amount than originally pre-

dicted. Rather than turning the corner, I found myself back in straitened circumstances.

In mid-April, Jones informed me he would no longer have the time to represent me in the Merrill Lynch case. Jones said he was going to be monopolized by other legal obligations, including frequent travel to Japan on behalf of a client and a looming deadline to complete a book on Oklahoma criminal law, practice, and procedure. He said he had not foreseen the situation when he initially agreed to serve as my counsel but it was unavoidable now.

In addition to what Jones told me, I suspected there was another reason behind his resignation from my case. I believed Jones withdrew because once he realized my case would likely go to binding arbitration, he lost confidence I would receive a fair shake. I believed he had the same concerns I did about the validity of the self-regulatory process. Jones knew the complexity of my case, given the voluminous information involved. He also knew it would be a hard-fought battle with Merrill Lynch. I believed, aware of all the other demands on his time, Jones simply weighed the probabilities of success in arbitration with the costs and decided he was not up for the risk. Also, since he was on a contingency-fee arrangement, except for the fees he would earn if I had the funds to pay him to file the action in state court, it is reasonable to speculate he figured it was in his best interest to walk.

Since I had a contract with Jones, I could have stood firm in insisting he at least take the case into arbitration. I elected not to do that. I wanted someone who had fight in his gut, not someone who wanted to walk away.

So there I was with no attorney and very poor financial prospects. Unbelievably, things were about to get worse.

The same month the oil wells looked less promising and Jones quit my case, my wife of 13 years filed for divorce. The financial circumstances and uncertainty following my termination from Merrill Lynch, as well as the stress the anticipated litigation was causing, had taken their toll. We had moved to Enid to try to regain financial stability through the opportunity with Merrill Lynch. Instead, our hope, marriage, and family had been destroyed as a result of that move.

I will never forget the emotional experience when Donna and I told our children—Tyler, eight, and Tara, five—we were separating. Tyler and Tara broke down and started crying uncontrollably. Donna and I did the same. We all cried like babies for 20 minutes before finally being able to get control of ourselves. That was the most excruciatingly painful emotional experience I ever had.

I was at my lowest point ever in April 1994. My marriage and family were breaking up. My hopes of financial success had disappeared overnight with the sudden decline in production of the two oil wells. I had no attorney to represent me in the Merrill Lynch case. On top of all that, I had less than six months before I would lose my right to file an action. I was in emotional and financial turmoil and did not know what to do. The sky had fallen, and I felt buried.

It was time to do some serious introspection to see what I was really made of and decide whether I could continue this fight. I had put two years into this endeavor against Merrill Lynch and was devastated to think I might have to abandon it now.

Outwardly I remained cheerful. Anyone who saw me on the street would truthfully report I said everything was fine. Yet inwardly, I was crushed. I was not suicidal, but I was certainly a broken man. I often found myself wandering aimlessly around my nearly empty townhouse.

During one of these wanderings, I happened to come across my Bible. I had been raised in the church but had not participated seriously in it as an adult. I would have periods where I would not go to church at all and then periods of heightened interest, where I would read the Bible occasionally. However, it never really held true meaning for me.

I picked up my Bible that day in 1994 out of desperation. I could not remember the last time I had opened it or even prayed. I do not remember which particular passages I read but I do recall getting encouragement from it.

Reading scripture and praying soon became part of my daily routine. It gave me an incredible source of strength, something I needed badly at the time. It also gave me the confidence and courage I needed to proceed with my journey. My faith helped me realize I was doing what I was supposed to.

Between my newly discovered spiritual strength and ingrained work ethic, my resolve to pursue my case against Merrill Lynch renewed. I was now more committed than ever. I was determined not to let Merrill Lynch's reprehensible and unconscionable actions concerning what I had reported, as well as its actions toward me, go unanswered. I knew I would go the distance no matter what obstacles I had to overcome— even including the disturbing thought of possibly having to arbitrate. If that was my only shot, I would take it and see what happened. I knew by now my situation with Merrill Lynch was dynamic and anything could happen.

Nevertheless, I had to face reality. I had less than six months to file my action, regardless of whether it was in state court or in arbitration, before my two-year statute of limitations expired on September 28, 1994. Time was short and I knew not only did I need counsel who would take the case on a contingency-fee arrangement, but also I knew my action against Merrill Lynch was not an ordinary lawsuit. It was not risk free, nor would it simply be a matter of filing a few legal briefs and making a few courtroom arguments. This was a war against the most powerful securities firm on Wall Street and it was clear neither side was interested in taking prisoners.

On April 19, 1994, something happened I had almost concluded would never take place. Clark, my former colleague in the Enid office who was still with Merrill Lynch in its Wichita office, called me. "I wish I was there to shake your hand," he said. "I think you did it. No, I don't think—you *did* it."

Clark had just been told by Barton that Ellis had been forced to resign his position as senior resident vice president of the Oklahoma City Complex. Ellis told Barton I got them both. "Well, Keith, it's been quite a ride, I tell ya," Clark said.

"Yeah and it's not over with," I responded. "I think people in New York still have some questions to answer as far as I'm concerned."

A little later in the conversation I said, "A lot's been accomplished and it took some guts by several people to get it done." Clark himself had fought several battles concerning pay issues.

"Your guts were hanging out all over," Clark said.

"Well, I predicted it was gonna be a coup d'état, I just thought it was going to be a little quicker," I responded. "But the job was done."

Ellis, an employee of Merrill Lynch for 22 years, was one of 174 RVPs in the Merrill Lynch organization who, collectively, had oversight for more than 12,000 FCs. When Ellis announced to his Oklahoma City office of about 75 employees he had been asked to resign, there was at first a single clap, then another, then a groundswell of applause. I suspect the applause was not out of appreciation, but was because his employees were thrilled to see him gone. Ellis was the kind of guy people loved to hate. Quinton Ellis, Jr., dripped arrogance and conceit. However, because of his power within Merrill Lynch, his brokers were afraid to stand up to him—until that trouble-making rookie FC came along.

Ellis told Barton and the Oklahoma City employees he was forced to resign his RVP position for losing market share. Ellis and Barton both had reason to know better. So did I. As Barton presumably knew, market share was not even one of the 14 critical review items on which Merrill Lynch RVPs are evaluated. Furthermore, Barton knew the purported 1 to 2 percent market share Ellis had lost for the Oklahoma City Complex could easily be explained by PaineWebber opening an Oklahoma City office. It was only reasonable to expect another large Wall Street securities firm to capture a share of the market.

Not long after Clark told me of Ellis' forced resignation, I heard a strange rumor Ellis had resurfaced in Merrill Lynch's San Diego office. Not only had he resurfaced but it appeared he was a district sales manager. I smelled a rat. First, I believed Ellis had not really been fired from his RVP position for losing market share. Second, San Diego was not exactly Siberia. I suspected Merrill Lynch had made an under-the-table deal with Ellis in preparation for what lay ahead. Why else would someone with such immense pride as Ellis ever say he was forced to resign based on less than satisfactory performance if it was not true? It looked to me like Merrill Lynch was willing to do whatever it took to win.

Clark also told me in that conversation Roepke was scheduled to retire as the district director of the Arkoma District at the beginning of May. A light went on in my mind. Merrill Lynch was getting rid of all the ones I had targeted. Thomas had resigned, Barton was terminated,

Ellis was forced to resign his position, and Roepke, who was not directly involved but was in the chain of command, was retiring. It looked like a shrewd move to me. The firm could now appeal to the NASD that all the people responsible for the problems were no longer with the firm (or in Ellis' case, no longer in the RVP position) without having to say they left because of my allegations, which would strengthen *my* case. If Merrill Lynch got off light with any actions or sanctions imposed by the NASD, then *its* position would be strengthened concerning my anticipated litigation.

With the clock running, I was working hard trying to find counsel to represent me against Merrill Lynch. I talked to many different attorneys over a six-week period who all said they liked my case but could not take it for various reasons. Most of them said their law firms did not make contingency-fee arrangements or the case was too complicated for the short amount of time remaining before the statute of limitations expired.

I thought I had tried everything and was beginning to feel worn out once again. I had almost given up for the second time when I remembered an attorney friend of mine, Dick Gore, who had invested in several of the oil and gas wells I had promoted. I had told Gore about my situation with Merrill Lynch sometime soon after my termination in late 1992, but Jones was already representing me at that time. Gore told me then it sounded like I had a good case.

I had not previously considered Gore as potential counsel because I had remembered Gore's law firm, Mahaffey & Gore, as predominantly practicing oil and gas law. Mahaffey & Gore was a medium-size Oklahoma City law firm of 13 attorneys located downtown in the prestigious Two Leadership Square. But since time was short, I decided to call Gore just to check it out. I was surprised to learn from Gore his law firm had significantly diversified its practice, and Art Schmidt, one of the partners, had been spending more than a third of his time practicing employment law.

Gore told me to send the most important documents to him for his evaluation. He would talk to Schmidt and the other partners and get back with me. I provided the requested information to Gore on June 3 and within days he informed me Mahaffey & Gore would represent me against Merrill Lynch on a contingency-fee arrangement. It would also file the cause of action in state court in an effort to avoid arbitration. Gore told me of all the cases his law firm had handled, the case against Merrill Lynch stood out. Schmidt told me he believed my action was a strong one for constructive discharge. I could not believe my good fortune. I was not out of bullets.

In June, I had an interesting and insightful conversation with Dicus, the NASD investigator. He informed me the NASD was in the final stages of its investigation. I probingly asked Dicus, "You think it's going to be all for naught?"

"Well, I think you know, if you look around, you can make that conclusion already," Dicus answered. "You've already seen some results."

Thinking of Thomas, Barton, Ellis, and Roepke all leaving, I said all that had happened was internal, and I was referring to the external perspective.

"Well, you just have to look at the big picture though," Dicus said.

"What do you mean by looking at the big picture?" I asked.

"If I were you I wouldn't feel like it were all for naught, regardless," Dicus answered. "I think, if nothing else, we've all gotten a little bit educated and maybe have a new perspective on large wirehouses and how they really do work."

"Well, are you suggesting what you've seen because of all this is something you were unaware of?" I asked him.

"I think it has changed my viewpoint if you will on how these large wirehouses operate," Dicus said. "I think I was maybe a little bit naïve going in with the assumption that these guys are pretty good at policing themselves and do a good job and now I'm not so sure that's the case. So I'll be looking a little bit harder at all the branch office exams I do. We'll just have to see on this one what happens but you know, it was an education. I've picked up on a few additional techniques they employ."

I was intrigued by Dicus' comments. They spoke volumes to me. Such an experienced NASD investigator had likely seen every trick in the book. And even he saw something new from Merrill Lynch.

On July 15, the NASD concluded its investigation of the Merrill Lynch matter. It decided the appropriate course of action in light of the allegations was to issue two letters of caution.

Letters. No fines or suspensions. No real punishment or penalties. The NASD dispensed a mild "tsk-tsk" and "don't do it again," like Merrill Lynch had been caught biting its nails. I was disappointed. Sure enough, in a legal proceeding in 1995, Merrill Lynch downplayed the seriousness of what I had reported and used the NASD's mild treatment to support its argument.

After a number of phone conversations with Dicus I realized the NASD's investigation was no more thorough than Merrill Lynch's two internal investigations. It appeared the NASD had not interviewed key people such as Barton, Hall, and others who were clearly knowledgeable. I was beginning to see the picture—self-regulators were not going to bite the hand that feeds them, particularly when that hand is the biggest one around.

The letters of caution concerned only three incidents out of all the wrongdoing I had reported. The first letter was issued to Merrill Lynch, and the second letter was issued to Barton.

I did not learn what wrongdoing the letter of caution issued to Merrill Lynch mentioned until I received it in a legal filing in 1995. However, I learned the contents of Barton's letter within weeks of it being issued. This occurred because of an incredible development I, even in my wildest imagination, could never have foreseen.

Barton, who had been fired by Merrill Lynch in January 1994, called me on August 4, 1994, and left a message on my answering machine asking me to call him. I knew my case against Merrill Lynch was dynamic, but Barton's call was almost inconceivable. I knew he either had something valuable to tell me or he just wanted to unload on me because my memorandum and letter to the board had ruined his career with Merrill Lynch.

I returned Barton's call not knowing what to expect. I was hoping my conversation with him might prove to be productive because I knew that Barton, as a former resident manager and sales manager of Merrill Lynch, had a perspective that I did not. I was not disappointed.

I quickly learned from Barton he was angry and bitter about his termination from Merrill Lynch and had revenge on his mind, but not against me. Barton was out to get Merrill Lynch. Barton believed he had been hung out to dry by the firm he had been employed with since

1987 and which he had been planning to make a career with. Barton wanted to talk with me to see if we could help each other in fighting our now mutual enemy, Merrill Lynch. While I was not having much success in finding oil with my drilling ventures, I struck gold with Barton.

I did not have a lot I cared to share with Barton, but that was not the case with him. He had a lot to say. I gave Barton my undivided attention, not only in this first conversation but in many more that were to follow. I could not believe that Barton, who had cussed out Kelli Metz at her 15th reunion in the summer of 1993 for talking to me, was now himself, one year later, doing that very same thing. The dynamic nature of the relationship between Merrill Lynch and me had been underscored once again.

What Barton shared with me was insightful and revealing. Barton confirmed my belief, time and again, that Merrill Lynch was willing to conduct itself with more expediency than integrity.

I learned Barton's letter of caution from the NASD was for the falsified seminar expense statements and the misrepresentation of the MuniYield fund.

Barton told me Merrill Lynch had told him his signature on his client's document was not enough to get him fired. The ongoing investigation by the NASD concerning what I had reported was, he said, the real reason he was fired. This was the case even though, according to Barton, Merrill Lynch had exonerated him after both of the internal investigations. Barton said Merrill Lynch was going to use his termination like an NCAA deal so it could say, "See, we let the bad coach go."

Barton also told me after the first internal investigation, Merrill Lynch did nothing to him. Then, because of my 31-page letter to the board of directors, Merrill Lynch reinvestigated and made him step down as sales manager, made him pay back his Tour de France trip to Lake Tahoe, and put him out of management for two years. Barton said when Merrill Lynch reinvestigated, it found everything concerning him the same as the first time. He thought the actions were taken against him after the second investigation for appearances.

When I asked Barton if Ellis' transfer to San Diego was a lateral transfer he said it was not. I asked if it was a demotion. He said it was a major demotion. Barton then repeated my belief Ellis' demotion for loss of market share was a pretense because market share was not even one of the 14 criteria by which management was evaluated. I asked how Ellis viewed the situation. Barton told me Ellis said Merrill Lynch could say whatever it wanted but he knew his demotion was tied back to Enid.

Barton informed me the NASD, during its investigation, had never contacted him. Later I would also be told by Barton that Ellis had never been contacted either. I could not believe it. Barton and Ellis were the two primary targets in my memorandum and my 31-page letter, but were *not* contacted by the NASD? I wondered, what kind of an investigation was that?

Barton said Ellis was the one who coached him not to say anything, and he was sure direction came from above. Barton told me he wanted to be in management and was willing to be the stand-up guy if that is what he had to do to get there.

I could not believe my ears when Barton made his next comment about taking the insurance exam. "I went to that Saturday morning session they had in Stroud and I was like, well God, if they had had a cheat sheet, why the hell would I have done that?" he said. With that comment, I thought Barton's termination was truly Merrill Lynch's loss since clearly he was a bottom-line kind of guy. It all fit the picture I had: Why waste time complying with rules, regulations, and laws when you can be generating commissions? The clients would never know the difference.

Barton told me Ellis thought he would eventually be back as an RVP. This bolstered my suspicion Merrill Lynch probably had made a deal for Ellis to lie low until the NASD investigation was over. Ellis knew too much and besides, he was one of the boys.

When Ellis and Roepke had to visit senior management in New York in August 1992 because of my memorandum, Barton said Ellis met off to the side with Sherman. Barton said it looked to him like Merrill Lynch had built a wall around Sherman.

Concerning his termination, Barton said, "I tried to resign, Keith. I was going to be offered a manager's job with Rauscher in Fort Worth. And we tried to get Merrill Lynch to let me resign and they wouldn't do that. They said, 'Oh no, this is the policy. Boom, you're fired.' They would not let me resign. They wouldn't even talk to my attorney. They just said that wasn't even a topic of discussion."

Barton shared with me he believed Merrill Lynch was scared of the NASD investigation and did not know what the outcome would be. The firm did its best, however, to make it appear to the NASD that it could deal with its own problems, and would. It had already removed or demoted all the major figures named in the allegations. The NASD could relax, which it did. So much so, in fact, it seemed it fell asleep.

It turned out Merrill Lynch really had nothing to fear from the NASD since the only admonition it received was a letter of caution. What Barton could not understand was why Ellis did not receive such a letter. After all, it would seem that if Barton and Merrill Lynch received letters, then surely the man in between would receive one too. The answer to this mystery would soon be revealed.

Barton believed he had become Merrill Lynch's scapegoat. He had been hung out to dry and was determined to prove it. If that meant he was going to help me with my case as part of his plan, then more power to him.

Merrill Lynch knew how to play hardball, but so did I. On August 7, 1994, my attorneys were two days away from filing the lawsuit against Merrill Lynch for wrongful termination. I thought maybe Merrill Lynch would like to receive prompt notice of the filing, so I made arrangements to meet with a reporter for *The Daily Oklahoman*, Oklahoma's largest newspaper. The reporter and I met the next day so he could review the lawsuit that was about to be filed. He was interested in the story and thought his editor would want to run it.

On the afternoon of August 9, I, along with my two children, filed the wrongful termination lawsuit in Garfield County. The next morning in the business section of *The Daily Oklahoman* an article appeared with the headline "Whistle-Blower Sues Merrill Lynch." Finally, the Merrill Lynch FCs in the Oklahoma City office learned that I did not just stop showing up for work, resulting in my having to be fired for job abandonment, which was what Ellis had told them.

The news article, which had the sub-headline "Ex-Employee Claims Wrongful Firing," reported I had filed suit against Merrill Lynch's retail division. It listed the wrongdoing I accused various levels of Merrill

Lynch management of committing. The article also mentioned that, as part of my employment agreement with Merrill Lynch, I was required to read the firm's *Guidelines for Business Conduct*, which said, "Employees are to be diligent in questioning situations they believe violate Merrill Lynch's high ethical standards."

The piece mentioned my original memo and that it had prompted an internal investigation by Merrill Lynch that turned up nothing that would result in criminal charges or terminations of employees. It reported I then wrote a 31-page letter to each of Merrill Lynch's 13 directors, which I was asked to discuss in New York City and upon returning from this meeting, was fired.

Merrill Lynch senior management did not have to wait for the customary service of summons for its notice of my suit. The article told all. Bruce Day, a prominent attorney with Day, Edwards, Federman, Propester & Christensen, an Oklahoma City law firm retained by Merrill Lynch, immediately sent someone over to pick up a copy of the petition at Mahaffey & Gore.

Day, who for years had been lead counsel for most of Merrill Lynch's Oklahoma legal matters, was a former Oklahoma securities administrator from 1975 to 1978, making him the youngest securities administrator in the state's history. Day was considered widely as one of the best securities attorneys in the state, and his firm's clients included the majority of large securities firms including the Wall Street giants of PaineWebber, Prudential Securities, Smith Barney, and of course, Merrill Lynch.

Day was also a strong Democrat and took great pride in his network of contacts. Soon Day would be elected as president of Leadership Oklahoma Inc., a group of statewide movers and shakers that each year selected 50 candidates for a 12-month program to energize Oklahomans to effect positive change through a network of leadership. Day was definitely connected.

Day was savvy and knew how to play the game. He had the reputation of being a tenacious and intimidating trial attorney. I remembered meeting him once in the mid-1980s when I was managing an oil and gas company owned by H. E. "Gene" Rainbolt, one of Oklahoma's most successful bankers. Day and I met in his law office, since he was handling a securities-related matter for the oil and gas firm. In meeting

Day for the first time, he struck me as pretentious; he even spoke with an affectation that belied his rural Oklahoma background.

Two days after *The Daily Oklahoman* article appeared, Barton called me again. "Guy, you made a splash in the paper, son," he said. "I thought, 'Hell, it might even show up in *The Wall Street Journal*.'"

He then proceeded to tell me Day was Ellis' best buddy. I was not surprised.

When I asked Barton if Thomas had taken a lot of heat from New York two years earlier when he threw me out and threatened to sue me, Barton said he had not. I found this extremely insightful because I assumed if Thomas had simply been acting unilaterally as Mandel had represented to Jones, then surely Merrill Lynch would have hung Thomas by his toes for such careless and reckless behavior at such a sensitive point in time.

Barton said he was a scapegoat for Merrill Lynch in the deal. He told me he would be more than happy to help me because of what Merrill Lynch had done to him.

I asked Barton why he was forced to step down as sales manager if Merrill Lynch had already concluded in its first internal investigation that he did nothing wrong. Barton answered it was because of the extra pressure I had imposed by writing to the board. "They did it for appearances, Keith," he said.

Barton said someone higher up than Ellis told him not to bitch, be quiet, and carry on as usual and according to New York, hope it would all blow over.

Barton complained about Ellis, saying he made empty promises and ignored his brokers. He said both he and Ellis kept quiet about any involvement Sherman had in any of the incidents in question.

Barton kept talking and I kept listening. "I was told to bite the bullet. I was told over on the side, there's no sense in dragging people higher up in this thing, we can just contain it right here; and it'll be remembered and kinda fall on the bayonet, take a little heat now and they'll make it up to you later. Be a good soldier."

I asked who was telling him that.

"New York didn't really say a whole lot," Barton said. "But everybody more or less insinuated, let's just get through this and let the storm pass and we'll get on back to amongst our stuff. This isn't a long-term deal, it's not gonna damage your career and kinda like you'll be remembered for being a good trooper."

Barton told me that after my memorandum and then the 31-page letter to the board of directors, "As you can well imagine, Quinton was hoping you'd get yours with a red hot poker. I think he and a lot of other people were like, he'll get his, everything will come around that goes around. Nobody thought it was that major that it was warranting the kind of publicity it was getting."

I was not surprised with what Barton was telling me. Everything he said fit the pattern I had already experienced with Merrill Lynch. The firm was brilliant in damage control strategy so far but I hoped it would really blow it when Meditz and Mandel testified as Merrill Lynch's witnesses in my wrongful termination case. Merrill Lynch may have thought the two parties in charge of its two internal investigations could go on record, under oath, and let whomever it may concern know the firm's investigations were *thorough*, especially concerning the alleged widespread insurance cheating scandal. If that was the strategy, I thought it would backfire.

Only a few days after I filed my suit against Merrill Lynch, Day visited Mahaffey & Gore's office and met with Gore and Schmidt. Through the attorneys, Merrill Lynch offered $10,000 to settle the case. Gore immediately dismissed it. The amount was so minuscule he knew I would not consider it to be a serious offer.

Soon after, Clark called me and told me Barton was going to write to the NASD in an attempt to have his letter of caution withdrawn. Barton had sent Clark a draft of the letter, which he read to me. The parts that interested me most read, "...nor was I even contacted by the NASD prior to the completion of their investigation of the allegations related to Merrill Lynch's Enid office," and "Because of litigation, which Merrill Lynch was expecting and which was, in fact, filed by Mr. Schooley on August 9, 1994, against Merrill Lynch in Oklahoma state court it was, and has been Merrill Lynch's intent to control and distort the facts in order to protect itself."

I was amazed the NASD would take action against any registered representative of a securities firm without first giving that person an opportunity to present his side of a matter. Furthermore, I liked the fact that Barton, a former resident manager and sales manager, who had always seemed a Merrill Lynch insider, would make a formal statement to the NASD representing the firm's intent to "control and distort" facts.

As Clark and I continued our conversation, talking about motions to be filed and a possible hearing date, he said to me, "Well, you knew it was gonna be a process."

"I've got all the patience it requires," I replied. "I don't care how long it takes. Period." I would prove I meant every word.

Then an incredibly interesting thing happened in early September 1994. I ordered that year's *NASD Manual* and was told by the SRO it was out of stock, but I could receive a free 1993 *NASD Manual*. When that publication arrived a few days later, I started reviewing it. Page 255 of the manual listed all the District No. 5 officials including the 10 District Business Conduct Committee (DBCC) members who decide disciplinary actions to be taken against securities firms and their registered representatives, and the five Nominating Committee members who *elect* these DBCC members.

As I read the listing of the DBCC and Nominating Committee officials, I was shocked at what I saw. One of the Nominating Committee members was none other than *Quinton H. Ellis, Jr.,* of Merrill Lynch, Pierce, Fenner & Smith. I could not believe it. This did not pass my smell test.

The NASD's District No. 5 was the outfit that investigated Ellis for being a primary target in both my memorandum and in my letter to the board. The investigation commenced in April 1993, when Ellis himself was serving as one of the District's Nominating Committee members. I had seen it all and now had an explanation for why Ellis' hide had gone unscathed in the NASD investigation.

I quickly learned Day was an appropriate representative for Merrill Lynch as he played the same game, not letting the rules interfere with the goal. Knowing that Day was best buddies with Ellis, I should not have been surprised.

My Garfield County lawsuit that was filed August 9 had been promptly removed by Merrill Lynch to federal district court in Oklahoma City, since Merrill Lynch was not an Oklahoma defendant. Judge Wayne Alley was the presiding federal judge for the case. I was still hopeful I could avoid arbitration and keep the case in court. I was encouraged by the legal research Schmidt had done and the fact he was cautiously optimistic.

Consequently, I called Alley's office to find out when he would be presiding over a civil trial. I wanted to watch Alley in action to get a feel for him and his courtroom style, should I end up getting to litigate my wrongful termination case in front of him. I was told Alley's next civil trial would begin on September 6. I cleared my calendar so I could make the trip to Oklahoma City that day.

Before going to Alley's courtroom that day, I decided to visit the court clerk's office and pull up my case on the computer that was on the front counter. I wanted to see if Merrill Lynch had made a recent filing to try to remove the case to arbitration, since my attorneys and I were expecting that to happen anytime. I looked at the bottom of the docketing information and when I saw there had been no such filing I decided to exit the program. Then, just before I did, I glanced at the rest of the display and a certain word toward the middle of the screen jumped out at me—*arbitration*.

I did a double take, and sure enough, the display showed Merrill Lynch had filed a motion to compel arbitration on August 19. I requested the file so I could look at the actual motion to make sure the computer information was accurate. It was. I did not know what to think but was concerned my attorneys had inadvertently failed to notify me of Merrill Lynch's motion. I was particularly worried that perhaps the deadline to file a response had expired. I received a copy of the motion and headed immediately to Mahaffey & Gore's office just a few blocks away.

Gore was away from the office but Schmidt was there. Schmidt looked at the copy of the motion I handed to him and said their firm had never received its copy from Day's law firm, which had filed the motion on behalf of Merrill Lynch. I showed Schmidt the last page of the motion where Day had signed off, representing to the court that he had sent a copy of the motion to Mahaffey & Gore by certified mail, return receipt requested.

It fortunately turned out that the 15 days I had to respond to Merrill Lynch's motion would expire later than usual. The 15th day was a Sunday and Monday was Labor Day, so the actual deadline was Tuesday, September 6—that very day. My response was due within hours.

Schmidt quickly prepared a request for a seven-day extension from Judge Alley and filed it right before the end of the day. I went back to the federal courthouse and visited Alley's courtroom as planned. Thankfully, Alley approved the extension request.

That afternoon when Gore returned to his law office, Schmidt told him about the development in my case. Gore called Day three times that afternoon to try to find out what had happened. The first two times, the receptionist said Day was out of the office. Day returned neither call. The third time, when Gore told the receptionist the call was urgent and involved litigation, she said Day was in but he was unable to take the call. The next day Gore and Schmidt told me they suspected that not receiving notice of Merrill Lynch's motion to compel arbitration was likely no accident.

Two days later, Schmidt told me he thought Merrill Lynch was scared and wanted Day to get my lawsuit into arbitration and out of the public's view as soon as possible. Schmidt also told me he was going to request a copy of the certified mail green card from Day since he had represented in the motion it had been sent by certified mail to Mahaffey & Gore.

That same day I had an extraordinarily insightful conversation with Barton. "I just heard through the grapevine, your deal had gotten moved over to arbitration," Barton said.

Still under the impression Judge Alley had approved the extension request, I said, "I'm not quite sure that's right."

"Oh, really?" Barton said.

"They filed a motion to arbitrate and we're gonna respond to it," I replied.

"*Oh, really?*" Barton said again. "The word I had heard was they have already got it moved over to arbitration. My news comes second-hand."

I had no doubt I had received a taste of what to expect from Day. I wondered whether Day was so proud of how easily he had removed my lawsuit to arbitration without a fight, or so he thought, that he was prematurely telling others it was a fait accompli. Since the deadline for my response was imminent, I figured he was confident he had pulled it off.

Schmidt wrote to Day and requested a copy of the green card that could prove if Day had indeed sent my attorneys a copy of the motion.

In response to Schmidt's letter, Day had his paralegal call Schmidt and tell him there was a mistake and the motion to compel arbitration was not sent by certified mail. I was pretty sure that not only was the motion not sent by certified mail, it was never sent at all; certainly it was never received.

Knowing that the NASD investigation of the Merrill Lynch matter hardly constituted a thorough investigation, and after having reflected for a few days on my discovery Ellis was a member of the NASD's District No. 5 Nominating Committee while he and Merrill Lynch were under investigation by the SRO, I decided it was time to share my views with the NASD. I did so in a letter to Dicus.

I told him I found it incredible the NASD did not seriously discipline the offenders in the Merrill Lynch case. I specifically cited the Tour de France CMA contest cheating as one clear and unambiguous example from many incidents that constituted dishonest and unethical behavior. I even named the NASD regulation under which individuals partaking in such behavior would be held accountable.

I criticized the NASD for failing to contact Barton, Ellis, or other parties in its investigation and told Dicus that relying essentially on one side of the story, Merrill Lynch's, as it did was a grave mistake.

I wrote, "I think it is a sad but insightful commentary about the securities industry when the brokerage firm with the reputation for being the cleanest on Wall Street, that is, Merrill Lynch, may not, in fact, according to you, be good at policing itself. If so, the first level of 'self-regulation,' that is, the compliance departments of securities firms, is not only abysmally ineffective but also, quite frankly, a farce."

I also suggested if the greatest penalty such violations received were letters of caution, then even the next level of the self-regulatory system, the SROs themselves, was also seriously flawed and needed to be examined by a higher authority.

To demonstrate I was not the only one with such criticisms, I quoted a *Wall Street Journal* article that appeared the same day I wrote the letter and was titled "Investors Say NASD Ignored Them in Prudential Case." The piece included comments that paralleled those I had just made including, "...the NASD appeared to ignore evidence, failed to interview potential witnesses," and "...self-regulatory organizations policing the securities industry seem to go easy on big Wall Street firms."

Lastly, I questioned Dicus about why the NASD did not formally question Ellis in its investigation. I asked if it had anything to do with the fact that, at the time, he was one of five Nominating Committee members in District No. 5 (which includes Oklahoma in its jurisdiction)—the same committee that elects the District Business Conduct Committee, which is in charge of disciplinary matters.

I never heard back from the NASD. I would learn the NASD's letter of caution to Merrill Lynch was for the Tour de France CMA contest cheating. However, those individuals who actually were involved with the cheating, including Ellis, did not receive letters of caution.

I followed up my letter to the NASD with another letter to Chairman Dingell. I enclosed a copy of my letter to Dicus and told Dingell, "Unless you believe it is acceptable for senior management of our nation's largest securities firm to conceal, distort, and cover up wrongdoings under investigation, and furthermore, for an SRO to conduct an investigation that could have been better conducted by a cub scout troop, I encourage you and your Committee on Energy and Commerce to 'stand up.'"

Dingell, in response, sent a letter to me saying he had referred my letter to the SEC. Dingell had passed the buck to the SEC once again. Soon I would realize just how slumbering the Washington bureaucrats were, or perhaps more likely, how they were influenced by the "powerful and mighty."

It appeared the last hope I now had for the regulators to come through was by way of the Oklahoma Department of Insurance. However, I would be disappointed once again when I learned just how toothless this public watchdog was.

In September I wrote to Paine, the department's chief investigator, asking what the department had determined in its investigation so far.

Not knowing Paine had sent me his response just the day before, I decided to call him on the 16th of that month. Paine told me, "We have pondered this thing for an awful long time. The one thing that really is wrong, that does not give us any authority, is the fact that testing is not required on continuing education. That is a requirement of the provider. Now we have had dialogue with Pictorial and they have changed their scheme of giving these tests or the courses in the testing.

"We're not the governing authority to establish fact questions. We're really handicapped, I'm gonna be honest with you."

I pointed out to Paine the ethics language in the Oklahoma insurance statutes mentions dishonesty, which should cover the FCs who cheated at the Saturday morning meeting.

"We realize there's probably a breach of ethics but without a statutory requirement of a test being conducted to qualify for continuing education, our lawyers just don't feel there is anything we can get a hold of," Paine responded.

Not believing what I was hearing, I asked, "Even though they perjured themselves?"

Paine disagreed that the brokers had perjured themselves to his department but rather, if they lied, they did so to Pictorial. However, I had talked to the Oklahoma Department of Insurance and Pictorial in November 1992 and was told by both that the *State of Oklahoma*, not Pictorial, was the one that required an affidavit be signed by those taking the continuing education examinations.

We went back and forth for a while. Paine kept saying just because FCs could attend a course instead of taking the exam to meet the requirements, that meant there was nothing the department could do. Paine and his colleagues ignored that it was irrelevant as to how many methods there were to get certified; if the exam was one's method of choice, they must take it within the rules.

"Perjury is a violation of law," I told Paine.

"But that's where you are going to have to get a judicial determination on it," Paine countered.

I said to Paine that surely they had enough facts to determine that. He said they did not know how to prove what happened.

It looked like I had to spell out how clear it looked to me. "On Saturday morning, Bill Hall stood before those people and walked them through the exam on a question-by-question basis and then they ended up signing an affidavit saying they had no outside help in taking that exam. That is perjury and I would suggest if that information was presented to you in that manner or a similar manner, you have what you need."

Paine did not disagree outright but said three lawyers had reviewed the facts and they did not see it as I did. I asked Paine how that could be.

"Because it's a fact situation," Paine replied.

"If the facts are undisputed?" I asked.

"They are not undisputed at this point," Paine said.

"Are you saying Merrill Lynch did not concede or admit that those FCs met on a Saturday morning and Bill Hall gave them an overview on a question-by-question basis and then they did, in fact, sign the affidavits?" I asked.

Paine remained evasive. "I think their statement would stand on its own merit."

When I saw Paine's letter the next day, I was incredulous. It said the department was closing its file on the Merrill Lynch matter and that if my lawsuit resulted in a judicial determination that would result in administrative violations, then I could contact the department.

I could not believe Paine had said the fact Hall lectured during the Saturday morning session was not undisputed. I was especially perplexed by this since, attached to Paine's letter to me was a letter dated January 6, 1994, from Mihaly to the department. In this document Mihaly admitted certain facts which clearly established that the manner in which the exam was taken was in violation of how Mihaly, himself, said it should be taken.

I wrote to Paine again in an effort to help the department better understand what it could do in light of what were, without question, undisputed facts. Merrill Lynch itself had even confirmed them.

I wrote that the lawyers I consulted had said the FCs who attended Hall's question-by-question run-through, and then signed the affidavits saying they took the exam without any outside help, had committed perjury. I then told Paine, "Categorically, this illegal conduct is fraudulent, dishonest, and untrustworthy, and according to Section 1428A.1, 'the Commissioner...*shall* [emphasis added] censure, suspend, or revoke, or refuse to issue, continue, or renew, any license issued...' for such behavior."

Soon Paine responded saying my letter had been reviewed by one of the department's attorneys who concurred with his original conclusion.

He wrote, "The complaint, as filed by you, is based on allegations resulting in your word against numerous others who are with Merrill Lynch. You have provided the Department with no uncontradicted evidence; therefore, Mr. Wiley directed me to close the file. Should you have any additional questions please feel free to contact Eddie C. Wiley of our Legal Division."

I did have a question for Wiley, so I wrote saying, "I found Mr. Paine's responses to be unresponsive to particular points I made in my recent letter to him, and would appreciate a straightforward response from you."

I asked Wiley, "Please responsively and without evasiveness tell me specifically how the necessary facts to prove wrongdoing are not present as they relate to said statute and said perjuries." Mihaly admitted to certain behavior, so it was not my word against numerous others with Merrill Lynch. I did not understand how the department could not see that. Wiley held true to form. He remained evasive, as much as someone could be. I never heard from him. I was amazed this was the regulatory watchdog that was supposed to be protecting Oklahoma citizens from fraudulent, dishonest, and untrustworthy practices by insurance agents.

So much for regulators, I thought. The NASD did not bother to interview Ellis, Barton, Hall, or others. It issued a letter of caution for the Tour de France CMA contest cheating but not to the individuals who actually cheated. The Oklahoma Department of Insurance said the facts regarding the Saturday morning insurance cheating were not undisputed when they were. The Texas Department of Insurance refused to even look at the alleged insurance cheating scandal even though by all appearances it was pervasive in Texas. Soon, I would learn the

SEC and NYSE, in their investigations, appeared to have relied exclusively on Merrill Lynch's inaccurate version of events. My last and only hope to make Merrill Lynch accountable for its actions was to bring such penalties against it myself, since it appeared the firm clearly had the regulators on its side. I was now more determined than ever to make my case as solid as possible.

I continued speaking with Barton on the phone quite regularly. On one occasion he told me, "Merrill is, you gotta understand, so protective of their image. They will sacrifice anybody and anyone at anytime for anything if they think it will help protect their image. But also, I'm seeing the sons-of-bitches are not above building a wall around people too, which I think they've done with Sherman."

On another occasion I asked Barton, "Considering how minor evidently New York seemed to think everything was, why was there so much damned paranoia? You got fired for that, Quinton told you, and Quinton himself believes he was fired because of Enid, and they've built a wall around Sherman, and they've covered up. I mean, why all the paranoia and all that stuff if everything was really just trivial stuff?"

"Well, Keith, that's a good question," Barton answered. "It's a damn good question. It's like Watergate. It's a third-rate burglary but it was a first-rate cover-up. It wasn't the burglary that was the problem, it was the damn cover-up that got everybody in trouble. It's almost like if you tell a little lie the first time then you've got to tell a bigger lie the next time, and a bigger lie after that. If they'd just come clean the first time it would have been a lot easier."

Barton's comment was interesting, but he was mistaken in one major way. I believed the reason for the "first-rate cover-up" was because it was a "first-rate burglary."

I also talked to Barton about his termination, supposedly for signing his client's name on a document. "I see a lot of bad faith on Merrill's part concerning your deal," I said. "That's so preposterous they would terminate you for that."

"I guarantee you, Keith, what it was done for was your deal," Barton countered. "It was positioning themselves for your deal. They're gonna say, 'Look guys, we got rid of that bad apple, we got rid of all them. Jack Thomas left, Brent Barton got fired, and we ran Quint off. And Leo's gone, he retired.' The only person who's still there is Bob Sherman and they're insulating themselves more and more. That's what they're trying to do, insulate Sherman."

Barton then talked about the Tour de France CMA contest cheating. "For them to say the things I did in the sales contests were against the rules, well, if that's true then we we're doing it with the okay of the firm," he said. "I did what Quint told me to do and in turn Quint notified Sherman in writing on what we did. It was with other people also. I'm sure it was done system wide if you go back and check, it was done at other places. But you're the only one who probably complained."

Barton filed a statement of claim against Merrill Lynch with the NASD arbitration department in September 1994. He was determined to show he had not been a renegade manager for Merrill Lynch but at all times, either Ellis or Sherman was aware of virtually all he had done. Barton believed he had been made the scapegoat. He wanted vindication and he was willing to fight for it.

I would never have imagined one day I would be fighting the same fight as Barton. We were the most unlikely of "bedfellows"; however, I did not mind putting aside my personal feelings for him for a time in order to hear any new information or insights he could provide. While he may not have been my greatest mentor, we were in similar boats on the same treacherous ride. Merrill Lynch had sold both of us down the river.

On September 28, 1994, Judge Alley granted Merrill Lynch's motion to compel arbitration. My worst fear had been realized. Arbitration it would be, with no chance to appeal Alley's ruling until after the arbitration decision was made. Even if I could overturn Alley's ruling I would still have to go through a grueling and I was sure, unfair, arbitration process first.

CHAPTER 9

NYSE Arbitration

Well, are you ready
to be thrown to the lions?

—DG

On February 10, 1995, my attorneys filed my statement of claim against Merrill Lynch with the NYSE arbitration department. I was seeking actual damages of $2.3 million and punitive damages in an amount at least equaling the actual damages. The arbitration process was in motion, and I could only hope I would get a fair hearing.

On February 28, Barton and I spoke again. Barton was preoccupied with his upcoming arbitration hearing that was to begin in about two months in Oklahoma City. "At this point in time, I'm just tired," Barton told me. "They're just gonna beat me down. I don't have an army of people behind me working for me to generate my income so I can keep on fighting these windmills. I can't do it anymore and I can no longer financially afford it. They're gonna drive me into bankruptcy." I understood exactly what Barton meant, but I was determined to go the distance no matter what.

"From the time this whole thing started, telling me it's over with, telling me it's fine and then coming back and saying, 'Oops, whoops, no, we were wrong, it wasn't fine and now we're gonna do this,'" Barton said. "The level of allegations against me never changed but then the determination of who they were gonna sacrifice does." Barton believed Ellis, Sherman, and Merrill Lynch had all betrayed him.

I knew Barton's arbitration hearing had the potential of providing important evidence that would support my allegation of a cover-up by Merrill Lynch. I asked Barton if he was going to have a transcript of his hearing made. When he said he had no such intention, I started thinking about how I could obtain a record of the proceeding for myself.

In April, I had another interesting conversation with Metz. Knowing that Metz still had friends in the Merrill Lynch Oklahoma City office, and that she was best friends with Barton's wife, I asked her, "What was the story behind Quinton's leaving, what have you heard?"

"The Enid thing," Metz answered. "But I really never heard any other details about it beyond that because I wasn't talking to Brent at the time."

"But you heard from someone that it was related to Enid?" I probed further.

"Oh, definitely," Metz replied. "I probably heard that from Debbie because Debbie is actually the one that called me and said, 'You won't believe it, Quinton was fired.'"

"And I know Leo, wasn't Leo given early retirement or something?" Metz asked. I confirmed for her that I heard he had and asked Metz what she thought about that.

"That shocked me," she said. "He's just such a by-the-rules kind of guy. Leo was the manager—well, he hired me and I just really respect him. He's a real family person. Maybe he just went to bat for Quinton and when they found Quinton to be wrong...." Roepke, prior to his tenure as RVP of the Little Rock office and promotion to district director, preceded Ellis as the RVP of the Oklahoma City office.

Next, I asked Metz about her arbitration hearing, and whether Merrill Lynch was forthcoming with discovery items she had requested. I received an eye-opening preview of what I could expect in my own proceeding.

"We would get like a file because there would be specifically something in there that I knew was in there and of course, we'd get it and it wouldn't be in there," Metz told me. "And then, be getting ready for this, documents that they presented in court, things in my file that they said they'd copied me on that I had never seen. And Quinton Ellis, under oath, got right on the stand and totally fabricated conversations he had with me that never even happened, with lots of emotion in his voice. He's an actor deluxe so get ready."

Metz then told me about two of her friends in the Oklahoma City office, a husband and wife team. "Cynthia and her husband left because they had had all of Quinton they could take. They love the manager over at Bache and they're really glad they went. She thinks she's in a different business, it's so different than working for Quinton Ellis. She says it's a joy to go to work."

Already having heard from Barton that a lot of FCs had left the Merrill Lynch Oklahoma City office in recent months, I asked Metz, "And you think Quinton Ellis is the reason why all the others quit too?"

"Oh, yeah," Metz responded. "He's bad news."

At this time Clark, still with Merrill Lynch in Wichita, was continuing to make an issue of the fact that Ellis had not kept his promise of delivering $5 to 10 million in assets to him. Clark got his attorney involved, who brought New York into the matter. Eventually a settlement was reached. As a result though, Clark believed he was now persona non grata with Merrill Lynch. Clark was promptly terminated in May 1995 for inability to perform to production standards. Clark was now considering his own wrongful termination action against Merrill Lynch.

On April 26, 1995, Merrill Lynch filed its answer to my statement of claim. Since the answer had been sent directly to my attorneys, Gore called me to let me know they had received it.

In a disappointed tone of voice, Gore told me Merrill Lynch had said a lot of things in its answer I had never told him or Schmidt, such as that I was a poor producer. I told Gore that was untrue and asked him to fax the answer to me so I could review it and respond to him and Schmidt about their concerns. I suspected Merrill Lynch and Day were simply executing their modus operandi, which was—why admit the truth when there is a more expedient way to handle the matter?

When I reviewed Merrill Lynch's answer I was floored at how inaccurate, misleading, and blatantly untrue many of its representations were. Merrill Lynch claimed, among other things, that the regulatory violations I alleged were without merit; no regulatory action ever resulted. I claimed I was in the top quintile in production but Merrill Lynch's records indicated otherwise. The Enid FCs were not promised $20 million in assets. The Enid office was not a hostile work environment for me, nor did I seek employment with other securities firms. And I had a duty to speak truthfully and was not going to be shielded by mixing false accusations with allegedly true accusations.

I knew everything I had alleged was true and was sure I would later prove it beyond any reasonable doubt at my arbitration hearing, less than five months away.

On May 9, Barton's arbitration case against Merrill Lynch began. I really wanted the proceeding transcribed because of its potential benefit to my own case against Merrill Lynch. However, Barton did not want to incur the expense of a court reporter and transcript. Since Barton and I had become friendly because of our mutual problem, Merrill Lynch, Gore was able to make an arrangement with Barton's attorney just days before the hearing began that if Barton would have a court reporter present, I would pay the expense. Barton's attorney agreed.

Soon thereafter, Barton's attorney called Gore and told him they had changed their minds. They thought the arrangement might compromise Barton's case in the eyes of the arbitrators. Gore asked Barton's attorney if he had any objection to my counsel showing up at Barton's arbitration hearing with a court reporter. Barton's attorney said that would be fine but he would, for the record, have to object to it to distance Barton from me. It was looking like part of Barton's strategy was to place a lot of the blame on me for what happened to him.

Schmidt showed up at Barton's hearing in Oklahoma City with a court reporter and requested permission from the three arbitrators to allow the reporter to stay throughout the entire hearing. The arbitrators denied Schmidt's request, telling him he could try to obtain the customary tape recording of Barton's NASD arbitration hearing through a subpoena. Schmidt countered by saying I would still be willing to pay for the cost of the court reporter and transcript and then only if I were successful with a subpoena would I receive my own copy of the transcript. The arbitrators went into an executive session to consider Schmidt's proposal and upon returning, told him his request was respectfully denied.

Schmidt, in showing up at Barton's arbitration hearing, got to meet Ellis, Roepke, and Alan Rockler, who was Merrill Lynch's expert witness from Los Angeles. Schmidt told me Ellis impressed him as a smooth salesman.

Barton's arbitration hearing was scheduled for three days but curiously only lasted one. Surprisingly, Merrill Lynch and Barton settled the case at the beginning of the second day of the hearing. Although Merrill Lynch had every opportunity to settle the case for months before the hearing began, it made no serious attempt to do so. I will always wonder whether the possibility that I could gain important evidence in what Barton, and others, might say under oath, may have been all that New York needed to decide to abruptly close the chapter on his claims.

In view of what surely had to be an unusual, if not unprecedented, move where my attorney brought a court reporter to Barton's arbitration hearing, Merrill Lynch knew I meant business. I was pulling out all the stops in my fight against Merrill Lynch.

I spoke to Barton four days after his settlement. I was curious to hear about his arbitration. He warned me, "It was a pretty intimidating line-up 'cause there was Bruce Day and Rod Heggy and Quint and Bruce's secretary and Brett Bernard, the manager, and Leo and this Alan Rockler were all there for Merrill sitting in the whole time. Just me and two attorneys in on my side. And as Bruce Day will tell ya, they've got more attorneys working up in New York in their legal department than McAfee & Taft has on staff. Merrill's got like 100, 150, 200 attorneys on staff up there."

"Were you able to get very much into your case on that first day as far as a lot of testimony?" I asked.

"Oh, yeah," Barton replied. "I was on the stand all day long. I'm telling ya, you're not gonna have much fun 'cause whatever you think, however bad you think it can be, it can get worse. You think you know how bad it can get. You don't."

"So did they have a chance to cross-examine you on that first day?" I continued probing.

"Oh, yes," Barton answered. "Oh, yes."

As the conversation ended Barton wished me luck. Little did I know by the time I would have my arbitration hearing four months later,

Barton would reverse his feelings, and his testimony would be filled with venom toward me.

On June 16, Day sent a letter to Gore saying Merrill Lynch would be filing an amended answer that involved more form than substance. When the amended answer came in, I would see it was significantly different from the original version.

The amended answer, as it turned out, was more accurate in its representations of numerous situations, which had been misrepresented in the first answer. I thought such a contrast was bizarre. Nevertheless, Merrill Lynch still represented, among other things, that I had a duty to speak truthfully and the Enid office was not a hostile work environment for me.

Merrill Lynch had also added something to the amended answer—Exhibit B. The document was Merrill Lynch's April 16, 1993, letter to the SEC, which discussed what its internal investigations had determined concerning the wrongdoing reported by me. I figured Merrill Lynch decided to disclose this letter because it had apparently just learned from the SEC that pursuant to the Freedom of Information Act request I made two weeks earlier, the April 16 letter, as well as other documents, would likely be released to me notwithstanding Merrill Lynch's request for their confidential treatment.

Merrill Lynch's letter to the SEC had a number of inaccuracies and its skewed version of the facts; furthermore, it appeared the letter was the predominant source of information the agency relied upon as it *carefully considered* all the alleged wrongdoing.

In June, Day sent a letter to David Carey, senior counsel of the NYSE, which had as an enclosure Merrill Lynch's amended answer. Day told Carey the original answer was filed soon after the Oklahoma City bombing which was near his office. He wrote, "Due to oversight, the answer was not reviewed by appropriate parties for Merrill Lynch prior to its filing and certain clarifications are necessary...."

It did not seem plausible to me that given the nature and sensitivity of the matter involving me that the appropriate parties for Merrill Lynch had not reviewed the answer. The Oklahoma City bombing had no effect on New York. If anything, Day should have been requesting an extension of time in which to file Merrill Lynch's answer because of the impact the bombing might have had on his law firm.

I later suspected the reason Merrill Lynch had submitted its highly inaccurate first answer may have been to try to kill a story that *The Wall Street Journal* had been planning to run. Shortly after I filed my petition in Garfield County on August 9, 1994, I had a number of conversations with Mike Siconolfi and Anita Raghavan, both *Wall Street Journal* reporters. Siconolfi told me my lawsuit warranted coverage, but before running it he would have to talk to Merrill Lynch and the NASD. Siconolfi soon handed the Merrill Lynch story off to Raghavan because he was busy working on some other developing stories.

Raghavan told me on September 23, 1994, the article should run the following week. Raghavan also told me Merrill Lynch, more than any other securities firm, would try to kill the story. I told her I had no doubt Merrill Lynch would try to kill the story especially since it had gone all the way to the board of directors with an allegation of a senior management cover-up. Raghavan told me in this same conversation the NASD was a rigged regulatory body.

I had several more conversations with Raghavan, with the last one being on November 8 when she told me she was currently busy working on other stories. *The Wall Street Journal* never ran the piece.

I suspected either Siconolfi or Raghavan contacted Merrill Lynch and was informed by the firm I was outrageous in my claims, could not be believed, and to run the story given those facts would not be fair to Merrill Lynch. Since Merrill Lynch had just filed its motion to compel arbitration on August 19, it would only be fair, I would guess the firm argued, to let it file an answer whether in court if its motion was denied or in arbitration if its motion was granted. Merrill Lynch's motion was granted on September 28, removing the matter to arbitration. I submitted my statement of claim to the NYSE on February 10, 1995, and Merrill Lynch after receiving an extension, submitted its answer on April 26. In its answer Merrill Lynch denied the truth. I speculated it was Merrill Lynch's answer, later amended, that contributed to *The Wall Street Journal*'s decision not to run the story.

In the same month Merrill Lynch amended its answer, Clark and I spoke again. Clark told me his attorney was negotiating with Merrill

Lynch concerning his own wrongful termination claim and if a satisfactory agreement could not be reached, he was prepared to take it to arbitration.

Clark and I discussed Barton's recently truncated arbitration hearing. Clark, in comparing Barton's case with mine, said, "You know what the big difference is though, Keith? You don't have any lies in your stuff. I just can't believe they wanna argue that in front of three independent arbitrators! I also think they don't know Keith Schooley. They just flat don't know him yet, and I think they think, 'Let's see if we can wear this guy out.'"

On July 1, I was surprised to hear from Clark he had just settled his wrongful termination claim with Merrill Lynch. Clark told me his attorney was dumbfounded. He could not believe what Merrill Lynch was willing to pay Clark to get the matter settled. Merrill Lynch's counteroffer to Clark's demand for damages was far greater than his attorney expected. Clark told me he believed Merrill Lynch just wanted to clear the decks by getting him and Barton out of the way so it could get ready for me.

I recalled Metz had told me in her successful federal pregnancy discrimination lawsuit against Merrill Lynch, Ellis, under oath, had been untruthful in a number of instances. I also remembered Metz saying the federal judge in the Western District of Oklahoma case, Robin Cauthron, had even said in her opinion Ellis was not a credible witness.

I decided to take a look at Judge Cauthron's opinion to see exactly what she did say about Ellis' credibility. In her opinion, Judge Cauthron wrote, "Mr. Ellis testified there was no such practice as counseling out of the business. This conclusion was contradicted by every other witness and circumstances surrounding the termination of other poor producers."

In a later section she wrote, "Ellis' testimony to the contrary is largely not credible." I learned nothing new from the judge's comments. I had already seen that Ellis had a serious problem telling the truth.

On July 25, I filed my first request for production of documents with the NYSE arbitration department. This discovery request would later come into play in a significant and serious way. Among other things,

I requested any documents detailing the meeting on September 22, 1992, between Thomas, Ellis, and a person believed to be named Paul who was from Princeton, New Jersey, and was employed by Merrill Lynch. I asked Merrill Lynch to provide information concerning this unidentified person's position with the firm. Merrill Lynch's response to my discovery request was "none." It claimed to have no knowledge of such a person named Paul, and therefore had no knowledge of a meeting he attended.

I was still under the impression Paul was someone who evaluated rural associate offices. I assumed he was some middle-level employee whose position could probably be capably performed by someone just out of college.

On August 1, Clark told me he had learned Ellis had recently been named the resident vice president of Merrill Lynch's Colorado Springs office. Now that the regulatory investigations were completed, perhaps New York felt it safe to reward Ellis for his sacrificial contribution in taking a fastball in the ribs for the sake of the team. Clark also told me he had recently talked to Barton, and it appeared as a result of his settlement with Merrill Lynch the firm had his cooperation concerning my upcoming arbitration hearing.

Between August 31 and September 8, Merrill Lynch and I provided documents to each other pursuant to our respective discovery requests. We also exchanged our lists of witnesses and exhibits. The arbitration hearing was to begin on September 18. Merrill Lynch and I, and our attorneys, were busy preparing our cases for what we knew would be an intense proceeding.

Just days before my hearing started, I received an unexpected phone call from Hall. The last time he and I had spoken was in November 1992 when he told me he was aware of cheat sheets floating around the Texoma District.

I had included Hall on my witness list I provided Merrill Lynch on September 8. However, I was not seriously considering calling him as a witness because my attorneys did not believe his testimony was really necessary. They felt my case was airtight in view of the extremely hostile work environment I was in when Thomas threatened to sue me and told me to leave his Enid office. Nevertheless, my attorneys wanted Hall on the witness list in the event they decided at the last minute to call him as a witness.

Day, thinking Hall would be a witness for me, called him to see what his testimony would be. Hall phoned me to tell me of Day's call. After a brief conversation about Merrill Lynch's interest in what he might have to say, I asked, "Well, did Merrill Lynch have anything else of interest to say?"

"Well, they had a whole lot to say," Hall replied. "I've spent a lot of time on the phone with their attorney and they feel that, of the points you've got, that the one they are going to spend the most time on is the one I'm involved in.

"Well, anyway," Hall continued, "I'm letting you know where I am if you need me."

"Oh, okay," I responded. "Let me ask what you mean by that. Are you suggesting you would like to testify and tell it the way it is?"

"Well," Hall said, "I think there is a lot of information that is not in there and I guess that basically is it, and I don't know how important…is your attorney working on a contingency?"

I answered yes and said, "When you say there's more information, do you mean there's more to the story than what you shared with me that one day?"

"Well," Hall said, "let's just put it this way, you didn't ask the right questions, Keith."

I told Hall I would talk to my attorneys and see if they wanted to make arrangements for him to travel from Austin, Texas, to Oklahoma City for my arbitration hearing. My mind was turning. If there was more to the insurance cheating than just cheat sheets and the Saturday morning meeting, I wanted to know what that was.

After talking to my attorneys, I called Hall back on September 15. Hall, no longer guarded in what he had to say, told me Gary Champion, another resident insurance specialist in Dallas, was the one spearheading the insurance cheating. "The abuse was rampant under his regime," Hall said. "His girls actually filled out booklets for the brokers and cheat sheets, if you want to call them that, were easily circulated around under his regime. But that's in Dallas. It never was in

Oklahoma. I even got crossways with a great big broker in the Dallas office because my girls and I would not fill out the booklets so they could have continuing education.

"What you need to do is get Gary's testimony, you need to get his girl's testimony, she was his right hand girl who really ran the office. Gary was a figurehead and the other girl was the gofer in the office, and the two girls were the ones who did all of this stuff and took care of it."

"How connected is this to the management level in Dallas?" I asked.

"I'm not sure the actual manager knew it was going on until I revealed it and told them I wasn't going to be coerced into doing that stuff because it would threaten everybody's license and I told Quinton that, as well," Hall replied. "Now upon revealing it and telling them what I was going to do and why, they verbally said they supported me and in fact, I think Quinton did support me because he showed for the motel thing, too." The motel thing Hall referred to was the Saturday morning meeting where he led eight Merrill Lynch FCs through the exam on a question-by-question basis.

"Well, but if Quinton were not, if Oklahoma management wasn't really involved in that aspect of it, why did you feel the need to visit with Quinton about it?" I asked.

"Protocol," Hall answered. "I reported to Quinton in that office. That is such a serious issue of potential compliance problems I didn't want any appearance that it was business as usual if you will, and I didn't even know it was, as usual, in the Oklahoma office because it had just happened in the Dallas office and I wasn't gonna have it so I was stopping it in all my offices."

"And who was the Dallas manager whose attention you brought this to?" I asked. Hall gave the name of the manager he had spoken to.

As our conversation was ending, I said, "Well, speaking of the other managers, what was interesting is a lot of them received credit for the *Estate Planning Training Course* all about the same time, in that same time-frame, and I suspect the girls were doing the same thing for some of these management people."

"Absolutely," Hall responded.

"Absolutely?"

"Absolutely," Hall said again.

"You have no doubt?"

"Guaran-damn-tee ya a manager's not gonna stop and fill out an estate planning thing when his focus is management," Hall said emphatically. "He could care less about that stuff." I had listed, in my 31-page letter to the directors, 14 members of management from the Texoma District who had received credit for the insurance exam. It looked like I was right in suggesting some had very possibly participated in the cheating.

I knew I wanted Hall to testify for me, even if his testimony was not needed to prove my wrongful termination case. Rather, Hall's testimony would show New York never even came close to finding the right answers, which I was still determined to find. Hall's testimony would be credible because he was far from beholden to me. In fact, I had implicated him in my letter to the board in connection with the Saturday morning session where he led the FCs through the exam. If anything, Hall would have had a personal incentive *not* to testify in a manner that would strengthen my case.

The Hearing Begins: Show Time

The *Keith A. Schooley v. Merrill Lynch, Pierce, Fenner & Smith* arbitration hearing was scheduled to begin on September 18, 1995, at the Medallion Hotel in downtown Oklahoma City. Both sides were reviewing and sorting through the voluminous information that had been exchanged in the discovery phase. Day had even commented to Schmidt several weeks earlier he had not personally worked this hard on a case in many years.

Both sides were sparing no effort in their preparation, and neither side was talking settlement. This was a conflict that would be fought to the bitter end. I was very much hands-on in my case. Schmidt called me a walking encyclopedia in regard to the factual situations of the matter. I had been preparing for a long time and was ready.

My attorneys and I were confident we had a compelling wrongful termination case, and in our minds the only question was how large the damages would be. In view of Merrill Lynch's behavior surrounding what I had reported, especially concerning how the firm had not appropriately dealt with the wrongdoing, I had one of the nation's leading authorities on punitive damages lined up to testify. I believed this was a case that begged for the defendant to be severely punished for its conduct.

It was show time. Everyone had their game faces on. This would be no ordinary securities arbitration case. The adrenaline was flowing, and the stakes were high. Merrill Lynch had to put to rest my allegation the firm's senior management had covered up widespread insurance cheating involving a multitude of FCs and members of management. Merrill Lynch had already gotten by the various regulatory authorities. My arbitration would be the last forum, and Merrill Lynch could not afford any costly mistakes. The firm knew, based on the last three years, that I, unlike the regulators, was a worthy adversary who would not be easily brushed aside.

I would soon learn part of Merrill Lynch's arbitration strategy would be consistent with how it had dealt with the regulators; that is, it would admit virtually all the alleged wrongdoing reported by me but put a spin on it so it would appear to be no worse than floating a stop sign. Most importantly, it would absolutely deny there was a widespread insurance cheating scandal. Merrill Lynch seemed to know all the other wrongdoing was manageable but the insurance cheating scandal, twice finessed by senior management, *had* to be shown to be nothing more than a malicious allegation contrived by me.

Another part of Merrill Lynch's strategy would be to ridicule my reporting of wrongdoing, notwithstanding the firm's own policy which not only encouraged the reporting of wrongdoing but required it. Merrill Lynch would paint me as a troublemaker.

As Gore, Schmidt, and I were walking down the corridor to the conference room at the Medallion, we approached Day and Rod Heggy, co-counsel with Day. They were standing outside the conference room visiting with parties who would be witnesses. All eyes were on me, the former rookie FC who had been at war with Merrill Lynch for three years. Day and Heggy would finally get up close and personal with Merrill Lynch's archenemy.

Knowing what Day looked like, I walked up to him and said, "Hi, Bruce. How are you? Keith Schooley."

As Day sized me up, he cordially responded and we shook hands. It appeared Day did not remember meeting with me about 10 years earlier.

I then walked over to Barton who was visiting with Heggy. Barton and I, even though we had many phone conversations in the last 14 months, had not seen each other since before my termination in 1992. We exchanged greetings and shook hands.

My attorneys and I went into the conference room to set up for the hearing. I was only a bit nervous. I mostly felt great confidence in my case and believed strongly in what I was doing. It was time to put all the preparation and hard work into action, and I was more than ready to begin.

In a few moments, Day entered the room, followed by Ellis. I had not seen Ellis either since before my termination in 1992. I broke the ice by extending my hand and saying, "Hello, Mr. Ellis, nice to see you."

Ellis, in the presence of everyone else, had no choice but to be a gentleman and accept my hand. He mustered up a cordial response. Two days later during a break and after much blood had been spilled, some of it Ellis' blood, Ellis and I would pass each other in the corridor with no one else present. Ellis' reaction would be much different than his cordial response at the beginning of day one.

The arbitration hearing began. Chairman Leslie Conner, Jr., an attorney and non-securities panel member, opened the hearing. He introduced himself and the other two arbitrators, George Barnes IV, a securities panel member, and John Preston, also an attorney and non-securities panel member.

Chairman Conner then asked all parties to identify themselves. After doing so, the arbitrators made certain disclosures for the record. Conner disclosed, among other things, that he, as president of the Oklahoma Bar Association in 1980, worked with Day when he was employed by the Association to incorporate the Oklahoma Bar and Professional Liability Insurance Company. The chairman also said he had attended seminars with members of Day's firm, both as participants and presenters. Conner could not recall any specific incident where he might have had contact with Gore's firm.

As the disclosures continued, I learned Preston served with Connor on American Arbitration Association arbitration panels, and Connor employed Preston as his attorney in the dissolution of his former law practice. Preston also disclosed, among other things, he had previously served on panels with Barnes.

Preston knew of the Mahaffey & Gore law firm, but did not know any of the attorneys. However, he did know Day. He also served as a mediator two years earlier in a matter at the request of one of Day's law partners.

Barnes disclosed, "I've been a New York Stock Exchange arbitrator for darn near 20 years now. I think it's fair to disclose that I have in the past worked for Merrill Lynch as an expert. I've appeared against Merrill Lynch as an expert. I have heard cases involving Merrill Lynch. I have seen Bruce Day what, once or twice a year somewhere."

I was already having concerns about my "day in arbitration," and binding arbitration at that. The three arbitrators, who were selected by the director of arbitration of the NYSE, were charged with deciding an extraordinarily sensitive matter that could reach not only the upper echelon of senior management but also the boardroom of Merrill Lynch.

Additionally, they were active arbitrators, especially Conner, and were paid a fee for their services. They were also very much aware of the peremptory challenge by each side in a securities arbitration case that could be wielded against them in the future.

What was of even greater concern to me was the fact the arbitrators, particularly Conner and Preston, had relationships with attorneys at Day's firm yet they had no relationships with attorneys at Mahaffey & Gore. In theory I knew that presented no problem but in reality, I was not so sure. I knew the arbitrators would never see me again but professionally speaking, they would likely be hopeful of continued interaction, in one way or another, with Day's firm—one of the most, if not *the* most, prominent securities law firms in Oklahoma. Surely they were also hopeful of seeing Merrill Lynch again either as arbitrators or as in the case of Barnes, as an expert witness.

I had my concerns not only because of what I perceived to be an inherent conflict of interest in securities arbitration as a result of the automatic peremptory challenge, but also because maybe the good-old-boy network was alive and well. Nevertheless, I was cautiously optimistic because I knew I had a strong case and I had expert witnesses that were exceptionally qualified to give powerful testimony. I could only hope when it was all said and done, that my concerns about the arbitration process, and in particular the makeup of my own arbitration panel, would prove to be unwarranted.

After Chairman Conner and the attorneys discussed a few procedural matters, it was time for opening statements.

Opening Statements: Bruce Day Does a Number

Gore presented his opening statement without affectation. He said I joined Merrill Lynch partially because of the high ethical standards it espoused. He told the panel I excelled in my training and performance with Merrill Lynch, and I was certainly not a disgruntled employee but rather extremely successful in everything I did with the firm.

Gore explained I was continuously confronted with what I perceived to be violations of those ethics. He mentioned the specific incidents of wrongdoing we planned to make clear. Gore also outlined how I had tried to use Merrill Lynch's internal system to properly report what I had witnessed. However, when that was not successful, after I learned the confidentiality of the hotline was breached, I decided to write the memo and then the letter to the board.

Gore told the panel that as a result of the letter to the board and second investigation, some action was taken, despite having primarily the same allegations to work with as were outlined in my memo.

Gore relayed how I had been confronted by Merrill Lynch investigators who indicated to me they did not like whistle-blowers. Instead of treating me as someone who had done exactly what he was trained to do by the firm's manual, I received the opposite reaction of hostility from every level.

The panel heard how Thomas had called me a cancer that had to be removed and threatened to sue me if I did not retract what I had reported.

Gore explained the opposing views of my termination situation, how Merrill Lynch had conceded and said it wanted me to come back to work, but the hostile environment would not be one in which anyone could realistically work. He explained how Merrill Lynch had erroneously put "job abandonment" on my U-5 form and as a result, more or less blacklisted me in the securities industry.

Gore demonstrated what I had gone through by saying, "Mr. Schooley, subsequent to that time, of course, has lost his employment, has had difficulty being employed as a result of his loss of that employment. He's gone through a divorce, more or less lost his family. He's suffered considerable and emotional distress. Of course, he feels he's been severely mistreated."

Gore went on to say, "I know Merrill Lynch considers Mr. Schooley some sort of extremist or fanatic, or something of that nature, because he reported these things and other FCs did not. But frankly, what you'll find is Mr. Schooley is just a very honest and very meticulous person who has certain principles and conditions that he lives by and refuses to live any other way and has the intestinal fortitude to proceed with that, even though it's cost him his livelihood, his family. Frankly, he's a very unusual person.

"He's paid a very, very high price for reporting these things, for being a whistle-blower, and that's why we're here, to attempt to make him whole with regard to his losses."

With that, it was now Day's turn to present Merrill Lynch's opening statement. Based on my limited but unhappy experiences with him to date, I suspected Day would have difficulty with the truth. I would not be surprised.

Day, in a pretentious manner not lacking for drama, said, "We're here today to conclude a three-year obsession by Keith Schooley with his 11 months as a stockbroker trainee with Merrill Lynch three years ago."

Day told the panel my complaints had been reviewed twice already by Merrill Lynch and "actively investigated" by the SEC, NYSE, NASD, the Oklahoma Department of Securities, Texas Securities Department, Alabama Securities Department, and Arizona Securities Department. He said as a result of these inquiries, no action was ever taken, that the arbitration was the last forum.

Day went on to claim I could not, in good faith, say I was actually or constructively terminated. Day said my complaints had been reviewed once, remedies taken. Then I filed a 31-page letter with the board making absolutely outrageous, baseless statements regarding a national 50-state conspiracy to violate state insurance laws, naming my manager among 50 others.

I was already amazed. Day's ability to butcher the truth was incredible. In less than two minutes Day, as an officer of the court, had represented that no regulatory action was taken when in fact the NASD had issued two letters of caution. He claimed I reported a 50-state insurance cheating conspiracy when in fact the allegation was the scandal occurred in the Texoma District, which covered only Oklahoma and most of Texas. Day had also represented I named my manager among 50 others in the insurance cheating scandal when in fact I named less than half that number.

Day continued, accusing me of trying to entrap Deline when I called him three days after I was fired and apparently in that conversation, I admitted I did not think I was terminated. This was another outright lie. They just kept on coming.

Day said when I showed up at the office the day after my termination, this implied it was a normal day and everything was functioning as usual. He talked about what evidence would be required to establish my being fired was a constructive termination of a whistle-blower. Day said the whistle had to be blown about constitutional, statutory, or regulatory violations that rise to the level of public concern. He claimed only one of my allegations could even potentially be a public policy concern and the employer's actions must be retaliating in a manner compelling a reasonable employee to resign.

Day then said, "And last, that employee has to be acting in good faith. That is, he cannot be acting out of spite, he cannot be acting out of malice, and he cannot be acting out of personal gain. All three of those elements cannot be satisfied here. None of them can be satisfied."

Day could not have been more wrong. I was not doing this for personal gain. I truly felt an obligation to other Merrill Lynch FCs I had seen treated unfairly, others that were likely being treated similarly in the firm, and to the millions of Merrill Lynch clients entrusting their money to an outfit that claimed to be ethical and have the utmost integrity.

Day then went into a brief explanation of each complaint. He prefaced this by saying the evidence included three years of documents and 111 taped conversations. Day said none of the parties knew I was recording the conversations and accused me of trying to entrap them. It was true that I did not let people know I was taping what they were saying; however, at no time did I "entrap" anyone or put words in their mouths. What I cared about was documenting the truth.

Day made light of the Tour de France CMA contest cheating saying just because there were no customer complaints, no one was abused. Day talked about the misuse of the country club list and said, "Now, the question before you: Does the country club care? Are they mad? Are they complaining? No." Apparently Day forgot that the whole reason I found out about this incident was because I had witnessed Barton telling Ellis and Sherman about the phone conversation Barton had with the country club manager when he called *to complain* about the list possibly being mass mailed.

Day spoke about the falsification of seminar expenses, claiming there was no tax fraud or embezzlement; therefore, it could not be a public policy issue. He also said the unfulfilled promises of assets were not of public concern, nor was the misrepresentation of the MuniYield fund since when the six clients who bought that product were offered rescission, no one accepted.

I was amused when Day said, "Brent Barton legitimately, honestly, because nobody really disputes this—any of this—there's no dispute. He believed this little mutual fund was pre-refunded." Barton, himself, had recently denied to the NASD that he sold MuniYield as pre-refunded, but was insisting he sold it as having call protection. Day was also wrong about Barton selling the fund to only six people; in fact, Barton had sold the fund to considerably more people.

Day was already showing cavalier carelessness with the facts and truth. Although, what did he care? This was binding arbitration. Besides, what he wanted to say would play better. I would soon realize there was a method to Day's inaccuracies. Of course, virtually every inaccuracy and misrepresentation was to Merrill Lynch's benefit; that was his job.

Day continued, saying there was no compliance issue regarding the out-of-state accounts because no transactions occurred, that the assets were taken but no security was bought or sold. Day was wrong again. Transactions did occur in the out-of-state accounts prior to proper registration.

To address the insurance cheating scandal, Day stepped up the theatrics. He implied the only evidence I had that the cheat sheet existed was my word. I thought Day must not care that Hall, who Day had interviewed just days before, would provide some powerful testimony as a former Merrill Lynch resident insurance specialist *insider,* not only concerning cheat sheets but also other ways in which cheating occurred.

Day told the panel I was a stockbroker for Merrill Lynch for 200 days; actually, it was 330 days. This was an irrelevant fact; however, it showed how Day was careless with the truth, both big and small.

Day tried to smear my character to make it appear I was going through this proceeding for nothing but my own personal gain.

"The first month he's in a dispute with his manager over…he wants a mass mailing," Day said. "He's 40 years old, it's his first time in the business. He's been in the oil and gas business all his life, by the way, not very successfully. It's not in the budget. He comes in and makes a mailing at night and he gets in a dispute with his manager."

Day either did not know, so he should not have made an assumption in a legal proceeding, or simply did not care that I had been a millionaire in the oil business at age 27, and later managed an oil and gas company owned by one of the most prominent businessmen in Oklahoma. Furthermore, Day misled the panel concerning the mass mailing. Barton had approved my personalized introductory postcard mailer, which he knew would be going out to a lot of people. Barton also informed me he had struck a special deal with Ellis, which would allow the Enid FCs to do the mailings at no expense to themselves.

Day kept on rolling. He told the panel that for the last three years, all I had been doing was working on my case. He continued to be reckless with the truth by ignoring the fact I had been actively involved in the oil and gas business putting deals together and drilling wells.

To finish things off, Day said, "Let this be the end of this matter, that we be compensated for our legal fees and our costs for being put through this proceeding one more time."

I could not understand how anyone could stand before an NYSE arbitration panel and proceed to tell one lie after another for almost 15 minutes. The only consolation I had was I knew the evidence I would present was the truth and surely the truth mattered.

Keith Schooley: The Earth Will Shake

It was time for Gore to call his first witness—me. Chairman Conner reminded me I was still under oath, as I had been sworn in prior to the opening statements.

I gave a brief overview of my educational and professional background prior to my employment with Merrill Lynch. I explained that in about 1990, after being through some difficult times in the oil business, my wife's mother told me she heard Merrill Lynch would be opening a new office in Enid. At that point I started considering the opportunity with Merrill Lynch since my family desperately needed some financial stability.

I told the arbitration panel I could see the Merrill Lynch opportunity was a good and unique one, especially because of the prominence my in-laws had in the Enid area. I said it was a good opportunity with a highly recognized firm that was known to be the best on Wall Street and to operate with high ethics and integrity. I thought this would allow me to turn the corner financially and have a successful career.

I then mentioned Merrill Lynch's *Guidelines for Business Conduct*, which each FC had to read and acknowledge in writing he had done so. I quoted from the document what it said about requiring every employee to make a personal commitment to the observation of the highest ethical standards and that employees should be diligent in questioning situations they believe violate such standards.

I then testified as to the effort I was putting forth with Merrill Lynch so I could have a successful career—including my score of 93 on the

Series 7 exam and my top 10 performance in production among my rookie peers in the Western Sales Division.

"At what point in time did you begin to notice or get involved in anything that you felt was not in line with the high ethical standards of Merrill Lynch?" Gore asked me.

"Well, I would say the first thing would be in November 1991 when I had to pass some continuing life insurance education to maintain a life insurance license," I answered. "I had to contact some people with Merrill Lynch Life in Dallas to find out what the procedure was and what I had to study and what test I had to take so as to achieve that. So I was in communication with a Sarah Graham with Merrill Lynch Life in Dallas. And in talking to her, she said, 'Well, let me send you a cheat sheet so you can pass that. What we have been doing is using cheat sheets so the FC can get the test behind him and study the materials at his convenience.' I know the context of what was said, how it was said, and that alarmed me that the cheat sheet was on its way, because she said that's how they do it."

I then discussed a number of incidents I had with Barton, but things soon returned to the subject of cheat sheets. "Could you identify exhibit 11 for us?" Gore asked me.

"Exhibit 11 is the cheat sheet that we just earlier discussed, or what was represented to be a cheat sheet by Sarah Graham," I replied.

"So you talked to her on the phone, correct?" Gore asked.

"Yes."

"And that's when she labeled this document, a cheat sheet; is that correct?"

"She orally labeled it a cheat sheet."

"Those are her words, not yours?"

"Right."

"And what is the second page?"

"The second page is her handwritten note saying, 'Keith, per our conversation Friday, 11–15. Thanks, Sarah Graham.'"

"And then what is the third page?"

"What she represented to be a cheat sheet."

"And what did that turn out to be?"

"It turned out to be an answer key to a practice exam." I had not learned this until months after receiving what Graham had called a cheat sheet.

"Did they send you the practice exam?"

"No, I never received a practice exam during the testing phase."

"Did this key ever relate to anything you were provided?"

"No, it did not."

Even though the cheat sheet I received from Graham went with a practice exam rather than the real exam, I had always believed FCs in the Texoma District had been using real cheat sheets for the real exam simply based on how Graham had phrased her words. I understood that my conversation with Graham had been about the real exam for the *Estate Planning Training Course,* and *that* was the exam to which she had been referring. I suspected that before Graham mailed a real cheat sheet, she spoke to her superior at the time, Hall, letting him know what she was about to do, which was what she had likely been doing for her previous boss, Champion. However, because Hall had just recently informed his superiors of wrongdoing involved in the insurance testing, he told Graham she was absolutely not to send a real cheat sheet to me.

I then discussed the time Barton had bragged to Ellis and Sherman in my office about using the country club list for mass mailings even when he did not have permission to do so, and how Ellis told Barton that was great and to keep on doing it. I went on to tell the panel of the time Ellis put his face in mine and said, "Don't worry about product knowledge. Just sell."

I discussed what Barton had characterized as an argument about MuniYield and how he had been selling it. I also shared how I had been informed that Barton was falsifying a number of seminar expense statements.

"As you see the pattern here," I then said, "I've been led to believe I've got a cheat sheet in my possession, Barton brags to Quinton Ellis and Bob Sherman about using a country club list, and Quinton has told me, 'Don't worry about product knowledge. Just sell.' Then we had the MuniYield deal and now, all of a sudden, I'm in my fifth week of production and I see seminar expenses being falsified."

Next, I told the arbitrators about the unfulfilled promise Ellis made to deliver $20 million in assets to the Enid FCs and distribute them based on how each FC did in the Tour de France CMA contest.

"What occurred on or around December 16, 1991?" Gore asked me.

"I went to Barton and I said, 'Brent, the insurance exam is certainly a lot more difficult than I thought it would be,' which was true. And I said I had to study pretty hard for that. And then he starts laughing. And he goes, 'Well, what I did with five or six other FCs is we got together on a Saturday morning and we had Bill Hall, who's the resident insurance specialist out of Dallas, Texas, walk us through that 25-hour continuing education exam. He walked us through.' And Brent also told me that was all with Mr. Ellis' approval.

"And the way Brent told that to me, I could tell he knew it was wrong. And he said, 'Well, we don't really sell life insurance, we simply need our life insurance license to get commissions.'"

I then explained exhibit 15 was the course book one had to study for taking the *Estate Planning Training Course* exam. It was 201 pages and contained extensive information on estate planning. Included in the exhibit was the affidavit of personal responsibility an exam taker had to sign that stated he or she had read the entire text of the course and had taken the exam without any outside assistance.

I went on to discuss my concern about management's cheating in the Tour de France CMA contest. I explained Ellis manipulated the headcount of the Enid office so he would look better in the contest. I discussed the effects of Ellis' cheating—how I could not properly service my clients.

I told the panel of my efforts to become a successful FC by bringing 70 out of 95 attendees to a professional money management seminar hosted by the Enid office at the Oakwood Country Club, which was a better turnout than all the FCs in the Oklahoma City office had for the same program that evening in Oklahoma City.

Next, I talked about my January 20, 1992, letter to Barton where I requested a certain pay arrangement for the near future. I said I knew Barton would have to talk to Ellis about the request and on the next to the last page of that letter, I had circled the reference I made to the cheat sheet I received from Merrill Lynch Life in Dallas. Neither Barton, Ellis, nor Thomas, who was then soon to succeed Barton as resident manager of the Enid office, came to me and asked me what I was talking about.

I then told the panel that on January 29, 1992, two days after Thomas became the Enid resident manager, Thomas forced me to sign an agreement that stated if I again rebated a commission to a client I would be immediately terminated. I explained the computer error that resulted in my refunding $15 to a client and that I had reviewed the NYSE, NASD, and SEC rules, as well as Merrill Lynch's policy manual, and could not see where I had violated any rule or policy.

"I would suggest...let me tie this in," I said. "Remember, the Tour de France contest started January 1, 1992, and I'm not helping management cheat in the contest, because on all my new accounts, I'm signing my name. They wanted me to leave my name off so they could put some other broker's name in there. Consequently, when I would sign my name to the new account form, they would have to squiggle over my name and then put someone else's name on top.

"So I had been opening a number of accounts in my name. They've had to do that to it, deface it, replace it. And I would suggest this rebate agreement was expressly for the purpose of trying to put Keith Schooley in line because he wasn't on the team of the Oklahoma City Complex helping them cheat in this contest.

"I was also aware that just days earlier I had, in writing, informed management of my receiving what I believed to be a cheat sheet. Oklahoma City management knew this rookie FC in Enid had to be whipped into shape, even if it required the threat of termination concerning a $15 refund which it would choose to, instead, call a rebate which was tantamount to kickback."

Next, I talked about the out-of-state accounts that had been improperly opened in Thomas' name and production number, and that Thomas told me it was okay to do that.

"And what then occurred on March 5, 1992?" Gore asked me.

"March 5, 1992, was my first hotline call to New York," I replied.

"And what was the nature of that call?"

"To report the contest cheating by Mr. Ellis and Mr. Barton."

"And why did you do that?"

"Because I felt like it was an abuse of me, of clients. It was an un-ethical violation on Mr. Ellis' part, to the best of my knowledge, and I felt like there was something that should be done."

I explained when I called the confidential hotline I would talk to Patrick Murphy, whom I believed held the position of director of world-wide security. I called the hotline a number of times in order to help Merrill Lynch figure out the contest cheating.

I said to the panel, "On March 11, 1992, when I made a hotline call to Mr. Murphy, we were trying to figure out the approach so he could catch Mr. Ellis cheating without jeopardizing who the caller was. In the course of discussing how to go about doing that to my satisfaction, he had some idea and it left me just a little bit uncomfortable because I told Mr. Murphy I didn't like that idea because I felt like Mr. Ellis could possibly determine who the hotline caller was.

"And I said because in the past, there have been a few things that have occurred that would suggest to Mr. Ellis, maybe I would rock the boat or tend to rock the boat. I said, for example, I disagreed with the use of cheat sheets. And what I'm trying to say here is I had told Mr. Murphy on the hotline, I made a reference to cheat sheets and Mr. Murphy certainly never contacted me concerning any follow up on cheat sheets."

At this point we adjourned for lunch for approximately an hour, then I went right back into my testimony. I discussed two other inci-dents that concerned Barton in March 1992, situations where the CPA of a client of Barton's and the wife of a client of Barton's asked me to help them with their situation. I obliged, and Barton hit the roof.

I briefly talked of an issue that involved how Thomas had solicited sales of Singapore Air stock, and then Gore asked me what occurred on April 9. I described how I had learned the hotline confidentiality had been violated when Thomas confronted both Deline and me about some-one complaining of being a mistreated trainee.

"But anyway," I continued, "the point to be made is, I had certainly not authorized Patrick Murphy to pass on what I was reporting confidentially, and sure enough Jack Thomas walked in and confronted me about it."

Gore continued inquiring about the violation of the hotline confidentiality. "And then did you make some other hotline calls that day?"

"Yeah," I replied. "I quickly called Patrick Murphy and had two separate hotline calls with him that same day discussing what happened, pursuant to Jack Thomas sticking his head in my office. Eventually Mr. Murphy told me he had shared the whole story with Bob Dineen, who was the national sales manager for the Western Sales Division and Bob Dineen had shared part of the story with Bob Sherman in Dallas and Bob Sherman spoke to Quinton Ellis about it, and then Quinton Ellis spoke to Jack Thomas."

I then explained how on the next day, Barton's administrative assistant in the Oklahoma City office called me and jumped all over me for a fax I had sent two days earlier. She obnoxiously reprimanded me for a lack of professionalism and improper behavior. She was upset over a note I had sent Barton requesting he send me his holding pages for a couple of his clients who wanted to keep their accounts in Enid, since he was now in Oklahoma City. After I talked to people in the Enid office and determined my request for the holding pages was appropriate, I sent her a fax saying my request was proper, so please send the holding pages. I also wrote telling her I would appreciate it if she and Barton would at least be accurate before making contentions.

I told the panel being confronted by Thomas the day before because of the hotline confidentiality violation, and now, indirectly, confronted by Barton over the holding pages request, I felt vulnerable. I was a superstar rookie FC who was doing everything by the book, but yet was getting reamed, much to the delight, I suspect, of the Oklahoma City Complex management. I did not believe in cheat sheets or cheating in contests, and I was calling the hotline. I was a troublemaker.

"And what occurred on June 16?" Gore asked.

I replied by telling the panel about how I had discovered Merrill Lynch's registration department had asked Ellis to look into my employment background.

"And when I saw that, I believed there might be a connection between my hotline calls and some further investigation into my background," I explained. "And my thought was perhaps if they could find some flaw in my employment application, some misrepresentation, whether it be intentional or unintentional, that they might be looking for a cause to terminate me. I didn't know, but I saw the wire and that concerned me."

Next, I discussed the event that triggered my June 29 memorandum. I described Thomas confronting me about opening an account and how I explained to him what had happened. I said Thomas did not accept my explanation and wanted to call the client to confirm my story, which we did and so it was confirmed. I described my reaction to the panel.

"And that just kind of rubbed me the wrong way. I just felt like he was totally not believing what I had honestly told him. So, you know, I'm just beginning to see there's not a whole lot I can do without just getting jumped on. I kept getting jumped on for one thing after another."

"Did you come to any conclusions after the June 18 incident with Mr. Thomas?" Gore asked.

"Yeah," I said. "At that point, I just felt like I was to the point where I needed to do something that resulted in some explanations. I've been saying, and we've been through them this morning, there've been a lot of things we've discussed. But I've seen time and again, these things that have happened, that appeared to me to be not right.

"And I'm hearing other things coming out of management's mouths, such as on my $15 rebate agreement, 'Well, that's really serious. If that ever happens again, you're going to be immediately terminated.'

"I know now Joe Bazzelle, who we haven't discussed this morning, he was fired for something where he was trying to help clients in this Pru-Bache VMS debacle where a lot of investors were taken advantage of and Joe got terminated just that fast for doing something that was really trying to help somebody.

"And I think we're about to talk about a situation where Barry Clark, this other Enid FC, had been made promises by Mr. Ellis, and those promises were not being fulfilled. And I'm just seeing a real double standard. I'm seeing people getting fired for almost no reason at all or threatened with termination. I'm seeing promises made and not kept.

"That's what prompted me to write my June 29, 1992, memorandum to Jack Thomas, which is kind of what kicked off—this is where Merrill Lynch alleges—'Schooley declared war.'"

My testimony continued. Among other things, I described certain exhibits and discussed the TGIF contest, how Meditz and Cordell had tried to persuade me the cheat sheet was not what it appeared to be, and how Ellis had acted disparagingly toward me in a sales meeting he called after I submitted my memo.

Gore's next question was, "What then occurred on July 28?"

"On July 28 of 1992, Quinton Ellis sent a memorandum to all the FCs at the Oklahoma City, Lawton, and Enid offices, and in that memo he appoints Brent Barton as the Oklahoma City Complex sales manager.

"And the significance of that is, here I am someone who has, in complying with company policy to report wrongdoing or the appearance of wrongdoing, I did that, and Helmuth Meditz had just been out to commence an internal investigation. One of the two primary people who would be targets of the investigation was Brent Barton. And the investigation's ongoing, it's not completed yet, but this memo is sent out.

"And when I see this memo, I say, 'Wow!' It blew my mind someone under an internal investigation had been promoted to the Oklahoma City Complex sales manager's position. I had reason to believe cover-ups were underway anyway. This even confirmed in my mind, they had no more intent in New York in coming up with the right answers, as evidenced by someone under investigation being promoted."

I testified how I had met with Meditz and Roepke at the Waterford Hotel in Oklahoma City and quickly learned the reason for the meeting was for them to inform me the investigation was concluded.

"And I just felt like I was twisting in the wind, because I had done that which was expected of me. But yet, New York didn't want the right answers, because, I guess being naïve at the time, I now see New York has one primary objective, and that's to do what's best for Merrill Lynch. And if what's best for Merrill Lynch means sweeping problems under the rug, so be it, and if that leaves me twisting in the wind, so be it."

I told the panel that after that unsatisfactory meeting, I felt tremendously disappointed and vulnerable, and that is when I came up with the idea to appeal to Merrill Lynch's board of directors.

"Now, at that point you've been working there for a year, about 13 months?" Gore asked. I replied that I had.

"Wait a moment," Day suddenly interjected. "You'd been a broker for how long at that point?"

"I started employment on July 1, 1991," I answered.

"You'd been a broker how long? Certainly, you're not misleading the panel?"

"I assume you'll have your chance at cross," Gore said. "Have you got a problem with—"

Chairman Conner interrupted, asking Day, "What is the purpose of your question?"

"Well, I think he was misstating himself."

Gore retorted to Day, "I said, 'How long have you been employed, about 13 months?' and you're asking a different question."

Gore turned to me and said, "Have you been with Merrill Lynch at this point since July 1, 1991?" I answered yes.

I knew by now this was just vintage Day theatrics, yet it galled me to hear him suggest *I* was misleading the panel.

We continued discussing my decision to write to the board. "Did you know it might ruin your career?" Gore asked.

"Yeah, I was aware of that," I replied. "I was aware that was a risk, yes."

I then discussed a multitude of things that had occurred, or not occurred, which supported my belief Merrill Lynch was covering up the wrongdoing I had reported.

With that, day one of *Keith A. Schooley v. Merrill Lynch, Pierce, Fenner & Smith* came to a close. Chairman Conner told the parties the hearing would reconvene at 9:00 the next morning.

The following day, Gore resumed his direct examination.

Gore reminded me I had concluded my testimony the day before speaking about why I believed senior management covered up. We spoke briefly of my letter to the board including why I wrote it and when it was sent. We also touched on the letter I sent to Ellis after he called me to say he had an open-door policy.

Next we discussed the issue of Paul, the man that visited Enid from Princeton the same day my letter to the board arrived in New York. I told the panel about Feightner telling my wife at the time I would not like what was being said in the meeting involving Paul. I explained I never got more information about exactly what Feightner thought I would not like, but my hope was her testimony would reveal what she had heard. Unfortunately, that was not to be. Feightner did not honor her subpoena to appear at my hearing.

I then discussed the comment my ex-wife had heard from Brainard, which was Barton saying I was the world's biggest liar and had a twisted mind. I added to that the remark Clark had told me Thomas had made about me being a cancer and he was not going to have me in the office infecting Deline and Stong, the other two Enid FCs.

There was absolutely no doubt that because of my letter to the board of directors, my superiors in the Oklahoma City Complex were livid, as evidenced by Barton's and Thomas' comments about me. Undoubtedly, the angriest of all was Ellis, whose behavior was highlighted in my hard-hitting letter.

We then got to the heart of the matter. I began to give the details of the incident when Thomas read his prepared statement to me, accused me of being a liar, threatened to sue me, and told me to leave his office.

"And how many people did you have in the Enid office at that time?" Gore asked me.

"I believe four: Jack Thomas, Michael Deline, Greg Stong, Kim Feightner, and me," I answered. "Is that five? Four or five."

"Do you have any idea what the size of the office is?" Gore continued.

"In square feet?"

"Yes, sir."

"Oh, golly, not really. A thousand plus or minus. Twelve hundred, maybe."

"Would you characterize it as small, large, medium-sized?"

"It's pretty small."

"Could you work in an office where the boss was threatening to sue you?"

"Personally, I would have a difficult time doing that. I would say no."

Gore then asked me what I did in reaction to Thomas' statement.

"Well, to be frank, at first, I didn't know precisely what he meant. He didn't come right out and say, 'You are hereby terminated,' so there was certainly some ambiguity to it. But I was also aware just a few days earlier he had told Barry Clark I was a cancer and he was not going to have me in the office infecting Michael and Greg.

"And I also knew Brent Barton was running around and at a minimum, telling Lisa Brainard I was the world's biggest liar and had a twisted mind. And I knew Kim Feightner had told my ex-wife this guy from Princeton had a meeting with Quinton Ellis and Jack Thomas. And evidently, whatever she overheard made her tell my ex-wife that Keith was not going to like what was being said. So as I tried to put everything into context, I felt like Jack was very possibly trying to fire me at this point in time."

I then explained the next day I went back to the office to collect certain documents in anticipation that Thomas would sue me since I knew I would not make a retraction by the 24-hour deadline or anytime thereafter. I also knew I might be filing my own lawsuit for wrongful termination and wanted to gather documents that might help me.

Gore proceeded to ask me if Thomas' prepared statement was on Merrill Lynch stationery. When I replied it was, Gore asked, "And is it correct Merrill Lynch stationery is not supposed to be used for personal reasons?"

"That's correct," I replied.

"Is that a rule or what is it?"

"I believe it's in the supervisor's manual."

"And there's a rule to that effect?"

"A very specific rule."

"So your interpretation of this was it was an additional act on the part of Merrill Lynch being on Merrill Lynch stationery?"

"I felt it was. It was a formal meeting. He called me in and he had Michael Deline come in and serve as a witness, and he explicitly states,

'It's for the record.' He underscores that. Yes, I felt like it was a direct action by my manager concerning my employment."

"And I believe he indicated here you are to get out of the office, maybe his office, maybe the whole office, something to that effect?"

"Right. I understand there's ambiguity concerning that. Merrill Lynch argues it's his personal office. I can't say for a fact. I do know it is his office, and he's evaluated on the Enid office, just as Quinton Ellis is evaluated on the Oklahoma City Complex, as other managers are evaluated based on their own personal office. So as I tried to make sense out of what just happened, when he tells me to leave his office—I mean, his office, to me, is the Enid office."

I then told the panel my attorney at the time, Jones, called Thomas to inform him I had nothing to retract and within two days, Jones and Mandel would be discussing the situation by phone and fax. Mandel insisted I had not been terminated and wanted me back in the office. Jones insisted I had, in fact, been terminated and would be pursuing my legal remedies. Consequently, Merrill Lynch, in its view, terminated me for job abandonment.

"And have you looked at job abandonment in any of your manuals?" Gore asked.

"Yes, I have," I replied.

"And what gives rise to job abandonment?"

"Merrill Lynch's policy definition of job abandonment is something to the effect of three consecutive days of absence without notification, i.e., it appears to me to be intended to be, if you just simply quit showing up, and they have no knowledge as to where you are or what the circumstances are, then that's abandoning your job. And it's in the section characterized as serious misconduct."

"Okay," Gore said. "Have you ever been notified of what serious misconduct you may have done?"

"Well," I replied, "I think the serious misconduct is the fact you just quit showing up for work. I mean, it implies you're derelict, you just—just quit showing up."

"And were there three consecutive days after September 29 when Merrill Lynch did not have notice of the situation?"

"No. At the latest, Stephen Jones was in contact with Barry Mandel on October 1."

I then discussed how Ellis had told his Oklahoma City FCs I just quit showing up. He did not explain any of the surrounding circumstances, which I felt put me in a negative light.

We returned once again to the subject of the insurance cheating scandal. I shared my phone conversation with Hall after my termination in which he told me cheat sheets for the insurance exam were floating around the different offices.

Concerning my conversation with Hall, Gore asked, "And that's the conversation you recorded?"

I confirmed that was true. Gore then asked if I had recorded any conversations prior to being terminated from Merrill Lynch. I replied I never had but began when I did, based on Jones' advice.

Gore and I then went through the efforts I had made, with Jones' help, to appeal to the various regulators and prove to them the representation of job abandonment on my U-5 form was inaccurate.

We briefly discussed my unsuccessful job search. We moved on to how Barton was fired, Ellis removed as RVP, and Roepke retired.

"Is there a connection between Brent Barton, Quinton Ellis, and Leo Roepke?" Gore asked.

"Yes," I replied. "Brent Barton reported to Quinton Ellis, and Quinton Ellis reported to Leo Roepke. And it's my belief that with the NASD investigation winding down around June of 1994, these three terminations or these three personnel moves, happened in quick succession so as to appease the regulators so they would take lighter regulatory action against Merrill Lynch."

I explained how the personnel actions by Merrill Lynch against both Barton and Ellis seemed suspicious as the reasons for them did not seem serious enough to warrant such consequences.

I shared with the arbitrators the insights I had received from my conversation with Dicus, the NASD investigator. This included that his investigation into this matter had opened his eyes regarding how large wirehouses really work and he was no longer sure his assumption that these securities firms were pretty good at policing themselves was correct.

I touched on Jones withdrawing as my attorney and my divorce before getting into the insights I gained from my numerous phone conversations with Barton.

I testified Barton had told me Ellis said he was fired because of Enid and Barton felt Merrill Lynch had built a wall around Sherman. I also said Barton had told me Ellis coached him into not saying anything that would implicate other parties.

I told the panel that, according to Barton, Sherman had instructed him to manage headcount in the Tour de France CMA contest and Ellis had promised assets to both Clark and Bazzelle but never delivered them.

I shared that the NASD never interviewed Ellis nor Barton and Barton had told me New York had told him hopefully the Enid situation would blow over. He was told to take a little heat, be a good soldier, and it would be remembered, but he ended up being the scapegoat instead.

I talked about the letter Barton wrote to the NASD in an attempt to get his letter of caution rescinded in which he said, "Merrill Lynch has intended to control and distort the facts because of expected litigation from Keith Schooley."

I continued, "Then on September 8, 1994, I had another conversation with Brent Barton. He said Merrill Lynch set him up and used him as bait, shark bait, and waited for the opportune time, when everything fell into place, and then took him out. Barton said Barry Mandel and Leo Roepke said the heat he was taking was pursuant to Keith Schooley's anticipated lawsuit."

I told the arbitrators Barton had been suspicious when Ellis and Roepke took him to a hotel room to demote him as the Oklahoma City Complex sales manager. According to Barton, Ellis also had told him the real reason he was fired was because of the situation in Enid and when that situation would not go away, it made everyone nervous.

Next, Gore and I went through Mandel's April 16, 1993, letter to the SEC and all its inaccuracies. This included his mischaracterization of the Saturday morning meeting where Hall took FCs through the insurance exam and the misrepresentation of when Merrill Lynch ceased to use Pictorial as the exam provider. I also presented my evidence that Mandel was wrong when he denied the improper use of the country club list; Barton lied to the country club manager; Sherman and Ellis told Barton how to falsify seminar expenses; and more.

I then briefly told the arbitrators about the letters of admonishment Ellis and Barton received from Tom Muller III, the senior vice president of the Western Sales Division of Merrill Lynch, and the letters of caution Merrill Lynch and Barton received from the NASD.

Next, I discussed the letter Mihaly wrote to the Oklahoma Department of Insurance. In this document, Mihaly, like Mandel, represented it was not clear the Saturday morning meeting was inappropriate and no evidence had been found supporting my allegation of cheat sheets, notwithstanding the transcript he had seen of my conversation with Hall that showed otherwise. I told the panel Mihaly accused me of putting words in Hall's mouth during that conversation but I believed when they saw the transcript they would see that was not true.

I then testified about my efforts to earn income after my termination from Merrill Lynch so the panel could see I had attempted to mitigate the damages I now was claiming Merrill Lynch owed me. I described the numerous oil and gas ventures I was involved in, my effort to work for other securities firms in Oklahoma City, as well as other efforts I had made.

I also discussed the difficult child custody fight I had been in with my then soon-to-be ex-wife in the last half of 1994. She wanted sole custody and I wanted joint custody. I explained both of us had retained a psychologist, and consequently, we attended numerous meetings with the psychologists as well as with our own attorneys. Thankfully, the matter was settled in December 1994, resulting in joint custody.

I then told the panel how I felt I had been damaged by Merrill Lynch as a result of my wrongful termination. I discussed my track record as a rookie FC for the firm. Based on Merrill Lynch's own production numbers for top 10 producers—which I was as a rookie—I calculated what I likely would have been earning had I been able to continue my employment with the firm. As a top 10 producer over the three years since my termination, which led up to the time of my arbitration hearing and over the next five years, I would have had a pay package averaging at least $240,000 a year.

"In reporting the wrongdoing you saw, did you do this out of revenge or was there any animosity or anything like that involved?" Gore asked me.

"No, I did not," I replied. "I know that's been alleged. I would say, emotionally, I had feelings of frustration or disappointment. I had come to Enid, Oklahoma, with the expectation and hope there would be an environment conducive of doing honorable business. I found that not to be the case.

"So when I wrote my memorandum to Jack Thomas on June 29, 1992, I was seeking some clarification. Because I'm having a difficult time understanding how the activities by Enid and Oklahoma City management that I've observed could be justified in light of how people were getting fired for other reasons, which seemed to me to be pretty minor. And I just simply wanted some clarification from Jack Thomas and that's when it hit the fan."

"Did you consult with Stephen Jones early on before you used the hotline?" Gore asked.

I responded that I did. "I consulted with Stephen Jones, I believe it was on November 30, 1991. I know Merrill Lynch would like for you to believe my memorandum to Jack Thomas was a result of my personal conflict with Brent Barton and Quinton Ellis perhaps, but what I'm here to say is, even before these 'personality conflicts' really developed, I had met with Stephen Jones."

"After this talk with Stephen Jones, did you work within the Merrill Lynch system?" Gore asked.

I answered I had, so Gore continued with, "Did you look in the rule book, or whatever, and follow whatever guidelines they gave you?" Again, I confirmed I had.

"And you abided by whatever guidelines they provided to you, is that correct?"

"To the best of my knowledge, I did, yes."

"And did you have a valid basis for everything you reported?"

"For everything."

"Why did you seem to increase the heat as time went by?"

"Well, after the first investigation, as a result of my memorandum to Jack Thomas on June 29, 1992, as I've already explained to the panel, it was clear to me cover-ups were taking place. It was clear to me New York had no desire nor any intention of coming up with what was a valid investigation or results related to it. It became abundantly clear.

"So that's when I decided I had gone out on a limb with my memorandum to Jack Thomas on June 29, and I decided prior to giving Jack that memorandum, I was going to do my best to see to it everything was handled as it should be, as I had been led to believe by Merrill Lynch it would based on its own literature. And part of that literature stated Merrill Lynch tolerates no violative behavior. And here I am providing my manager a litany of things that, to me, appeared to be significant improprieties or wrongdoing. So when I saw the cover-up ensue, that's when I decided to go ahead and write the board of directors."

"Why did you not tape any conversations until after you were fired?" Gore inquired.

"The thought never crossed my mind to do so," I answered. "I mean, basically, I was hopeful Merrill Lynch would come up with the right answers. I just didn't tape-record until Stephen Jones said, 'If you want to pursue this you better start tape-recording.'"

Gore then went back to the confrontation with Thomas. "On the date you felt you were discharged, was Mr. Thomas…what was his attitude?"

"He was cold, he was hostile," I replied. "When he read his termination letter he was belligerent, he would frequently look up every line or so to make eye contact with me, and in an intimidating manner."

Gore probed further. "How did the witness to this act?"

I responded that Deline told me afterward the whole time he was thinking to himself, "Wow!"—and he just could not believe what he was observing.

"Are you obsessed with this case?" Gore asked.

"No, I am not," I answered. "I'm not obsessed with it; I'm focused on it. I believe a lot of abuse has occurred, and I made the decision when I gave Jack Thomas my memorandum…I knew the serious nature of it, and I made the decision then, and I was concerned then, it might not be handled as it should be. Yeah, when I gave Jack Thomas that memorandum on June 29, 1992, I had a concern it might not be dealt with appropriately.

"But I had made the mental decision then if it wasn't, I, as a person of my convictions and principles, was going to do whatever I felt I could do, within the boundary of reason, to see to it things were done right. And that's what led to the letter to the board of directors and so forth."

"Did things you saw happen and the things that happened to you, did they affect the public?" Gore asked. "Not just you, did they affect the public?"

"Yes, they did," I answered.

Gore asked me to explain. "Well, the contest cheating affected the FC's ability to service his client. The insurance fraud, when FCs are representing themselves to the public as being knowledgeable about life insurance, and part of that representation is based on meeting statutory requirements of continuing education, and in this case, it involved the 25-hour Pictorial *Estate Planning Training Course*, which if you look at that book closely, there's a lot of content.

"I felt like the public was being abused when brokers hold themselves out as being knowledgeable about something they really are not knowledgeable enough about to duly maintain a life insurance license. So I see that as a disservice to the public."

Gore, in response to a comment made by Day in his opening statement, asked me, "Did you make the statement 'If I'm not a wealthy man out of this hearing, the earth will shake'?"

"I did," I answered.

"And in what context did you make that statement?" Gore asked.

"I haven't seen the transcript, at least not recently," I replied. "That's my understanding of what I said, so I think I did say that. I think it's been taken out of context. If I'm not incorrect, I think it was said to Barry Clark shortly before we filed my petition in Garfield County in August of 1994.

"So I'm talking to Barry, here I am in a position where the adrenaline's flowing, and we're about to file a lawsuit, and I say, 'I'm going to be a wealthy man.' And what I meant by that was, either we're going to settle it—and I knew to settle with Merrill Lynch it wasn't going to be for $2, because I feel I had been wronged. I feel like there's been a lot of abuse.

"And I just knew, my, oh my, I wasn't going to settle cheap. So either I was going to have a lot of money in the way of a settlement or else 'the earth was going to shake.' That's obviously a figurative expression. And what I meant by that was—I knew the content of our petition and the content was not insignificant, it was serious. I mean, the content included allegations on my part of a senior management cover-up. So in respect of 'the earth's going to shake,' I was figuratively saying, 'What we're going to file is going to have some substance to it.'"

Next, Gore asked me, "And did you notify or request congressional hearings related to what you reported?"

"I did," I responded. "I did. And I did that simply as a matter of conviction. In my view, I think I've expressed in this hearing up to this point, I have absolutely no doubt senior management has covered up a lot of improprieties and wrongdoing, and I think that's abusive.

"And I think when they have a policy in their own manual that suckers people into reporting wrongdoing, whether it be on a confidential basis or otherwise, and they represent that they will not tolerate violative behavior, but then they intentionally sweep things under the carpet—quite frankly, I think that's a serious abuse by senior management of a major corporation.

"The letter to Dingell, if I'm thinking of what Mr. Day has alluded to, I also made comments about the board of directors. It's my view that when I sent my letter to the board of directors, to each of them individually, in the first page or two pages, I made reference to the fact the first internal investigation was flawed either intentionally or because of incompetence. So I had the expectation, at that point, the board of directors, given its fiduciary responsibility, would surely think, 'Well, we're not going to have the same senior management do a second investigation because of the obvious conflict of interest.'

"Common sense tells me, if you have the same people redo the investigation they're not going to conclude there was a cover-up in the first one, because to do so would incriminate themselves. I mean, that defies logic. So I felt the board had the responsibility at that point, given the seriousness and the widespreadness of the allegations, they would need to obtain outside independent counsel to come in and do that which needed to be done.

"So I was disappointed with the board of directors. I feel like it did not fulfill its responsibility, and consequently I did communicate with Chairman John Dingell of the House Energy and Commerce Committee, encouraging him and his committee to take a look at what I perceived to be an abuse of power."

In closing his direct examination of me, Gore asked, "And you feel you've been wronged?"

"Yes," I answered.

"And you feel you should be compensated for it, is that correct?" Gore asked.

"Yes, I do," I replied.

Gore had no other questions. Chairman Conner adjourned the hearing for lunch and requested all parties return at 1:00 P.M.

After lunch, Gore and I were walking back to the hotel when he asked me, "Well, are you ready to be thrown to the lions?"

Knowing that Gore was partly serious, I ignored his comment. I was mentally steeling myself for what I knew would be an intense cross-examination. Even the thought I was about to be thrown to the lions was not acceptable to me because I intended to win the cross-examination duel.

When I did not respond, Gore said, "Huh?"

"We'll see," I replied.

As Schmidt had earlier predicted, Day, in his cross-examination of me, would have a tiger by the tail. Day and I were about to engage in a combative cross-examination. Day had a reputation for being tenacious and intense, which Barton confirmed to me. However, I was just as tenacious and intense and would not cower because of Day's intimidation tactics. As a matter of fact, I felt confident I would have Day off balance much of the afternoon, something to which, I assumed, he was not accustomed.

Day took understandable pride in his cleverness as well as in his ability to play games with words, but he would have his work cut out for him with me. I would not be an easy mark.

The first thing we haggled over was the length of my employment with Merrill Lynch, similar to what had already taken place during my earlier testimony.

Day moved on to my meeting with Meditz and Roepke. He asked me, "And you were advised of the results of that interinvestigation on August 13, 1992, by Leo Roepke and Helmuth Meditz, is that correct?"

After I confirmed that was correct, Day continued, "And you were advised at that meeting, were you not, they would take appropriate remedial action? Is that correct?"

I again responded yes. Day then asked, "Now, did they advise you of what all remedial action they were going to take?"

"No," I answered.

"Did you go into that meeting with any preconceptions, any attitude toward what you might hear?" Day inquired.

"I went into that meeting not expecting it to be the conclusion of the investigation," I replied.

Day was already having trouble with me. I sensed he was trying to establish the first investigation was ongoing—an *interinvestigation*. Of course, I expressly sent my letter to the board because I knew the first investigation had concluded without the right answers.

Day, as in his opening statement, was again having difficulty with the truth. Merrill Lynch's documents supported my position that management had addressed the matter and considered it over.

Next, Day waded into the most serious allegation I had made— that of the widespread insurance cheating scandal. Referring to my letter to the board, Day asked, "And Mr. Schooley, you didn't write this letter irresponsibly, is that correct?"

"That is correct."

"And you didn't write this letter and make accusations maliciously?"

"That is correct."

"And you didn't make allegations in here spitefully; is that correct?"

"I believe not. I believe that is correct."

Day then discussed how the cheat sheet Graham sent to me was, in fact, not a cheat sheet for the real exam but something that went with a practice exam. He said I knew that when I sent my letter to the board.

I explained to Day and the arbitration panel my allegation in the letter to the directors read, "what appears to be the widespread use of cheat sheets *or* other improper means concerning the self-administered examinations to maintain a life insurance license."

"But you have no hesitation on September 17, 1992, in writing to the board of directors and telling them unqualifiedly, 'I have the cheat sheet'?" Day asked.

"That's absolutely correct," I responded.

"But you have repeatedly referred to Ms. Graham's statement," Day said.

"Correct," I replied. "I had an impression based on how she said it, what she said, cheat sheets were being used, that's correct."

"And now you've also testified she didn't send you a cheat sheet?"

"No, I testified she sent me what she called a cheat sheet."

Moving on, Day asked me about my affidavit to the Oklahoma Department of Insurance dated April 20, 1993. Day requested I turn to the second page and read the second paragraph. This section basically said if Merrill Lynch's senior management failed to determine FCs were using cheat sheets to fraudulently meet state law requirements concerning life insurance continuing education, such a failure was due either to a flawed internal investigation or a need to deny the activity in an effort to avoid any penalties.

"And you signed this affidavit under oath, is that correct?" Day asked.

"Yes, I did," I answered.

"And signing affidavits under oath is a very significant thing to you, isn't it, Mr. Schooley?" Day asked.

"Yes, it is."

"At the time you made that allegation, had you ever seen a cheat sheet?"

"I had seen what Sarah Graham had said was a cheat sheet, that is what I had seen."

Day, now annoyed, asked, "Mr. Schooley, in direct response to the question, at the time you sent this affidavit in to the insurance department, had you ever seen a cheat sheet?"

Gore objected. "Well, I'm going to have to ask you to define a cheat sheet if you're referring to something other than what he's already testified to as a cheat sheet."

Day, directing his question to me, asked, "Do you remember what you defined as a cheat sheet?"

"Refresh my memory, if you will," I requested.

"You said it was an improper document. You didn't know if it was unlawful, but it was used to cheat on something, used to do something improper," Day said.

"That's one definition, yes," I responded.

"Okay," Day replied. "Mr. Schooley, are you wanting to change your definition at this point?"

"No, sir. That's my definition but Sarah Graham may have a different definition. I can't speak for her."

"But you never went back to ask her?" Day asserted.

"That's correct."

Day, seeming to become impatient with my lack of cooperation, said, "I'm asking you very directly, when you submitted this affidavit alleging this 50-state insurance conspiracy, nine months after you admitted you did not have a cheat sheet, did you have a cheat sheet?"

Gore interrupted, objecting to the form of the question and saying Day was misquoting me.

"Let's use your term," Day said. "I don't want to misstate you at all." Chairman Conner asked Day if he was going to rephrase. He said he would.

Day, turning to me, asked, "Did you suggest in this paragraph here, in your affidavit to the insurance department, there was a potential nationwide use of cheat sheets by Merrill Lynch?"

"No," I bluntly answered.

"Okay. Would you read it one more time, please?"

"I can tell you what I said, if I may."

"I'd rather you read it."

I read the paragraph again. This time I emphasized the words *by financial consultants in the Texoma District* when I got to the part that read "what appears to be a widespread conspiracy and scheme to violate state insurance law which perhaps resulted in the sale of variable annuities and life insurance products in possibly all 50 states *by financial consultants in the Texoma District* who maintained their life insurance license under false pretenses."

"Are you alleging, at least, a Texoma-wide conspiracy used cheat sheets to violate insurance laws?" Day asked.

"I'm alleging what appears to be a widespread conspiracy and scheme," I answered.

Day followed up, "So is it your position, Mr. Schooley, so long as you say 'appears,' it doesn't make any difference what you say?"

"No, I didn't say that," I replied.

Day, seeming to think he had me trapped, asked, "Mr. Schooley, when you wrote this memorandum, when you submitted this affidavit under oath to the insurance department, had you ever seen a cheat sheet for an in-state insurance exam?"

"I had spoken to Bill Hall," I answered.

This was not the answer Day was looking for. Day asked Chairman Conner if he could get a direct response.

"In cross-examination, we would ask the witness to answer the question that is asked of the witness," Chairman Conner said. "Would you restate your question, Mr. Day?"

"Mr. Schooley, when you submitted this affidavit and made the allegations contained on the second page you just read, second paragraph, had you ever seen a cheat sheet you felt had been used to violate state insurance law?"

I answered no.

"In point of fact, Mr. Schooley, didn't you admit in a telephone conversation, less than 60 days later, that you taped with the National Association of Securities Dealers, didn't you admit that not only you had never seen a cheat sheet—but you didn't know anybody who received one? Is that correct?"

"I would have to see the transcript, but that sounds to be correct," I responded.

Day handed me the transcript of the NASD conversation. He asked me to identify the document and direct my attention to a particular section.

At Day's request, I read one of Dicus' questions from the transcript: "Do you know of anybody specifically that maybe got a cheat sheet or knows somebody that got a cheat sheet?"

Then, reading my answer to Dicus, I said, "I don't, I personally don't. But that is why I would be hopeful that between Bill Hall and Gary Champion's secretary, that if a few stones were turned over maybe some of that would present itself."

Day asked me, "As of this date and as of your affidavit to the state insurance department to initiate investigation, all you had to support your outrageous allegations were the cheat sheet that you didn't have and a tape-recorded conversation with Bill Hall, is that correct?"

"I'm not agreeing to your categorization of outrageous allegations," I responded. "But if you're asking me if Sarah, the cheat sheet she had sent me, and my conversation with Bill Hall were the only two things, that's correct, yes."

While these were the only two direct items of evidence I had concerning the use of cheat sheets, I had already testified or submitted evidence there were also four indirect corroborating situations: (1) when Graham said cheat sheets were being used so the FCs could get the exam behind them; (2) when Ellis, Barton, and Thomas ignored my reference to cheat sheets in my January 1992 letter; (3) when Murphy ignored my reference to cheat sheets during one of our confidential hotline conversations; and (4) when the executive vice president of Pictorial told me he found the insurance exam scores by the Merrill Lynch FCs and members of management to be suspicious given how many had about the same score at the same time.

"Is it your position that this tape of Mr. Hall substantiates your allegation of violations of state insurance laws by Merrill Lynch?" Day asked me.

"It's my position that it supports that cheat sheets were being used," I answered.

Day then asked me to read part of the transcript of my conversation with Hall on November 20, 1992.

Repeating Hall's words, I read, "Well, I didn't know anything until probably a month or month and a half ago about the insurance department complaint...and indicated the people who came to the estate planning seminar had to go back and take the test and redo the work because it was perceived that was an invalid seminar. But because I was already away from the company, I wasn't involved in it. Had they contacted me, I could have said it was a valid seminar because of the work that people had to do before they got there, but that's neither here nor there. The part about the cheat sheet. Those things were floating around the Complex offices. I don't know where they started. I know where one started in Tulsa."

"Do you believe that testimony, those statements by Mr. Hall constitute a violation by Merrill Lynch management or knowledge by Merrill Lynch management of violation of state insurance law?" Day asked.

"By management?" I asked.

Day said yes and I replied, "Possibly."

"And how would that be possible?"

"Because in the Texoma District, as I enumerated in my letter to the board, I listed several management parties who were, at a minimum, in proximity to what appeared to be the widespread use of cheat sheets."

"In point of fact," Day asserted, "you named everybody in management by name in the Texoma District, including the insurance department, including the insurance officials, didn't you?"

"I can't say I named everybody," I replied. "I wouldn't know that."

"Everybody's name that you could think of, didn't you?" Day said.

"Everybody's name who I recognized on that computer-generated printout from Pictorial that was maybe 80 pages, close to an inch thick, that showed those Merrill Lynch employees who took the *Estate Planning Training Course* from 1990 to 1992," I responded. "Those parties who I recognized as being members of management I listed as being people the board of directors might want to talk to in trying to get to the bottom of what appeared to me to be the widespread use of cheat sheets."

As Day continued his cross-examination of me, at one point he said, "Mr. Chairman, I feel I've been buried in Mr. Schooley's documents for two weeks."

Day had been buried in my documents and was doing his best to build a record favorable to Merrill Lynch based not only on misleading interpretations but also on what I saw to be misrepresentation of the facts. Day was Merrill Lynch's spin doctor and the firm was looking for an immediate cure. The Schooley matter had already gone on much too long.

For the time being, Day was finished with his cross-examination of me concerning the one issue where Merrill Lynch could be hurt if the word got out. I had not been as cooperative as Day must have hoped for. In fact, in my direct testimony coupled with my cross-examination testimony, I believed I had painted a pretty clear and convincing picture that cheat sheets aided many Merrill Lynch employees in passing the 25-hour *Estate Planning Training Course*.

Day continued with his cross-examination of me concerning the other relatively less significant wrongdoing committed by management—the Tour de France CMA contest cheating; the misuse of the country club list; the misrepresentation of MuniYield; the falsification of seminar expenses; the non-performance of oral promises; and the improper opening of out-of-state accounts. In every instance Day did his best to trivialize the wrongdoing and in every instance, through my testimony as well as through the testimony of later witnesses, I showed the accuracy of each and every one of these allegations.

Day then informed the arbitrators how appreciative Merrill Lynch's investigators were for all the wrongdoing I had reported. I knew better. Merrill Lynch knew how to posture when necessary, and with me, whom senior management had to fear, appeasement was the name of the game.

"When Mr. Helmuth Meditz and Leo Roepke met with you on August 13 and told you the essence of the interim report, they extended their appreciation for your bringing the issues forward and expressed a great appreciation to you, didn't they, Mr. Schooley?" Day asked me.

I answered yes.

"And told you that you had done a good job and you had abided by the guidelines as you were supposed to do." Day continued. "And did you have any reason to believe they weren't sincere, Mr. Schooley, other than you disagreed with them for not firing Mr. Ellis, Mr. Sherman, and Mr. Barton?"

"Yes," I responded. "I had reason to believe they were insincere."

"Is that because you felt they were covering up?" Day asked.

"It's—yes. Plus more."

"I hate to do this," Day said hesitantly. "What more, Mr. Schooley?"

When I confirmed we were speaking specifically about August 13, 1992, I continued. "Yes. Mr. Meditz, on that occasion, twice emphasized how very, very serious my $15 'rebate' was. He also said, 'Why the memorandum? You had to know it would go all the way to senior management.' It was kind of like, 'Why did you do this, buddy?' I mean, he was not happy with that. So I believe the posturing was what you said, they thanked me and showed appreciation, I felt it to be insincere."

Day, attempting to regain his lost ground, asked, "You testified earlier your admonishment for giving $15 out of your pocket back to the customer was part of the initial conspiracy. Is that correct, Mr. Schooley? I don't mean to misstate you." I replied I thought he had done just that.

Day, trying again, said, "Okay. Was that part of an initial effort to fire you, Mr. Schooley, beginning back in February 1992, by the Merrill Lynch managers?"

Amazed with Day's twisting of the facts, I replied, "Excuse me. I think it was to intimidate me, because I wasn't helping management cheat in the Tour de France contest."

Day, not lacking audacity, responded, "But you did help them, Mr. Schooley."

"Not really," I replied. Even though Ellis had taken away my production number for purposes of cheating in the contest, I had signed many new account forms against management's request. I was hardly helping management cheat. To the contrary, I was making its cheating more difficult and obvious.

Day then asked, "After you filed your 31-page letter to the board of directors, you were interviewed by Orestes Mihaly, Robert Dineen, Barry Mandel on September 24 in New York City, were you not?"

"Yes."

"And they expressed great appreciation for you bringing these issues forward after they conducted that interview. Is that correct, Mr. Schooley?"

"They did."

"Did you believe them, Mr. Schooley?"

"No, sir."

"Did Robert Dineen call you on Monday morning, September 28, to see how you were doing?"

"Yes. Or at a minimum, to check in to see if I had an answer to one of his questions."

I believed when Dineen called me the Monday morning after the Thursday meeting in New York, the real reason for the call was to see what my next move would be if I thought Merrill Lynch would cover up the first cover-up. Dineen was not my guardian angel, as Day would attempt to have the arbitrators believe.

At that point, Chairman Conner adjourned the hearing for a 20-minute afternoon recess. When the hearing resumed for the remainder of day two, my testimony would be interrupted by Clark's. Gore had to work him in as soon as possible as he was scheduled to leave the country on business.

Barry Clark: Thomas Says Schooley Is a Cancer

Barry Clark had a good understanding of much of the wrongdoing I had reported and also knew Ellis very well. After some preliminary questions, Gore asked Clark about the Bazzelle situation. Clark told the arbitration panel he did not think Bazzelle ever hid anything from Barton concerning the letters that were sent to his former Prudential Securities clients, as supported by the fact that several UPS boxes containing the letters sat for awhile right outside Barton's office.

Clark explained he did not like the fact that Bazzelle got fired for sending out the letters because he was truly doing what was in the best interest of his clients.

Clark's testimony supported the allegations I had made against Merrill Lynch. He said Barton had represented to both him and me that he had sold MuniYield as pre-refunded. Clark told the arbitrators Ellis had promised him $5 to 10 million in assets that were not delivered.

Clark testified about the Tour de France CMA contest cheating, saying he knew it was not proper to do what Ellis and Barton had instructed him to do and sign his name to accounts opened by another FC.

Clark explained that the $20,000 in production credits he had earned during the Tour de France CMA contest for being the FC of record for the new accounts Deline and I opened had later been taken away from him. As a result of this, Clark had to go to Oklahoma City to demand they be returned. Ellis' position was he did not think Clark was entitled to the production credits, but after Clark argued he was, Ellis agreed to return them.

"Brent Barton told me after the meeting, after I got back to Enid the next day, he said Quinton was just testing me to see if I would fight for those assets," Clark testified.

Clark backed up my claim that the Enid FCs had been promised assets in connection with the Tour de France CMA contest, which were never delivered.

Clark also said he had heard Ellis had made derogatory remarks about me in an Oklahoma City meeting of FCs and staff personnel as a result of Meditz' visit to the Oklahoma City Complex.

Gore asked Clark, "Do you recall Jack Thomas' comments about Keith while he was in New York on approximately September 24, 1992?"

"What I definitely recall is Jack said he was very tired of Keith's stuff, a troublemaker, he had had it, and he didn't want him infecting the people in the office, and he mentioned Greg Stong and Michael Deline," Clark responded.

Later, Gore again visited this subject, asking Clark, "When you had your discussion with Jack Thomas and you related that conversation to Mr. Schooley in a phone conversation of October 2, 1992—I'm just going to read from the transcript. It says: Keith says, 'How did you put that?' And you said, 'And you know, he's a cancer and I'm [not] going to have him in this office.' Mr. Schooley said, 'I mean, do you think he was talking about his own personal office or the office in general?' You said, 'Oh, no, he was talking about the Enid office.'

"When Mr. Thomas said that to you, did you get the impression, in other words, he was going to get Mr. Schooley out of the Enid office?"

"There was something—and I can't even tell you what it was," Clark responded. "There was something Keith had done, some letter. I don't know if it was the board letter or what it was, but Jack was, he was irate over it, and he said, 'I don't understand why he's doing this, but I've had it, and I don't want him infecting Michael and Greg.'"

As Clark's testimony continued, Gore asked, "Do you know what announcement was made by Quinton Ellis in the Oklahoma City office after Mr. Schooley was either fired or whatever?"

"Just hearsay," Clark replied. "It was told by two or three different people they heard he had walked away from the job, that he had abandoned his job."

"Did you have a conversation with Brent Barton in which he tells you, after Quinton Ellis' termination as the RVP of the Oklahoma City office, Mr. Ellis had indicated Mr. Schooley had gotten both Brent and Mr. Ellis?" Gore asked.

"Yes, he did," Clark answered.

"What was the context of that conversation, what did he mean by that?" Gore continued.

"He just called and said Quinton had been fired or moved from the Oklahoma City office," Clark replied. "And when Brent called him, he said one of the first things Quinton said was, 'Well, he got us both.'"

"Do you know anything about the reaction of the Oklahoma City employees when Mr. Ellis announced his resignation?" Gore asked.

"No," Clark responded. "There again, hearsay. Two people said there was applause, but I don't know that."

"People said there was applause—" Gore inquired.

"Uh-huh," Clark interrupted.

"When Mr. Ellis indicated he would no longer be there?" Gore continued.

"That's correct," Clark said.

Gore asked Clark his thoughts about me. "Was he professional?"

"He was."

"Did he work hard?"

"I thought he did, very hard."

"Was he pleasant?"

"He was. We weren't really social friends. One time my wife and I went to a ballgame of his son's and I really think that's about the only social thing we did with him. We had lunch a few times."

"Was he pleasant to work with?"

"Absolutely."

"Did you perceive he had an opportunity at the Enid office?"

"Very much so."

"What's your impression about him?"

"He came across well with people, and he was—I think he was direct. I think people liked his manner."

Gore had just a few more questions for Clark. "Did you get the impression Mr. Schooley was there to be as good an FC as he could?" he asked.

"That was my impression," Clark replied.

"Did he ever give you the impression he was there for any other reason, like to make trouble for Merrill Lynch?"

"No."

"Did he just want a good place with a good atmosphere to work in?"

"I think that's what we all wanted, just a good place."

"Did you perceive his complaints to management as being nothing but trying to clean up the place so it would have a good spirit for working there?"

"I think he had legitimate concerns."

With that, Gore was finished with his direct examination of Clark. Chairman Conner told Day he could cross-examine.

Day quickly established Thomas became the resident manager of the Enid office during the Tour de France CMA contest. Therefore, this cleared him of any responsibility related to the headcount management. Day also established Thomas was not involved in several of my other allegations.

Day said to Clark, "So the only conflict you could be aware of Mr. Thomas might have had—I'll direct your attention to the board up here. We just went through six of them. The only conflict Mr. Thomas might have been reacting to would be an allegation regarding the use of cheat sheets?" On the display board was a summary of most of my allegations. Before Clark had a chance to answer, Day moved on.

Day conveniently failed to mention that in my letter to the directors, I named Thomas in other areas of wrongdoing and misconduct including the improper opening of out-of-state accounts, the threat to terminate me if something like the $15 "rebate" were to happen again, and his justification of the Tour de France CMA contest cheating. According to Day, Thomas was simply reacting for being unjustly accused by me of being involved in, or aware of, the insurance cheating.

Day then asked Clark a series of questions to establish he observed no hostile environment in the Enid office toward me. However, Clark had transferred to the Merrill Lynch Wichita office more than two weeks before Thomas' confrontation with me on September 28. He could not testify regarding the most critical time except for his visit to the Enid office on September 24 when Thomas was angry and made his cancer comments about me.

Day asked his last question of Clark. "And again, I don't want to beat this up, and I want this clear on the record. Insofar as Mr. Thomas' comments to you about, 'We did not want Mr. Schooley infecting Mr. Stong and Mr. Deline,' the speculation could just as easily be he didn't want Schooley's allegations that Jack Thomas was part of a cheat sheet scheme to infect their relationship with him?"

"That could be the take on it, yes, sir," Clark responded.

Had Clark known it would be Thomas' sworn testimony he did not know about, nor had he seen, my 31-page letter to the board of directors until *September 28*, I do not see how Clark could have said, "That could be the take on it." Thomas could not, according to his own testimony, have known on *September 24* (when he made the cancer comment to Clark) about the allegation he "was part of a cheat sheet scheme." Also, while Clark was saying Thomas was angry and upset on September 24, Thomas later testified he was not angry until he saw my letter on September 28. However, it seemed to me what Day did make clear on the record by virtue of his last question to Clark was Day, himself, knew Thomas was, in fact, aware on September 24 of my letter to the directors.

Once Day concluded with Clark, Gore wished to redirect. "Was there a hostile environment for Mr. Schooley from other people besides Mr. Thomas?" Gore asked Clark.

"Well, I never saw him in conversations with Quinton Ellis," Clark responded. "But when Brent came down it was certainly cool, because Brent maintained his clients after he left and went to Oklahoma City. He would come back almost on a weekly basis, a day or two, and it was certainly a very cool and uncomfortable relationship between Keith and Brent Barton."

"So a possible hostile environment created by Brent Barton to Mr. Schooley?" Gore asked.

"Yes," Clark answered.

"Was Mr. Thomas hostile on September 24, 1992, when he was describing his feelings of Mr. Schooley to you?" Gore asked.

"Well, he was upset and angry," Clark answered.

"Is it possible Jack Thomas intended to terminate Keith Schooley with his comment to you?" Gore asked.

"That's certainly possible," Clark replied.

Gore once again read from a transcript of the conversation between Clark and me on October 2, 1992: "And Mr. Schooley says, 'How did he put that?' You said, 'He just said, "Hum, you know, he's a cancer and I'm not going to have him in this office."' Mr. Schooley said, 'I mean, do you think he was talking about his own personal office or the office in general?' You said, 'Oh, no, he was talking about the Enid office.'"

Gore continued, "Was that a conversation between you and Jack Thomas?"

"Yes, it was," Clark answered.

Gore was finished with Clark but he was not yet excused. Day wanted to recross.

After a few less important questions, Day asked Clark about Thomas' comments to him on September 24. "Could it have been anything as to what he intended by that, including that you were tired of him calling you an insurance cheat sheeter…a cheat sheeting…I'm sorry…a cheat sheet insurance violator? Did you think he might have been just concerned and reacting that he didn't want Mr. Schooley to be telling

Mr. Stong and Mr. Deline that he violated state insurance laws as part of a management conspiracy?"

"Well, I want to be real clear," Clark replied. "I didn't have any idea why Jack Thomas was upset. I just know what he said. I just know he said he was angry and upset, and he didn't want him infecting the office."

After this, Gore wanted to redirect again.

"Mr. Clark, regardless of whether you knew or didn't know you were being taped, whether you were or you weren't, do you tell the truth when you talk to anybody?" Gore asked.

"Yes, sir, I do," Clark answered.

"And were you telling the truth, as far as you know, as far as your recollection when you were talking to Mr. Schooley on October 2, 1992?" Gore asked.

"Yes, sir," Clark replied.

"Thank you," Gore said. "No other questions."

Arbitrator Barnes had a few questions for Clark. "Mr. Clark, did Keith ever come to you and ask counsel or your advice? Or did you all chat in general about these matters and their degree of gravity and that sort of thing?"

"Yes, sir, we did, on several occasions," Clark responded.

"Recite that," Barnes requested.

"Well, I think my thoughts on it were they were rule violations," Clark replied. "I really did not want to get involved. I really felt it was a no-win proposition for me. I felt if I challenged, it would not be to my benefit. And I really did not want to try to question the system on it."

"The system was the system you were going to try and work with?" Barnes asked.

"I did not want to take that risk of losing my job," Clark answered.

Clark's appearance was significant for two reasons in particular. First, Clark testified Thomas was angry and upset with me on September 24. That was two days after someone named Paul was in Enid for a meeting with Ellis and Thomas. It was four days before Thomas supposedly even knew about my September 17 letter to the board of directors. Second, Day was suggesting Thomas' reaction to Clark on September 24 was a result of being accused of participating in the insurance cheating scandal when, according to Thomas' later testimony, he did not even know of any such allegation until September 28.

Schooley Continues: There Will Be No Violence

After the conclusion of Clark's testimony, Day resumed his cross-examination of me. Chairman Conner reminded me I was still under oath, then Day began.

He asked me about part of my letter to the board. "Now, Mr. Schooley, when you name Mr. Thomas in this letter to the board of directors, along with all these others—let's stick with Mr. Thomas. Based on the evidence you've—the testimony you've given, when you made this allegation to Mr. Thomas' ultimate boss, did you think he might adversely react to your allegation?"

"Did I think Mr. Thomas might adversely react to the allegations?" I responded. "I don't believe that thought crossed my mind."

"You just didn't care, did you?" Day asked.

"No, I simply stated the facts," I replied.

"And the facts were?"

"The facts were—"

"I'll pose a question, Mr. Schooley," Day interrupted. "And the fact was Mr. Thomas was aware of or participated in the cheat sheet scheme. Is that correct, Mr. Schooley?"

"That is correct."

Later, Day asked, "Now Mr. Schooley, did you write your 9–17 letter, not just because you felt compelled to, but were you trying to set yourself up for a wrongful termination case?"

"Absolutely not," I answered.

"Did you make the reckless and unfounded allegations regarding Jack Thomas in your letter to the board of directors with a view toward enraging Mr. Thomas so he would react here?"

"Absolutely not."

"Did you care about what Mr. Thomas' reaction would be to you naming him in your cheat sheet conspiracy language?"

"I can't say I addressed that. I didn't have that as a thought. I simply stated the facts, and I stand by the facts at this moment and what I say in my letter to the board."

"You just didn't care about the impact on the individuals you named in that letter of September 17?"

"Excuse me, Mr. Day, I cared about the truth, and I spoke the facts as I knew them, and I believe what I said in that letter is accurate and you've said nothing to make me believe otherwise. And I was very careful in how I phrased what I said, and I'll be happy to go back and dissect it with you." Day did not accept my offer.

"Did you care about the impact on Jack Thomas of making those allegations against him to the board of directors of Merrill Lynch, that he was aware of or participated in a nationwide scheme to violate state insurance laws with cheat sheets which you never saw in your life?" Day asked.

"Again, I cannot say the thought of whether I cared or not went through my mind," I answered. "I simply stated the facts."

Day would add a touch of drama to the hearing with his next series of questions concerning an exhibit of my handwritten notes of a phone conversation between Clark and me in June 1994.

Day asked me to read a certain excerpt. I read, "I told Barry Clark in July I would suggest either I would be a relatively wealthy individual or the earth will shake."

"And if you don't become a relatively wealthy individual out of this trial, that doesn't mean you're going to do anything violent, does it, Mr. Schooley?" Day asked.

"Violent?" I asked.

"Yes."

"I don't understand your question."

"Well, we just happen to be sitting in a city where we're conscious of those kind of remarks."

"I see," I responded. "There will be no violence."

Even though Day had already heard me explain my comment, he had brought it up again anyway. I had already said it was a figurative expression meant to imply the lawsuit I was about to file against Merrill Lynch would have some substance to it. What Day tried was to connect my comment to the recent bombing of the Alfred P. Murrah Federal Building just five months earlier. Of course, my figurative expression was made almost a year before the Oklahoma City bombing—but that was irrelevant to Day's purposes.

Late in the afternoon, even though he was almost finished with his cross-examination of me, Day indicated he was tired and ready for the hearing to be concluded for the day. Chairman Conner agreed and adjourned until 9:00 the next morning.

It seemed a long day for Merrill Lynch's attorney. Despite his misuse of important facts, Day had been unable to break me as he had hoped. I was a tough witness.

As everyone was leaving the conference room, Day was walking immediately in front of me as we approached the door. He turned to me, and in a sincere and complimentary manner said, "You did a good job."

"Thanks," I replied. "I thought you'd never stop coming at me." We shook hands. We both knew we were combatants in a major war with a lot at stake.

The next morning Chairman Conner began the hearing by asking Day to introduce a new party to the proceeding. It was Alan Rockler, an expert witness for Merrill Lynch. Day then returned to his cross-examination of me. He only had a few questions. When he was done, Gore wished to redirect.

"What did Sarah Graham call the document she sent to you?" Gore asked me.

"She called it a cheat sheet," I answered.

"Is that the reason...why did you call it that?"

"Why did I call it that?"

"Yes."

"Because that's what she called it."

"Did you receive subsequent confirmation, the use or existence of cheat sheets anywhere else?"

"Yes, I did."

"Where was that?"

"In a telephone conversation with Bill Hall on November 20, 1992."

"To your knowledge, did Merrill Lynch require the taking of the insurance test?"

"Yes, it did."

"To your knowledge is that insurance test required to sell insurance?"

"Yes, that is correct."

"Was that represented to you by Merrill Lynch?"

"Yes."

"Were some FCs required to retake the insurance examination?"

"Yes, they were."

"Was that as a result of your reporting the cheat sheet situation?"

"The cheat sheets and/or other improper means of taking the exam, yes."

"And did anyone from Pictorial make any statements concerning the test-taking by Merrill Lynch prior?"

"Yes, someone did."

"Who was that?"

"Mr. Don Fischer."

"What did he say?"

"He's the one that produced the 77-page computer generated printout, which had all the Merrill Lynch FCs that took the exam from 1990 through August 26, 1992. And once he came up with that information, he told me, by way of telephone, that the scores looked highly suspicious."

"Did this further confirm whatever your thoughts were about the possible use of cheat sheets or other means of improper taking of the test?"

"Yes, it did."

Gore continued, asking me a number of questions about the cheating in the Tour de France CMA contest, the improper use of the country club list, the falsified seminar expenses, and the improper opening of out-of-state accounts.

Getting back to the incident with Thomas, Gore asked, "Did Jack Thomas ever retract his letter in any way to you?"

"His letter dated September 28, 1992?"

"Yes, sir."

"No, sir, he did not."

"Did he ever indicate to you he would not sue you?"

"No."

"Was there ever any offer by Merrill Lynch to protect you from his lawsuit or transfer you?"

"None whatsoever."

"When they offered to rehire you, did they offer to protect you in any way from him?"

"No."

"Is there any circumstance Merrill Lynch could have arranged for you to where you could have gone back?"

"Well, I think that possibility exists, but just nothing was ever offered by Merrill Lynch to even make it a realistic consideration."

Gore was done; however, I was not off the hook yet. Day wanted to recross.

"You're not testifying now you weren't repeatedly asked to come back to work after you left, are you?" he asked me.

"Mr. Mandel did a couple of times, I believe, several times perhaps, make an offer to come back if that's what you're asking, yes," I replied.

Day had no further questions; however, Gore now did.

"Mr. Mandel did not say if you did come back, Mr. Thomas wouldn't sue you, did he?" he asked.

"He did not," I responded.

"Nor did he say Mr. Thomas wouldn't continue to be your direct supervisor, manager, boss, or whatever?" Gore asked.

"That's correct," I replied.

Finally I was finished testifying. I was pleased with how it had gone. I knew Day had come at me with his best shot in an effort to break me under pressure and destroy my credibility. I did not back away from Day at all and in fact, felt I had exposed the extraordinary difficulty of his case.

Gary Champion: I Can Guarantee You...

The next witness was Gary Champion, a former resident insurance specialist for Merrill Lynch in Dallas. Hall had told me five days earlier the insurance cheating was extensive during Champion's tenure. My attorneys had subpoenaed Champion but decided to release him from it upon interviewing him just before his possible appearance at my hearing when they realized he appeared unwilling to testify in my favor. However, Day wanted Champion to testify so he was now Merrill Lynch's witness.

It was established Champion now worked for PaineWebber but was previously employed with Merrill Lynch from 1982 to 1993. My curiosity was piqued when I heard Champion's employment with the firm ended in 1993. I wondered if his departure was in any way related to the wrongdoing I had reported.

Champion told the panel he and Hall were working for Merrill Lynch in Dallas at the same time, albeit in different offices. At one point, they switched offices resulting in Hall going to the San Jacinto location downtown where Champion had just been. San Jacinto was where Hall told me he had first learned from a big broker of the improper taking of the insurance exam and where Graham worked in November 1991 when she sent me what she called a cheat sheet.

"Did you provide, condone, participate in the utilization of cheat sheets so Merrill Lynch securities, insurance agents could pass or comply with state insurance laws in Texas?" Day asked Champion. "Do you understand my question?"

"I understand your question and my answer to that is, absolutely not," Champion answered. "Can I expound on it a little here?"

"Okay."

"'Cheat sheets' was terminology used by a young lady who was making reference toward a practice exam for Texas insurance licensing. The lady was incorrect in making that statement. She had no idea what she had said. She was a nice lady, but she had no business being in that department."

"Do you deny the allegations made by Bill Hall regarding your conduct in violating the state insurance laws of Texas while you were employed at Merrill Lynch?"

"I deny these allegations and I don't believe they were made. I can't believe Mr. Hall would say something like that. And this never occurred in Texas, this never occurred in any of my offices."

"And as far as you understand, no secretary or clerical employee under your supervision ever violated or assisted or condoned any violation of any state insurance laws?" Day asked.

"That's correct. My administrative assistants and my secretaries, one, they don't have any access to do that. They don't have time to do that. We did not do or have anything to do with the doing of their exams, period."

I believed Champion was skirting the truth when he said his administrative assistants and his secretaries did not have the accessibility or time to assist in cheating. To cheat in the manner Hall had described to me would not be difficult or time consuming. I thought Champion was lying between his teeth.

"Mr. Champion, based on your review of the allegations made here by Mr. Schooley, in your experience, while employed with Merrill Lynch, is it true there was open and brazen cheating on state insurance examinations by Merrill Lynch?" Day continued.

"There was no open cheating at all by Merrill Lynch."

"Was there any cheating, period?"

"To my knowledge, there was no cheating that I know of. All I can do is supervise and oversee and make sure the process follows. This was an open-book test. Everyone should make 100. So I can't see why there would be any cheating involved in something like this. And to my knowledge, there was no cheating. Now, if something happened that I don't have any control over, I have no information…I have no indication there was any cheating done."

Champion was wrong again. The exam for the *Estate Planning Training Course* was not an open-book test. Champion had confused the real exam with the practice exams throughout the course book where the solutions to the questions were immediately available by placing a red transparent card over encoded answers.

Day was done with Champion. It was Gore's turn to cross-examine.

"Mr. Champion, the nice lady in Dallas you were referring to— would that have been Sarah Graham by any chance?" Gore asked.

"Sarah Graham, yes."

"Who is Sarah Graham?"

"Sarah Graham was a 20-year employee with Merrill Lynch who was a nice lady, who got promoted from one office to another office instead of being fired. She was a nice lady, but she basically had no business being in our operation because she knew nothing about life insurance."

Gore then asked Champion if it was possible Graham sent an answer sheet, which was identified as a cheat sheet, to me prior to the exam.

"Yes, sir. She did that a lot. I mean, yes. I would assume that's exactly what happened."

Concerning the meeting where Hall led eight FCs through the examination on a question-by-question basis, Gore said, "The parties who take that test sign an affidavit where they swear under oath they had taken the test without any outside assistance; are you familiar with that?"

"No."

"If they were required to sign such an affidavit, then they would have to take a test without anybody giving them the answers?"

"Yeah, that's true."

"And if you found out later somebody walks some folks through the test and gave them the answers and then they signed an affidavit saying they did it without any outside assistance, do you think that might put them on notice there's a problem, or they might be concerned about something?"

"If someone were telling me Bill Hall held a class and gave the brokers the answers, I can guarantee you, they knew the answers before he gave them," Champion responded.

I was incredulous. I had heard it all now. If the FCs—five from Oklahoma City and three from Tulsa—knew the answers before Hall gave them, why then would they, Ellis, and Hall meet in a small town between Oklahoma City and Tulsa on a Saturday morning?

"And I take it from your testimony your relationship with Bill Hall is not a good one?" Gore asked Champion.

"Bill Hall...I don't have a bad relationship. As far as a working relationship, we're fine. We don't socialize together."

"I understand. So Bill's not that bad?"

"Bill's not a bad guy. He's basically very smart, and he's got an ego to go with it. I don't have any problems with him. He's not a bad guy. He just doesn't say nice things about me."

With that, Gore had no further questions and Day did not want to redirect so Champion was free to go.

I would later learn that three years after the hearing, Champion was terminated by PaineWebber pursuant to an internal review for violating the firm's policies regarding reimbursement for travel and entertainment, receipt and distribution of gifts, and unapproved outside business activities. From what I had witnessed, I knew Champion lacked integrity and I also knew leopards do not change their spots.

Lisa Brainard: Mistaken Identity

The next witness Gore called was Lisa Brainard. Brainard had worked for Barton in the Merrill Lynch Enid office for a few months in late 1991.

Brainard testified Barton was supposed to use the country club list on a one-time basis only but did not honor that promise. He had also expected her to help him minimize the misuse of the list.

Brainard also testified she overheard a conversation between Barton, Ellis, and Sherman in the Enid office where Barton told them he had obtained the list from the country club manager. Brainard said Barton was bragging to Ellis and Sherman about how he was using the list.

Gore asked Brainard what she thought of me, if she thought I was a professional and pleasant to work with. She answered yes to both.

Gore then read a part of the transcript of a conversation Brainard and I had on October 1, 1992, when she told me Barton had told her I was the world's biggest liar and had a twisted mind. Unfortunately, Brainard was unable, now almost three years later, to remember telling me what Barton had said to her.

Day had just one question for Brainard. He asked her if she remembered being interviewed by someone from his firm several months back. She did not. Day said maybe he had confused her with someone else and had no further questions.

I suspected it was Feightner who had been interviewed by someone in Day's firm. Feightner was the administrative assistant who was sitting at her desk just outside Thomas' office when he was meeting with Ellis and Paul. Feightner did not honor her subpoena to testify at my arbitration hearing, and I wondered if she had been interviewed a few months earlier by one of Merrill Lynch's attorneys and whether that had scared her off. Merrill Lynch certainly had a motive to keep Feightner from testifying because part of its defense was the position there was no Paul in Enid, Oklahoma, the day of and the day after Merrill Lynch's board of directors received my letter.

Bill Hall: Cheat Sheets Absolutely Existed

The next witness on my behalf was Bill Hall, a former resident insurance specialist for Merrill Lynch in Dallas. Hall would have a lot to say that was in direct opposition to his former counterpart, Champion.

Hall gave a summary of his educational and professional background. He then told the panel he worked for Merrill Lynch from August 1990 to June 1992 as an estate-planning specialist (EPS).

Gore requested Hall to describe the circumstances surrounding his departure from the firm.

"I went to work for Merrill Lynch and within a two-year period, I was terminated, in June," Hall replied. "And I thought I had an exemplary track record in production. I was number one in the firm for a couple of months in the last year. No one had done that before. So my production was excellent, and I was terminated. And I couldn't understand it."

"Okay," Gore said. "And while you were with Merrill Lynch, did you have a role in continuing education for insurance purposes?"

"Yes," Hall replied. "EPSs were responsible for the continuing education tracking, training, teaching, making sure all the licenses were secured for the product before a broker FC would write the product or solicit the product. And on an ongoing basis, make sure all the t's were crossed and the i's dotted, basically, in the insurance in that area."

"Was the emphasis more on securities or life insurance?" Gore asked.

"Well, obviously, securities," Hall responded. "We were told many times the securities business drove 97 percent, on average, of the office's gross revenue, and insurance was only 3 percent. And consequently, we couldn't expect a whole lot of top-down support, programs, things like that, from the management. And we had to, based on that, develop and cultivate the brokers ourselves to the extent they would invite us into their book, invite us to do business with their clients."

Gore then asked, "And how did you go about getting people maintaining their licenses? Did you send them study materials or how did you handle that?"

"My staff maintained a file on who was licensed and who was not," Hall answered. "And we continually tried to get the people who were not licensed, licensed, and then attract, also, those that were coming up for renewal, to find out which had continuing education credits and which were delinquent and needed those before a certain date. We then contacted those people and talked to them about, this is the date, you've got to have this many credits...try to arrange for either a correspondence course or encourage them in some way to get involved in a course to get those credits taken care of. After they did that, then we would just mark it and keep track of it. We had a tracking system."

"And these brokers you were doing this with, were they busy selling securities?" Gore asked.

"Oh, absolutely," Hall replied. "Tremendous pressure to create gross, to do their business. So unless you developed a very personal relationship with a broker, you really didn't get a lot of time. They are busy."

"So was the continuing education for insurance purposes something on the back burner, so to speak?"

"Yeah."

"Were you ever approached by anyone to do anything other than provide them with study materials?"

"When I came to work for Merrill Lynch, I was hired by the manager in the Central Expressway office," Hall said. "And within about a year, I was moved over to the San Jacinto office, which is the downtown office in Dallas, and the largest office. The way we were taught to do our business is to talk and work with the biggest brokers and work down. And based on that, one of the large brokers in the San Jacinto office came up for continuing education. When I went back to talk to him, because he hadn't responded to my office's reminders, he indicated, in the past, the staff took care of that. And I said, 'What do you mean?' And he said, 'Well, they just take care of this. I guess they fill out the books or whatever.' And I'm in a pretty precarious position at that time, because I have got to solicit the relationship with the big brokers, but I can't step on their toes or I won't be given any business, and I'm on straight commissions. But that's a clear violation of the law. And I really don't think this broker—because he's a very good broker and a very highly ethical person—felt like that was something other than the norm. And I explained to him that was not the norm, we were not doing that. That was against the law. It could cost all of us our licenses. He would have to do the study course, but I would help him pick the course, based on what his business plan was and what we were trying to do in the estate planning area. And so it came to my attention at that time there was something other than the proper manner for acquiring continuing education training."

"Did you look into it any further?" Gore asked.

"Well, I didn't look into that, no, because if, in fact, that's the culture, it was my responsibility to do it correctly. So I then went to the manager, and I said, 'This is what's not been done and I have pressure from this broker, and I can't do that.' And I explained to him this would jeopardize everyone. And that, in fact, we're going to do it the right way, and he supported me. And at that time, I also had Oklahoma City and I came to Quint, and I sat down with Quinton, and I can remember it like it was yesterday, and Quint supported me 100 percent. He says, 'We don't want any problems. We're not going to do it that way. I don't know anything, and I'll support you 100 percent.' I remember that. And I had to have the support of the managers from a protocol perspective. Everything revolved around these managers. They were God in their offices. So I didn't want them hit from the blind side either. Because as sure as shooting it, I walked into that broker and said, 'Well, I don't know what's happened in the past, but here's the way we're going to do it in the future.'"

"And did you find out what the broker meant who came to you and said to have the staff do the test?" Gore asked.

"Well, the broker just indicated to me the girls filled out the books for them, that was what he told me," Hall replied.

"Do you know how widespread this was in the past?"

"You mean, prior to this broker saying this? This was the only occasion and the initiation, if you will, to me something was wrong, that I had to change it. So I just assumed it was the methodology. So I just followed with the change and didn't look back."

"Were there any cheat sheets or anything of that nature being used, that you're aware of?" Gore asked.

"Well, none came out of my office," Hall answered. "The brokers would get together and work together and I would hear certain things and I would just tell them, you know, we can't be a party to that. But there were no cheat sheets I condoned or endorsed or that ever came out of my office."

"Okay," Gore said. "Do you believe they existed prior to your regime?"

"Absolutely."

"And why do you think that?"

"Well, the brokers worked together, and one in this office will know brokers in other offices. And they attend conventions together and they're close comrades and they call one another, and they share marketing ideas and all kinds of ideas, and it's just a constant communication. Well, obviously, if you're under the gun and you've got to create 35 continuing education credit hours and you've got a week to do it, you just call a compadre and say, 'What did you do?' So, you know, things could be faxed around real easily."

"Do you have any idea or any knowledge of this occurring anywhere outside the Dallas office?"

"In the Tulsa office, one broker approached me, and I told him I didn't want to hear anything about it and he just said he would take care of it."

"And when you said he approached you, what did he approach you about?"

"Well, about getting...same thing. You wait until the bottom of the 9th inning and you've got to get the continuing education credits done, and what's the shortest distance between two points?"

Gore, probing further, asked, "And when you said, 'Wait until the 9th inning,' what does that mean?"

"Well, the continuing education credits, if 30 credits were due by the end of a given period and they had neglected to do the study or accrue those credits, then it's got to be done or they're going to lose their license. So there's some pressure, all of a sudden, it becomes from a C priority to an A priority, an urgent. And I was approached, if you're talking about this Tulsa incident, I was approached by a broker about how is the most expeditious way to get this out of the way. And I explained to him I had been telling him all along, and he had received a series of letters that you have got to get this done. And he said, 'Well, this isn't the way we've done it in the past.' And I said, 'Well, I don't want to hear about it in the past.'"

"Did the staff you were informed took the test for them in the past, was that under Gary Champion?" Gore asked.

"In the Texas area," Hall answered. "Gary never came out of Texas, Gary was only in Dallas—well, during my regime, he was only in Dallas."

"And do you know which staff members were involved in that situation?" Gore continued.

"In Texas?"

"Yes."

"It would have been Gary and his staff. My girl used to be on his staff, Sarah something, I can't remember, it's been so long ago."

"Would 'Sarah Graham' ring a bell?"

"Yeah, Sarah Graham. She was one of my girls."

"All right. And do you have any idea what the others did for Gary?"

"Well, yes. One did all the underwriting and illustrations and the proposals. She was the brains behind the operation and Gary was a figurehead. And the other was kind of a secretary. And a larger broker indicated to me that she was the one that filled out the books."

"And when you say, 'she filled out the books,' what did you mean by that?"

"She filled out the continuing education books for the continuing education credits when they were due."

"Was she filling out the tests that were counted for credit?"

"Sure."

"Was this procedure widespread or do you have any idea?"

"Well, I have no knowledge of it beyond just that Dallas office and that one situation. When that came to my mind, I just stopped it right there."

"Was anybody in management involved in that situation, to your knowledge?"

"No, not to my knowledge."

"And you're indicating that there were some improprieties going on with the taking of these certification tests prior to your regime; is that correct?"

"Yes, absolutely."

"And do you have any idea of the number of people that would have taken advantage of that situation?"

"I don't have an idea. But I can just imagine that if you're in a pressure cooker culture to produce, and you're inundated with all kinds of information that you've got to read and you don't have enough time, and this is either none of your business or very little of your business, but it's going to take 30 hours of your time, I would suspect that any common-sense person would pick the shortest distance between two poles."

"And if you're certified in Texas, without taking the test, let's say, in the manner you were describing with the secretary taking the test for you, can you then use that to get certified in another state?"

"You can get appointed to other states as long as you have an active and current resident Texas license. A nonresident appointment, is that what you mean?"

"Correct. Can you then get appointed in another state—conceivably you could use that test then to get appointed in all 50 states?"

"Correct."

"And then you could sell life insurance in all 50 states; is that correct?"

"Correct." In fact, 49 Merrill Lynch employees who resided in Texas had, as of 1995, nonresident life insurance appointments in Oklahoma.

"In your opinion, was Gary Champion familiar with this situation where the secretaries were taking the tests for the brokers?"

"Oh, absolutely. He had to have known."

"That was under his regime that you're referring to, is that correct?"

"Sure."

Gore then asked Hall if he had discussed his testimony with Bruce Day. Hall confirmed he talked to Day for maybe two to three hours. Gore inquired if any discussion of money had taken place. Hall explained he told Day he wanted the $15,000 in severance pay he felt he was owed by Merrill Lynch when he was terminated. Day told him they could not pay a fact witness.

Gore had some more questions for Hall. "Do you know if Sarah Graham ever sent out answer sheets and called them cheat sheets, or would you even be familiar with that?"

"I know Sarah Graham, and Sarah is a very honest person," Hall responded. "And to my knowledge, and my girls knew how I felt about any kind of an impropriety, and I have cautioned them to not take shortcuts, and this was even when brokers didn't want to study for the insurance exam to take it, but they wanted to sell an annuity, so they'd come down and they'd try to jerry-rig or talk the girls into doing something, and I made it crystal clear we're not going to do that. So that same principle transposed to the continuing education. We just don't take shortcuts."

Gore continued, asking, "Did an investigator from Merrill Lynch ever contact you in relation to these cheat sheets or whatever?" Hall answered no.

"Were you ever contacted by a Merrill Lynch investigator for any reason in the last couple of years?" Gore asked. Again, Hall's reply was no.

"Or since 1992, maybe I should say?" Gore clarified. The answer was still no.

Hall added, "And Bruce said they didn't have my right address and they've had my permanent address all along."

"Do you feel that Mr. Schooley did have some basis for saying there were improprieties going on with this test?" Gore asked.

"Yes, very definitely. There was plenty of fire."

"To your knowledge, was any management aware of this situation with the secretary doing the test, or whatever...any improprieties in relation to the insurance test?"

"Well, the managers I talked to, which were the managers I reported to, were aware of it because I made them aware, if they weren't aware prior, and then made them aware of my plan of action for curing the problem."

"And which managers did you report that to?"

Hall answered he reported that to Ellis, another RVP, and a superior up the other line.

At that point, Gore had no further questions for Hall. It was now Day's turn to cross-examine.

"Now, is it your testimony here today, that you have, during your tenure—during Mr. Schooley's tenure—that you never saw a cheat sheet, never heard of a cheat sheet, no cheat sheets or any violation of any state laws up here occurred? Is that correct?" Day asked as he limited the scope of his question to Oklahoma.

"Correct," Hall replied. "Except for the Tulsa situation."

"Did somebody ask you for a cheat sheet in Tulsa?" Day asked.

"Yes."

"And did you provide that cheat sheet?"

"No."

"Did anybody else ever ask you for a cheat sheet in the state of Oklahoma during Mr. Schooley's tenure?"

"No."

"Now, the fact that FC asked you for a cheat sheet, does that mean there were multiple uses of cheat sheets in the state of Oklahoma prior to your time?"

"I would say that request supports the fact that, yes, there was use in the past, but I haven't seen them. And I think a lot of them knew my rigidity and perhaps wouldn't even approach me."

After a few other related questions, Chairman Conner interrupted to ask Day where he was going with his line of questioning. Day replied, "I just want the record clear on this, that nothing happened here in the state of Oklahoma." Day, looking at Hall, asked, "That is your testimony; isn't that true, Mr. Hall?"

"You just said nothing happened, yet the prior questions were about something that did happen," Hall answered.

"One single FC asked you for a cheat sheet; is that correct?" Day asked.

"Yes, yes."

"Very well. And Sarah Graham, your employee, it's your opinion that she never sent anybody a cheat sheet, including Mr. Schooley; is that correct?"

"Yes, that's correct."

"So all of your allegations here today all relate to Gary Champion's actions; is that correct?"

"Now, I'm going to have to object," Gore interrupted. "He's not making any allegations here today, he's testifying." The chairman asked Day if he wanted to rephrase the question.

"The statements as to improper actions in violation of state insurance law in Texas were all done by Gary Champion and/or his clerks; is that correct?" Day asked.

"Correct, in Texas," Hall answered.

Day was finished with Hall.

Day's cross-examination of Hall did not last long and accomplished little, except for partial confirmation of what Hall had already testified to during Gore's direct examination.

Gore wanted to redirect, so he asked Hall, "Is there any doubt in your mind that cheat sheets were coming out of Gary Champion's office?"

"There's no doubt in my mind that improprieties were done in Gary Champion's office," Hall replied.

"And what type of improprieties would those have been?"

"I've already stated his staff was completing the books for the big broker."

"If you received credit in Texas for continuing education, can you apply that to Oklahoma for credit?"

"You don't need continuing education credits in Oklahoma, to my knowledge, if you're a resident in Texas and you're in good standing. But there's an indirect transition, if that's what you're saying."

"So if you're licensed in Texas, in other words, you don't need to take a test in Oklahoma?"

"Correct."

"And did you tell Keith Schooley about either cheat sheets or some improprieties that were going on in the Texas office?"

"Yes. I felt he should have the same information I'd given Bruce."

"And did you also tell Keith Schooley about some improprieties, cheat sheets, whatever, several years ago, actually, when he talked to you on the phone?"

"I'm not sure if I related to him all that I've related today."

"Correct. And I'm not asking if you related everything. I just asked if you had related that cheat sheets were floating around to him."

"Yes."

At this point neither Gore nor Day had any further questions.

In my view, Hall, as a former resident insurance specialist in Dallas, had shattered beyond any reasonable doubt Day's repeated assertion that my allegation of a widespread insurance cheating scandal was baseless and malicious. Not only did reasonable statistical analysis of the Pictorial 77-page computer printout strongly support my allegation, but it was also confirmed by Hall's sworn testimony as a former *insider* who was in a position to know.

Brent Barton: It Was Starting to Look Like Watergate

Gore called my last witness for day three of the hearing. That witness was Brent Barton. He described his educational and professional background for the arbitration panel, including his employment with Merrill Lynch until January 1994 and since that time as a financial consultant for another securities firm.

It was immediately clear how Barton planned to present his testimony. Right off the bat, when Gore asked him about misrepresenting MuniYield, he denied ever having sold it as pre-refunded even though Merrill Lynch informed the regulators he did and the NASD had felt it necessary to send him a letter of caution for doing just that. Barton also claimed an oral rescission offer was made soon after the first investigation to clients who bought the fund. However, I had been told by Dicus of the NASD that he contacted some of Barton's clients and none could remember being offered the right of rescission concerning the purchase of MuniYield.

Barton testified about the country club list saying he purged it from his computer. He then testified he had submitted falsified seminar expenses—admitting that not only did Ellis know he was submitting them, but also he was soliciting the country club manager's complicity in covering for him (since the seminars had supposedly taken place at the country club). He also admitted Ellis never delivered the assets he promised to the Enid office for the Tour de France CMA contest, and only after attorneys got involved was Clark made whole on the assets Ellis promised to Clark.

Getting to the insurance cheating, Gore asked, "Did you participate in any Saturday morning meeting involving insurance exams?"

"Yes," Barton answered.

"And were you walked through the test?" Gore asked.

"I guess you could say 'walked through the test,' I guess." Barton then briefly explained how the group would have discussions involving the various questions.

"And the answers were not given to you in that discussion, is that correct?" Gore asked.

"I guess you could figure them out after the discussion happened," Barton responded.

"So what you did, you discussed each question one at a time, the answer would be somewhere in your discussion and when you covered that, you'd go to the next one, is that correct?"

"That's how I remember it."

"Who walked you through that?"

"I think it was Bill Hall."

Gore asked Barton if he recalled who was at the meeting. After Barton mentioned a number of FCs were there, as well as Ellis, Gore asked if Ellis knew how the meeting was being conducted, to which Barton answered, "I would guess so."

"To your knowledge, did everyone there then sign an affidavit stating that they completed the test without any outside help?" Gore asked.

"I don't remember what was signed or what wasn't signed," Barton answered. "I guess, if you say so."

"Was it issued by Pictorial?" Gore asked.

"Uh-huh."

"So everyone there would have executed their affidavits; is that correct?"

"I'm sure they did."

Moving on to the Tour de France CMA contest cheating, Gore asked, "Did you participate in any way in the Tour de France contest cheating?"

"If taking their production number away was cheating, I guess that's how I cheated," Barton answered.

"Do you know if this was occurring in other offices?" Gore asked.

"It was pretty well known that other offices managed their headcounts to whatever degree," Barton replied.

Barton then explained managing the headcount meant reclassifying FCs, either by taking away their production numbers, making them associate FCs, bringing them into a partnership with other brokers, or even terminating them.

Gore asked about Sherman, getting Barton to confirm he held quite a senior position and that he was the one who told Barton how to manage headcount. Barton also conceded that he assumed this situation was occurring throughout Merrill Lynch. He testified Ellis, Sherman, and Tom Muller III, one of the top four senior executives of Merrill Lynch's retail division, would all benefit from managing the headcount. Barton also told the panel that both he and Ellis had to pay back the trip they won in the contest as a result of the headcount activities.

At that point Chairman Conner ordered a 10-minute break. During this recess, I left the conference room and was walking down the corridor when I saw Ellis coming toward me. Our paths were about to cross for the first time since shaking hands before the start of the arbitration hearing.

As we approached each other, I extended my hand and said, "How are you, Mr. Ellis?"

With no observers in sight, Ellis glared at me and said, "I'm not going to shake your hand." As Ellis spoke he pulled his right arm up and behind him as high and as far back as he could. We both continued walking. Quinton Ellis, Jr., once a god in the Oklahoma City Complex, was not about to shake hands with his former rookie FC who had caused him tremendous personal and professional trouble and affected his stature and future within Merrill Lynch.

After the break, Gore resumed his direct examination of Barton. Gore inquired about my January 20, 1992, letter where I mentioned being provided a cheat sheet from Merrill Lynch Life in Dallas. Gore asked Barton if he had seen the letter and he said he had. Gore asked him about the paragraph with the cheat sheet reference and what his response to it had been.

"I told Keith I'd read it and I'd send it on down to Quinton to handle," Barton responded. "But I left and went back to Oklahoma City as a sales manager. And Jack Thomas and Quint handled it, and I wasn't there when they took their action, so I don't know how they responded to him." Although Barton went back to Oklahoma City in late January, he was not officially named sales manager until July.

"To your knowledge, was anyone in the Merrill Lynch company aware of any cheat sheets being used in relation to the insurance test?" Gore asked.

"No," Barton replied. "My response was, if I had a cheat sheet, why in the hell would I have gone to the seminar?"

Moving on, Gore asked, "Do you have any knowledge of Mr. Schooley using the hotline to call New York?"

"I have been made aware of it, after the fact," Barton responded. "I mean, a year or so later I was made aware of the fact that he had called the hotline."

"Were you aware or are you aware that Quinton Ellis might have been informed of his using the hotline when he did it?" Gore asked.

"No," Barton answered. "In fact, I was informed by Helmuth some time later at the end of all this or something, or when I read Barry Mandel's letter or something."

Gore asked Barton about the timing of his promotion to sales manager, and whether it occurred during the first investigation. "I was under the understanding that they had pretty much completed it, I thought," Barton replied. I would notice that despite the evidence to the contrary both Day and later, Meditz, would try to persuade the arbitrators that the first investigation had not been completed at about the time of Barton's promotion, but was, in fact, ongoing.

Gore then asked, "Have you ever made any derogatory remarks to Lisa Brainard about Mr. Schooley?"

"I don't recall them, but—" Barton began to reply.

"Would you have called him the world's biggest liar and said he had a small twisted mind?" Gore interrupted.

"I don't remember making it, but there were times I felt I'd claim authorship to them."

"Are there times that you felt that way?"

"Yes. But that's not something I would have said. I've been ready to claim authorship."

"But you don't disagree with them?"

"No, not too much. Not after the last three and a half years, I don't disagree with them at all. In fact, I think they might be kind of mild."

When I heard this, I had to laugh to myself. Barton had the nerve to claim calling *me* a liar was mild. This coming from a man who was first against me, then with me, then against me again. He seemed to choose sides however it suited him best at the time. He appeared to have no real conviction or commitment to his position. He just jumped on whatever bandwagon was going his way.

Gore moved on to the issue of the unknown Paul. He asked Barton, "Do you have any knowledge of a meeting in Enid on September 22, 1992, between Quinton Ellis, Jack Thomas, and someone named Paul from New York?"

"No," Barton answered.

I was surprised by Barton's answer. On the morning of September 24, 1992 (the day I met with Mandel, Mihaly, and Dineen in New York), Clark had told me Barton knew about my 31-page letter to the directors as of Tuesday afternoon—September 22—the day Paul met with Thomas and Ellis. I figured that when Ellis returned to Oklahoma City after meeting with Paul, he informed his second in command of why there had been a meeting in Enid and with whom. However, when Thomas later testified he, too, could not remember any such meeting, my surprise turned into suspicion.

"Did Quinton Ellis say to you that he wanted Keith Schooley to get his with a red hot poker after Keith Schooley sent a letter to the directors on September 17, 1992?" Gore asked.

"I don't remember Quinton saying something like that," Barton answered.

"All right," Gore continued. "Would you have told Keith that in a phone conversation?"

"That sounds more of something on what my opinion would have been more than Quint," Barton replied.

"Okay. So you might have said that?"

"I might have said it."

"Did Jack Thomas tell you that Keith was a cancer in the Enid office?"

"No."

"Did he indicate to you he didn't want him around?"

"No, not at all."

"Did Jack never have any derogatory remarks about Keith, is that correct?"

"Not to my knowledge."

"And how about Quinton Ellis, did he ever make any derogatory remarks about Mr. Schooley?"

"No, not to me."

It was now obvious to me Clark was right. After Barton's settlement of his arbitration case with Merrill Lynch, the firm had his cooperation in regard to my case. To believe Ellis and Thomas had never made any derogatory comments to Barton about me in view of all that had happened would be like believing Americans had never made any derogatory comments about the Japanese immediately after Pearl Harbor.

Gore asked Barton about his run-in with Kelli Metz at the class reunion in the summer of 1993, asking him if he yelled and cussed at her. Barton responded, "I know I got loud with her; I don't remember cussing. But if you say I did, I did."

Gore, after asking Barton several questions about when he signed his client's signature on a document, asked, "Did you ever tell Mr. Schooley that you did not think you were terminated for that, but for Enid?"

"Oh, I'm sure I did," Barton answered. "I probably told him I thought it was because of Enid, and I still believe it was because of that."

"And did Quinton Ellis indicate to you that he was fired for Enid instead of the reason put on—the official reason?" Gore asked.

"I don't remember if he did or not," Barton replied.

"Did he ever indicate to you, 'Schooley got us both'?" Gore asked.

"He might have said it, I don't remember," Barton said.

"Would you have communicated that to Keith in those words—'he got us both'?" Gore asked.

"I might have, I don't know," Barton answered. "I felt like that was the basis on mine, I may have said that."

Continuing to inquire about Ellis, Gore asked Barton why Ellis lost his position in the Oklahoma City office.

"I understood it was for loss of market share," Barton replied.

"Is that a valid reason?"

"It could be. They make decisions for whatever they want to."

"Did you ever indicate to Keith that you thought that was not the real reason?"

"I might have."

"That's not one of the factors they evaluate managers on, is it, loss of market share?"

"To my knowledge, it's not."

"And wasn't there a new PaineWebber office in the Oklahoma City area that opened around—before that time?"

"Uh-huh," Barton answered.

"And didn't you say it would be reasonable to anticipate a 1 or 2 percent loss of market share?"

"There are reasons you could explain it, yeah," Barton replied.

Gore moved on to the NASD investigation. Barton told the panel neither he nor Ellis were ever interviewed by an NASD investigator. Gore had Barton read from his own letter to the NASD he wrote to fight his letter of caution, in which he said, "Because of litigation, which Merrill Lynch was expecting and which was, in fact, filed by Mr. Schooley on August 9, 1994, against Merrill Lynch in Oklahoma state court, it was and has been Merrill Lynch's intent to control and distort the facts in order to protect itself."

Barton proceeded to tell the arbitration panel the only thing Merrill Lynch had distorted to the NASD was its representation that he had sold MuniYield as pre-refunded. Barton asserted he did not sell MuniYield as pre-refunded. I now had no doubt Merrill Lynch had Barton's cooperation in my arbitration hearing.

Gore then asked, "Did you ever make the statement that what had occurred was a third-rate burglary, but a first-rate cover-up?"

"I don't know if I said that or not," Barton answered.

"Do you recall what context you said it, if you said it?"

"Probably making it look like, at that time, it was starting to look like Watergate. They were just like, probably Watergate. Third-rate burglary and a first-rate cover-up."

"Did you state, 'It's almost like if you told a little lie the first time, you got to tell a bigger lie the next time, and a bigger lie after that, and that if Merrill Lynch had just come clean the first time, it would have been a lot easier, and I don't think they really came clean the first time'?"

"I don't remember saying that," Barton responded.

"Did you state you bit the bullet because you were led to believe you would be rewarded for it?"

"I might have thought that."

"Did you make the statement that Merrill Lynch has built a wall around Bob Sherman?"

"I might have made a comment like that."

"You made the statement that you felt like you were hung out to dry?"

"Yeah."

"Were you made the scapegoat in this situation?"

"Yeah."

"And who did that to you?"

"I think Merrill Lynch did it to me."

"And nothing happened to you after the first investigation, correct?"

"Yeah, nothing at that time."

"It was only after the letter to the directors, is that right?"

"Yes."

"Did Merrill Lynch try to make the Enid office look like a renegade office?"

"I felt they did."

"You personally don't like Mr. Schooley, correct?"

"That would be a pretty good assumption."

"Did you have a severe dislike for him?"

"That would be appropriate."

"As far as his professional habits were concerned, was he a hard worker?"

"All the reports I was getting back from the trainers, he was doing extremely well. He did fine in the training phase."

"Was he thorough?"

"From what standpoint?"

"In his work habits."

"Yeah, I would say so. He scored real high on his test. He seemed to apply himself to the test. I would say you would have to be pretty thorough to do that."

"Was he professional?"

"I think so."

"Do you wish he had never been hired?"

"In hindsight, yeah."

I certainly agreed with Barton there. Even though the opportunity with Merrill Lynch held such promise at first, it had never brought me anything positive. In hindsight, part of me also wished I had never been hired.

Gore was finished with Barton and Day had no questions for cross-exam. I was pleased that having recordings of my many conversations with Barton had kept him in check and did not allow him to be as friendly a witness to Merrill Lynch as he seemed to want to be.

As I heard it, Barton's testimony established a number of things, including that both he and Merrill Lynch made efforts to cover up; Ellis broke promises; Sherman gave orders to manage the headcount during the Tour de France CMA contest; Hall provided answers to the eight FCs for the insurance exam; Barton, Ellis, and Thomas were aware I had received what I believed to be a cheat sheet from Merrill Lynch Life in Dallas as reported in my January 20, 1992, letter; Barton learned from New York that I had used the confidential hotline; nothing happened to Barton as a result of the first investigation; Barton believed he and Ellis were fired because of Enid rather than the official reasons; and Barton had hostile feelings toward me for reporting the wrongdoing.

Day three of my hearing was complete. I was feeling good. Most things were going just as I had hoped.

Ellis Edwards: Merrill Lynch Needs to Terminate Some People

It was now the last day of my arbitration hearing. Merrill Lynch and I would both present some high-powered witnesses to support our respective positions. Gore would call an expert witness, a former president of a securities firm who later served as treasurer of the State of Oklahoma. Gore would also call possibly the nation's leading authority on punitive damages. Day would call Merrill Lynch's manager of internal reviews, its assistant general counsel, and a securities expert witness from Los Angeles. Day would also call Thomas.

This was a unique day in my arbitration hearing—one that was loaded with extraordinary witnesses who would raise their right hands and swear to tell the truth, the whole truth, and nothing but the truth. I would be shocked at what I was about to hear from the Merrill Lynch witnesses and would come to believe in their view the truth was disposable. The primary objective was to win the war.

The first witness for the final day was my securities expert witness— Ellis Edwards. Edwards provided the arbitration panel with his educational and professional background, including that he had been president of the brokerage firm R. J. Edwards and had served as the treasurer of the State of Oklahoma. Gore's direct examination of Edwards would be brief but powerful.

He established that Edwards had managed a securities office and was somewhat familiar with securities rules, regulations, and laws.

Gore asked Edwards if he had read my 31-page letter to Merrill Lynch's board of directors, and Edwards said he had. "If one of your employees gave that to you, reported that to you, what would be your reaction?" Gore asked.

"I would be appalled and would really take measures to investigate right away," Edwards responded. "If I found them to be true, or I thought they were to be true, I'd probably terminate some people immediately. But in the meantime, I'd suspend some people."

Gore confirmed that Edwards would follow through with the investigation to ensure everyone was interviewed and if he found there was any substance to the allegations, he would terminate the people responsible for it. Edwards also said he would report his findings to the NASD and consult a lawyer to be sure he had done everything he should.

With that, Gore concluded with Edwards and Day began to question him.

"Mr. Edwards, is the scope and extent of your knowledge about this case the reading of one letter?" Day asked.

"Yes, sir," Edwards replied.

"I have no further questions," Day said.

Edwards then said, "I should re-answer that. Reading probably several letters that are in that exhibit that I was given to read."

"What he's referring to is, there are some letters attached to the board of directors letter that are exhibits to it," Gore interjected.

Day then asked Edwards if he agreed that in terms of regulatory violations, the insurance cheating allegation might be, in terms of intentional violations of the law, the most significant.

"I don't know that would be the most substantive, but I think it would be something that would probably violate the law," Edwards responded.

Day asked Edwards of all the allegations I had made, which he considered to be the most serious. Edwards replied he felt not doing the best for your customers might be the worst thing, referring to what happened as a result of the Tour de France CMA contest cheating, and that the misuse of seminar expenses would be quite significant, especially within the firm.

"So if Merrill Lynch investigated that, audited that, and they took remedial action they thought was appropriate against that manager, it would depend upon what action they took as to what your opinion might be?" Day asked.

"That's correct," Edwards answered.

"And that would be true with regard to each and every one of those allegations?" Day continued.

"Well, one of the things they need to do is terminate some people," Edwards replied.

"Would you wait until you found out if they were true or not?" Day asked.

"Yes, I would," Edwards responded.

Day had no further questions. Edwards had established that in his expert opinion, terminations should have taken place if the allegations were true. It seemed obvious to me the evidence was substantiating every one of my allegations. Since no one was suspended by Merrill Lynch, let alone terminated after my first report of wrongdoing, I hoped the panel got the message I had reason to be concerned about a cover-up.

Helmuth Meditz: Why the Memo? You Had to Know It Would Go All the Way to Senior Management

Chairman Conner recognized Gore had called all my witnesses with the exception of one that would arrive later in the day. The arbitrators were now ready to hear from the rest of Merrill Lynch's witnesses, having already heard from Champion. Conner asked Day to call his next witness. He called Helmuth Meditz.

Meditz had flown in from New York to demonstrate to the arbitrators that Merrill Lynch had responsibly and thoroughly investigated all the wrongdoing reported by me. However, what I heard was that Merrill Lynch's star witness demonstrated the one allegation that had serious potential for the firm—the allegation of widespread insurance cheating—was covered up.

Meditz provided the arbitration panel with his educational and professional background including that he had been employed in a number of securities firms' compliance departments since 1972. Meditz said he joined Merrill Lynch in 1987 to head up a unit called internal reviews.

"How did you become aware, Helmuth, of Keith Schooley?" Day asked.

Meditz, in reference to my memorandum, answered, "This is a letter that I received a day or two after June 29, 1992, a letter from Mr. Schooley to Mr. Jack Thomas that was faxed to me, I believe, by Oklahoma City management."

"And your reaction to this correspondence?" Day asked.

"Well, I was certainly surprised and disturbed by this letter," Meditz replied. "He raised numerous issues—most of which were not your typical issues I might be involved in."

Meditz explained he immediately made plans to visit Oklahoma to investigate my memorandum and flew to Oklahoma City on July 6, 1992. "I was down here within days of receiving this letter," Meditz said. "We made every effort to immediately jump on this and try to resolve it."

Meditz told the arbitrators he interviewed Ellis, Barton, Thomas, and me. He also talked about the meeting he had with me at the Enid Best Western. "I found Mr. Schooley to be a very intelligent person, very bright, very articulate," Meditz said. "It was interesting that very quickly through the conversation that developed, in my opinion, a strong dislike he had for the management of Enid at the time, Brent Barton, and the Oklahoma City office, Quint Ellis, calling them arrogant and using other words, as I found in my notes in reviewing them. I think at one point he called them con artists, thugs, bullies. And Mr. Schooley went over his concerns, there were about seven or eight different ones. Mr. Cordell and I listened, we asked him questions, he responded, and we took notes and we told him we would look at this and we would get back with him at a later date."

"Did you give Mr. Schooley a progress report in your investigation?" Day asked.

"On July 16, I called Mr. Schooley to advise him of the internal progress we made and what I had found so far," Meditz responded. "Mr. Schooley, subsequent to my conversation with him on July 16, wrote a July 18 letter to me, which troubled me to no end, in effect, considering this to be a cover-up and that if I'm having difficulty finding the right answers, he would assist me in finding the right answers."

"Did you need Mr. Schooley's help to find the right answers?" Day asked.

"I don't need Mr. Schooley's help to find the right answers," Meditz answered. "And I've done this all my life in my profession. I take great pride in what I do, and I was deeply offended when the letter came in. And well, needless to say, it bothered me."

Day asked Meditz what his investigation determined. Meditz told the arbitration panel his investigation had determined local management had made misjudgments in the Tour de France CMA contest that were not in conformity with Merrill Lynch policies and guidelines. As a result of these misjudgments, Meditz went on to say I had not been paid bonuses that were owed to me or sent to New York for additional training to which I was entitled. The training Meditz alluded to was actually held at the Princeton corporate campus, headquarters for the firm's retail division. The Princeton campus was only 50 miles from New York City. Consequently, in Merrill Lynch parlance, New York and Princeton were virtually synonymous.

Day then asked what Meditz determined about the cheat sheets. "The cheat sheets originally were very disturbing," Meditz answered. "Certainly just the phraseology of the cheat sheet was disturbing to me. Having contacted the numerous individuals, having done a lot of work on this, the bottom line was, it was a nonevent. There were no cheat sheets. The way I determined that was in conversations with people at Pictorial who ran the testing procedures, conversations with the person who supposedly made the allegation to Mr. Schooley that there was a cheat sheet."

Meditz went on to address a number of my other allegations, conceding that wrongdoing had occurred in the instances of the seminar expenses, the MuniYield fund, and the opening of out-of-state accounts.

"Senior management of Merrill Lynch is very concerned about one person in the department trying to make a decision affecting a big issue," Meditz told the panel. "Therefore, the general counsel of the firm, Mr. Hammerman, set a procedure in place, going back to the time when I joined Merrill Lynch, actually it kind of started when I came, what we call a review committee. I call it 'the white heads and the baldies.' But these are the senior members of the law and compliance department. We gather around in a conference room and we discuss major issues. Now, these are: the director of compliance, the head of litigation, the head of human resources, the head lawyer, a former head of the New York State Securities Commission, the former SEC regional officer, a former head of the New York Stock Exchange enforcement area. These are people who sit around a table that listen to the issues, okay? And then obviously we don't call them together every time we have to make a decision, but when there are unusual circumstances, significant issues, as this was, because it was so unusual."

"Mr. Meditz, let me ask you something," Day said. "You bring these people together for big problems. You just described this as not being a big problem?"

"I was—you were interrupting me. I was just leading up to the point. While this was rather unique, this was different. This was addressing issues I, in all my years, really had never gotten into as your typical compliance investigation. And I wanted the benefit of other people's thinking in reviewing this. So on August 5, we met. We talked about it. It lasted several hours, and the committee asked me to do a detailed memo, since I think it was confusing to them also, or unusual to them."

I felt Meditz was dissembling—acting as though the wrongdoing reported in my memorandum was difficult for someone with his compliance expertise to understand. What was difficult to understand about the contest cheating, the cheating on insurance exams, the improper use of a country club list, the falsified seminar expenses, the misrepresentation of MuniYield, the improper opening of out-of-state accounts, and the promise of assets to FCs? It was unlikely Meditz needed the help of the distinguished review committee to understand the issues.

I believed the reason Hammerman had the review committee get involved was for the same reason Meditz asked me on July 7, "Why did you do it—why the memorandum to Jack? You had to know it would have to go all the way to senior management" and "What does Keith Schooley do after the movie?" Merrill Lynch had a major problem on its hands. A critical decision had to be made by senior management since I, in my memorandum, put in writing my allegation of what I believed to be "the apparent acceptance and encouragement within the District of what appears to be the widespread use of cheat sheets or other improper means concerning the self-administered examinations to maintain a life insurance license." I believed the decision the review committee would have to make would be how to deal with this particular allegation.

Meditz told the arbitrators he and Roepke met with me on August 13, 1992, to let me know the findings of the investigation. Meditz said he told me the matters reported did not rise to the level of terminating someone at Merrill Lynch, and I strongly disagreed.

"Now, I do this for a living," Meditz said. "I interview over 100 people a year where I do major investigations, most of them are done in New York. On occasion I come out to a branch. And this was rather surprising to me that Mr. Schooley who had a short career in the business at that point, wanted someone who has been with the firm for 21 years with an unblemished record, terminated."

"And the next time you heard about this?" Day asked.

"The next time was the big letter, the [September 17] letter to the board of directors, a 31-page letter that was addressed by Mr. Schooley to every member of the board at Merrill Lynch," Meditz replied. "Needless to say, that caused quite a stir. And in meeting with the senior members of the law and compliance department in New York, when this letter to the board came in, it was decided that another investigation should be done, independent of me, by another person. And that person who was assigned that task was a senior attorney in our litigation department, Mr. Barry Mandel, and assisted by Orestes Mihaly, a former chief of the New York State Securities Department. They began an investigation into this whole matter."

"Did you engage in a cover-up as Mr. Schooley alleged in his correspondence to the board of directors?" Day asked.

"I did not," Meditz answered. "I was deeply offended by that. I take great pride in the job I do at Merrill Lynch. I think the firm stands for integrity. We believe it."

Day had no further questions so it was Gore's turn to cross-examine the witness. Gore wanted to establish that as a result of Meditz' investigation of my memorandum, virtually no action was taken against those individuals who were parties to the wrongdoing. Consequently, I sent my letter to the board effectively accusing Meditz of a cover-up.

"On August 13 when you met Mr. Schooley, nothing had been done, and didn't you tell him the investigation was concluded and whatever happens was—" Gore asked.

"No, no, no, no," Meditz interrupted. "The investigation was an ongoing investigation. I was in the process of preparing a memo, which was requested of me by the review committee to pull all these pieces together. I wanted to give him an update of where we were. And yes, we met with the review committee and I think I wanted to communicate with him, the most important point that I thought was in his, Mr. Schooley's mind—that was, he wanted two management people terminated. I wanted to tell him that was not going to happen, and that we were still reviewing other matters and cleaning it up."

Gore then asked, "A few minutes ago you testified your investigation was completed when you met on August 5 with the review committee, and you met on August 13 with Mr. Schooley to tell him the results of the investigation. Is that not what you said a few minutes ago?"

"The investigation, I would say, has been completed," Meditz replied. "But in order to resolve all the issues—one thing is to find out what each paper said, and something else to ever come to a conclusion, what should be done about each and every item."

Following up, Gore asked, "Mr. Meditz, is this your memo in the conclusion of your investigation on August 5?" He was referring to one of Merrill Lynch's exhibits.

"This is a status report that I prepared as a result of the review committee meeting on August 5 where they asked me to put together and present my findings," Meditz answered.

"So the only things, in other words, that were left to be done were the things you've listed under resolutions?" Gore asked.

Meditz asked Gore what page he was referring to and Gore reminded him after each issue he wrote a resolution paragraph. Gore asked, "And you just said your investigation was complete with the exception of completing whatever action was going to be taken, which appears to be what you've listed under resolution, is that correct?"

"Why don't we go over it," Meditz responded. "I think it speaks for itself."

"Well, I'm just asking you," Gore said. "Is it correct that the only thing left to be done was action taken? You had already gathered all the facts, the only thing left was whatever action was going to be taken on those facts. Is this the action that was going to be taken listed in the resolutions?"

"That was the resolution of the fact, yes," Meditz replied.

Gore and Meditz continued to go back and forth. Gore was attempting to establish that the only actions taken, or to be taken, by Merrill Lynch were those listed as resolutions in Meditz' report. Meditz was saying they were only the "immediate resolutions" to my concerns and senior management was still in the process of determining what additional actions might result from the investigation. Meditz said, "The sanctions and the ultimate resolutions on some of these issues had not all been concluded at that point. I wanted to go back to Mr. Schooley as quickly as possible to report back to him that, yes, we had a meeting of the review committee, and the recommendation was not to terminate two people as he had demanded or requested we do. But the sanctions had not all been imposed at that point in time."

I was amazed at how important Meditz and his superiors evidently felt I, as a rookie FC in 1992, was, as suggested by Meditz saying, "I wanted to go back to Mr. Schooley as quickly as possible to report back to him." Not only had Meditz flown to Oklahoma in July to meet with me but he flew to Oklahoma again in August to report back to me "as quickly as possible." I remembered Meditz' direct testimony only minutes earlier when he said, "I interview over 100 people a year where I do *major* investigations. *Most* of them are done in New York, on *occasion* I come out to a branch." I also remembered the many deep breaths Meditz and Roepke took on August 13 when they came on a mission to put the matter to rest but could not accomplish this goal.

"We tried to correct as much as we could by the time I sat down with Mr. Schooley on August 13," Meditz continued. "I reported back to him that we reviewed it, we found at this point that they should not be terminated, and we will take—I think my notes reflect—that we will take whatever appropriate sanctions or remedial action the firm sees fit to take. That's in my notes, and that was done. It was not all done by the 13th, it was not all done by the 5th. It was done at a later time.

Some was resolved by the time I met with Mr. Schooley on the 13th, some done later on."

Meditz, manager of internal reviews for the largest and most respected securities firm on Wall Street, seemed to be doing all that he could to obscure the reality that Merrill Lynch considered the matter over until my September 17 letter to the board hit.

"So the things that occurred after September 17, 1992, would be as a result of the second investigation. Is that correct?" Gore pointedly asked.

"Not correct," Meditz replied. "It's fair to say some of the things that I brought up in my investigation, ultimately, the sanctions were imposed during the reign of the second investigation."

"Okay," Gore said. "Is it your testimony here that on August 13, 1992, when you met with Mr. Schooley, you did not tell him the investigation was over and whatever action was going to be taken has been taken and it was closed and over with?"

"I told Mr. Schooley what the facts were as we investigated so far," Meditz answered. "I told him the firm will take whatever remedial action needs to be done. I made that quite clear to him."

Meditz' testimony continued as he addressed a number of the other allegations I had made. Chairman Conner interrupted Gore's questioning at this point, asking him to help the panel understand how his cross-examination related to the case of wrongful termination.

"The respondent is trying to say there's no basis for any of Mr. Schooley's complaints," Gore replied.

"Well, focus me on how that bears on the wrongful or constructive termination?" Chairman Conner asked.

"If a whistle-blower makes frivolous complaints, he's not a whistle-blower," Gore responded. "He wouldn't be subject to public policy wrongful termination."

"All right," Chairman Conner said. "So the cross gauges toward whether or not they were frivolous or legitimate complaints?"

"Exactly," Gore answered.

As Gore continued his cross-examination, he asked Meditz if certain allegations I had made were valid. Meditz responded, "I told Mr. Schooley when we met on August 13 that I appreciated him bringing these matters to our attention. I told him he was right in many of the issues. He was wrong in some."

"Which issue was he wrong on?" Gore asked.

"Cheat sheets," Meditz answered.

"Okay. Let me ask you about that. You said you interviewed Sarah Graham; is that right?"

"I did not."

"You never interviewed Sarah Graham?"

"I spoke to her on the phone. I believe Mr. Mandel may have, I did not."

"You never interviewed her?"

"I spoke to her on the phone. I never personally interviewed her."

"Okay. You talked to her on the phone?"

"Yes."

"Okay. Well, an interview on the phone is good enough. Okay. You did interview Sarah Graham, you talked to her?"

"Yes."

"Who else did you talk to?"

"People at Pictorial."

"That's the people that give the test?"

"That's right."

"Were they going to tell you there were cheat sheets?"

"I asked them what this cheat sheet represented, and they told us this was an answer sheet to a practice exam. It was not an answer sheet to any exam they were administering. It was an answer sheet to a practice exam."

"All right, sir. You're talking about a piece of paper that was given to Mr. Schooley by Ms. Graham?"

"I believe that's where he got it from."

Gore asked Meditz who else he talked to in relation to his cheat sheet investigation. He told the panel the only other people he spoke to were several of the FCs who attended the meeting with Hall and had to retake the exam.

I could not believe the testimony Gore had just gotten from Meditz. His investigation was clearly a lackluster effort. Gore probed further,

"Who was in charge of giving those tests in the Dallas office where Sarah Graham worked?"

"I don't know who the head was at that unit, or whose insurance area, who would head that up," Meditz replied.

"Would it not be good to talk with them?"

"The person who allegedly gave the sheet was Sarah Graham. We spoke to Sarah Graham. I spoke to the people that took the exam."

Gore asked Meditz if he talked to Graham's boss, or Champion, or Hall. His answers were no, no, and no again for Hall because he was no longer with the firm at the time.

"Does that prevent you from interviewing them?" Gore asked.

"Typically—no, but if a person is no longer with Merrill Lynch, I generally don't reach out unless it was a major issue," Meditz said.

"You're an investigator and when you do an investigation, your investigation is limited to Merrill Lynch employees?" Gore asked.

"I didn't say that," Meditz answered.

"I'm sorry, I misunderstood," Gore said. "What did you just say?"

"I said, typically, I will review Merrill Lynch employees and generally not go outside the firm unless it was a major issue where I felt it was necessary."

"So this wasn't a major issue and you didn't feel it was necessary?"

"I believe Mr. Hall was gone. I think an effort was made to contact him. I don't think he could be reached. One of the persons that works for me, Tommy Boyd, I think, did try to reach out and could not contact him. He had left. He had been terminated prior to that."

"Is there any other issue that you think Mr. Schooley didn't have a valid basis for besides the cheat sheets?" Gore asked.

"Mr. Schooley raised legitimate concerns in these other situations," Meditz answered.

Gore then asked Meditz about the results of the second investigation. Meditz said he had a general knowledge of what happened, including Ellis and Barton having to pay back their trips; that Ellis' year-end bonus was severely impacted; the letters of caution the NASD issued; that Ellis was admonished by his senior person; that Barton was admonished, stripped of his sales manager title, and prevented from going to a training program necessary for advancement within the firm.

Next, Gore asked, "Did you ever make the statement to Mr. Schooley, 'Why the memo? You had to know it would go all the way to senior management'?"

"I believe I may have asked him that question," Meditz replied.

"Did you threaten Mr. Schooley with any action in accordance with a $15 rebate he supposedly made?" Gore continued.

"I pointed out to Mr. Schooley many of these issues he was raising are matters of degree, on what's severe and what isn't severe," Meditz responded. "In his mind, all these issues that he raised were severe. I said to him, in my opinion, they're not all severe. I pointed out to him that rebate, that $15, under New York Stock Exchange rules, one could consider that to be sharing in the losses and profits in a customer's account. They could take some serious action. To them, forget the 15 bucks, the fact that you paid a customer off, in their eyes, is a major violation. I'm sure in Mr. Schooley's eyes it's not a major violation. So I wanted to point out to him, it's a matter of degree. I've been around 27 years. I sit on the disciplinary panel at the New York Stock Exchange. I sit on arbitration panels. I know what the rules and regulations are. I know what the New York Stock Exchange demands, what kind of action they want to take when you have a rebate or you pay your customer back. I'm familiar with that, because I sit on that table. So I wanted to point out to him that, yes, in some eyes it's serious. It was not a threat. I don't threaten anybody. I'm a very nice person."

Gore asked Meditz if he knew why Barton was terminated and Ellis lost his position as RVP of the Oklahoma City Complex. Meditz stuck with the company line on Barton, saying he was fired for signing a client's name even though he had a faxed signature from the client approving it. Regarding Ellis he said he had no idea what the reason was behind the action.

Meditz' testimony came to an end. It was a powerful performance, but not for Merrill Lynch, for me. I believed it had now been established by the firm's own manager of internal reviews that my allegations of wrongdoing were accurate—except, of course, the allegation of the use of cheat sheets.

Yet what was even more powerful was the transparent fact that Meditz, presumably under the supervision of Hammerman and the review committee, skirted my allegation of the apparent widespread use of improper means in taking the life insurance examinations.

Meditz testified that in his investigation of the cheat sheets he interviewed several FCs who attended the Saturday morning meeting led by Hall. However, those eight FCs were not even alleged to have used a cheat sheet as proven by the fact that they attended the Saturday morning meeting. Meditz said he interviewed people at Pictorial, but they were not alleged to have been party to the insurance cheating. The *only* person Meditz interviewed who was likely to have been a participant in, or knowledgeable about, the insurance cheating scheme was Sarah Graham.

Meditz did not interview Champion, the resident insurance specialist in Dallas during the investigation, nor did he locate Hall, a former resident insurance specialist in Dallas. Hall had already testified Merrill Lynch had his permanent address all along. Day certainly had no difficulty in finding Hall three years later just prior to my arbitration hearing. Furthermore, Meditz did not even know who Graham's boss was. I felt even after this Meditz might need my help after all in finding the right answers.

Barry Mandel: I Don't Know if I Could Work in an Office Where My Manager Is Threatening to Sue Me

Day's next witness was Barry Mandel, assistant general counsel of Merrill Lynch, the firm's other star witness. Mandel had been the one in charge of the second internal investigation.

Mandel gave a brief overview of his educational and professional background and stated he joined Merrill Lynch in April 1992. Mandel said he was in the firm's litigation department where he handled various litigation and regulatory matters. Mandel explained his first serious contact with my case was when I sent my letter to the board. This prompted Mandel to begin an inquiry that would determine if the previous investigation had been thorough and allow him to advise the board in what actions would be appropriate.

"Mr. Mandel, would you briefly summarize your investigation, the conclusions, remedial action that was taken?" Day asked.

"What we did was, we spoke with people involved in the matter," Mandel replied. "We spoke with Mr. Schooley, reviewed the documents. I reviewed many of the materials gathered by Mr. Meditz. I spoke with Mr. Meditz. And ultimately we focused on the issues raised by Mr. Schooley before his letter to the board and then the new issues that we perceived as being raised in the letter to the board. They fell, for example, into a category of an alleged violation of the insurance laws. And the principal issue that we understood Mr. Schooley to be raising, was one of the use of cheat—what he has referred to as cheat sheets. And we were unable to confirm the use of cheat sheets. We had found that there had been an answer sheet distributed, but that was to a practice exam. And we'd also found some evidence that seemed inconsistent with the use of cheat sheets, meaning that we had determined there had been some meetings with insurance personnel explaining the insurance laws, and that seemed to have occurred at or about the same time as the exam, and so it didn't seem, at least to make sense to us, that those kinds of meetings would take place if the same personnel was simply using the answers to the test. And so one of the things we concluded was, that at least someone might raise a question as to whether or not it was proper or appropriate to have such meetings at the time of the exam, and so we required the people, who we were able to identify as having attended those meetings, to take the exam again.

"On the issue of falsification of seminar expenses, we concluded that what Mr. Schooley had pointed out was, for the most part, accurate and then there were some details to it that we ultimately required Mr. Barton to pay back some money. With respect to the alleged misrepresentation of MuniYield, we concluded that it was likely that Mr. Barton had made misstatements to customers about MuniYield about whether it was pre-refunded and we required that the customers be offered the right of rescission. Then there was a question about registration violations, about opening accounts in states people were not registered. We found that really occurred essentially in two instances. With respect to the contest headcount manipulation, we found that Mr. Schooley had described the situation accurately. We took some steps with respect to that, such as, requiring Mr. Ellis and Mr. Barton who had received a certain free trip by virtue of that contest to pay for their own trip. And then there was an issue of the purported unregistered sales of Singapore Air stock. I think that issue was raised for the first time in Mr. Schooley's letter to the board. And we concluded, at least, with respect to some of these situations, that it was accurate. Offers of rescission were made to the purchasers. And then ultimately we took some steps with respect to letters of admonishment in demoting Mr. Barton and taking him out of the management track for a period of time. I think that's sort of a summary of the things we found and the steps we took."

Mandel then told the arbitration panel that Merrill Lynch's legal department had no involvement in Thomas' termination statement he read to me, and it was his understanding Thomas prepared it by himself. Mandel said he had conversations with Stephen Jones starting on October 1 where he told Jones there was a misunderstanding and Thomas did not terminate me. Mandel explained that Jones' position was Thomas *did* terminate me.

"Was there any subsequent conspiracy to cover up any of the matters raised by Mr. Schooley in response to the regulators?" Day asked.

"Absolutely not," Mandel replied.

"Isn't it the truth, in fact, there was basically, by virtue of the lack of regulatory action, determined to be no substance to those claims or that your remedial actions you took were proper?" Day asked.

"Yes," Mandel responded. "We certainly viewed the fact that several regulatory authorities looked at what we found, which in some instances, was, in fact, a confirmation of what Mr. Schooley had told us that there had been certain, either misconduct or wrongdoing, and had concluded that the actions Merrill Lynch had taken were satisfactory to address that kind of wrongdoing, misconduct."

"I have no further questions," Day said.

Gore began his inquiry of Mandel. He established that Mandel conducted a review of the prior investigation and he found it to be thorough. Mandel said he had found two of my allegations, the improper use of cheat sheets and the country club list, to be unsubstantiated but that the other issues had some basis in fact.

Mandel explained to investigate the matter of the cheat sheets, he contacted the personnel involved. This meant the insurance personnel who would have been the ones giving out the cheat sheets, so it seemed obvious to me they would deny it. He said he also contacted other financial consultants in the office to see if they had cheat sheets, which they denied. Mandel concluded that since FCs were walked through the exam, then likely there were no cheat sheets available since they would probably chose to use them over attending a seminar if they had the chance.

"You said you contacted the person who handed out the cheat sheet," Gore said. "Is that correct?"

"Yes."

"Who was that?"

"I believe that was—well, I think we contacted a Mr. Hall and Sarah Graham."

Gore, surprised, responded, "Oh, you contacted Mr. Hall?"

"I didn't, my colleague Orestes Mihaly did. I believe he reached out for him. I believe he ultimately contacted him."

"Can you verify that?"

"He just testified to it," Chairman Conner interjected.

"How can I verify it?" Mandel asked. "At least to my recollection, I mean, I could go ask him. As I'm sitting here, I believe that was the case. My recollection is Mr. Schooley told us that he had actually gotten the cheat sheet from a Sarah Graham. And I know I spoke to Sarah Graham and she denied it."

"All right, sir," Gore said. "Bill Hall testified here that cheat sheets were floating around some offices and were available. Did he tell you that when you interviewed him?"

"No. We did not have that information, no. That was not told to us."

"So anyway, Mr. Hall didn't tell you the same thing he told us, is that what you're saying? Is that correct?"

"Well, if you're saying Mr. Hall told you that, in fact, they used answer keys to the test or cheat sheets, no, that was not told to us."

"Did you interview anyone else?" Gore asked.

"I think we interviewed Mr. Ellis, Mr. Barton, and maybe Mr. Thomas on the subject, this financial consultant, Sarah Graham, I believe

Mr. Hall, and Mr. Schooley. I don't believe there was anyone else, nothing that occurs to me now."

Concerning the country club list, Gore informed Mandel that Meditz had already testified the country club manager indicated the list was to be used only for the open house mailing.

Mandel soon conceded that Barton might have made three or four mass mailings with the list. Mandel also said he thought the list had been purged from Barton's computer and would not be used again.

Gore then had Mandel look at his April 16, 1993, letter to the SEC. Gore had a number of questions for Mandel about his representations to the securities regulator.

Concerning the issue of the meeting where Hall walked eight FCs through the insurance exam, Gore said, "You indicate the take-home examination has to be done without assistance from any outside source and you said, 'It was determined William T. Hall did spend several hours lecturing several financial consultants as the employees answered the questions.' That is your drafting of this letter, correct?"

"Yes."

"And then your next line says, 'It's not clear that taking the test under such circumstances was illegal.'"

"Yes."

"The parties who take that test have to sign a sworn statement or affidavit that they took that test without assistance from any outside source, do you know that?"

"Yes."

"How could that not be illegal, for them to be given the answers during the test?"

"We did not reach a conclusion they were given answers. It was not clear to us that was the kind of outside assistance that one would conclude was prohibited. And in any event, when we heard that, what we concluded was, there could at least be an argument that in fact that was the kind of outside assistance that was prohibited, and that's why we required the people who took the exam, under those circumstances, to retake it separately, under different circumstances. We didn't want there to be any question about that." Of course, Barton had already testified there was a discussion before each exam question which provided the answer.

Gore continued, referring to the paragraph in Mandel's letter where he claimed the Pictorial system was no longer used as of January 1992.

"I have a letter from Pictorial that indicates 157 of your FCs took the same exam they were taking before, between January 1, 1992, and August 26, 1992," Gore said. "Under those circumstances, is this paragraph accurate?"

"I couldn't reach that conclusion," Mandel replied. "I just don't know."

I was amazed. Mandel, who was in *charge* of the second internal investigation, seemed to be unsure about lots of things. Mandel *thought* his investigation of the insurance cheating scandal included an interview with Ellis and Barton and *maybe* with Thomas—none of whom had focused on the comment in my January 20, 1992, letter where I had made reference to being provided a cheat sheet. Mandel *thought* his investigation included an interview with Hall. He *thought* Merrill Lynch no longer used Pictorial as of January 1992, but he was not sure.

Gore moved on to the specifics of my termination. Mandel insisted job abandonment was not put on my U-5 form to blacklist me, but because it was the best description they could find for my refusal to return to work. Mandel said he had been given a copy of Thomas' statement and was aware of the lawsuit it threatened. He also said he knew the Enid office was small.

"And is it reasonable to expect someone to work in an office where the boss is suing them?" Gore inquired.

"Well, I don't know, but he hadn't sued him and I don't know if he was in fact suing him," Mandel responded. "I understood that he was shortly considering it. As of that point, he hadn't, and I don't believe he ever did commence a lawsuit."

"Could you work in [an office] where your manager's threatening to sue you?" Gore asked.

"I don't know if I could," Mandel replied. "If I could work out the problem, if I gave it a chance, maybe I could work it out. I can't tell you that everyone I've ever worked with I would socialize with, but I found a way to work with them."

Gore established that Mandel never offered to protect me from Thomas' threat of a lawsuit. He asked Mandel, "So, essentially, you just wanted Mr. Schooley to come back and continue or attempt to work with Mr. Thomas, correct?"

"Yes," Mandel responded. "I certainly wanted him to come back and we would hope we would resolve what certainly appeared to be a dispute between these people. But it wasn't going to get resolved by his not coming back to work."

That was all Gore had for Mandel. Again, I felt Merrill Lynch's witness had done more for me than for the firm. Mandel established that my reporting of wrongdoing was accurate—except, of course, the allegation of the use of cheat sheets. Mandel also showed his second internal investigation was even more lax than the first. He had failed to interview any of the 14 members of management or 281 FCs in the Texoma District I named or referred to in my letter to the board as having had taken the exam as indicated in the information Pictorial sent me. In addition, Mandel was mistaken in his recollection that Hall had been interviewed. Mandel's own letter to the SEC represented that Hall's whereabouts were unknown to him at the time, even though, according to Hall himself, Merrill Lynch always had his permanent address. Again, and not surprisingly, neither Mandel nor Mihaly interviewed Champion, the resident insurance specialist in Dallas at the time of the second internal investigation. As was the case with Meditz in the first internal investigation, the *only* person who was interviewed who was likely to have been a participant in, or knowledgeable about, the insurance cheating scheme was Sarah Graham.

However, even more important in terms of my wrongful termination case were two things. The first was Mandel's excuse for placing job abandonment on my U-5 form, saying Merrill Lynch could not think of any better way to describe the situation. Second, Mandel had responded to Gore's question concerning if he could work in an office where his manager was threatening to sue him by saying he did not know if he could. This was exactly what I was trying to establish—given the environment that existed, it was unreasonable to expect me to return to work in the Enid office.

Jack Thomas: I Was Going to Sue Schooley for Anything I Could

Next up was Jack Thomas. Merrill Lynch would attempt to show that Thomas, learning on September 28, 1992, of my 31-page letter to the board of directors, simply reacted as any normal person might have when he or she was accused of wrongdoing—called me a liar, threatened to sue me, and told me to leave his Enid office.

Thomas provided the panel with some personal background information. He said he went to work for Merrill Lynch in 1990, became the resident manager of the Enid office around February 1992, and left the firm in 1993. Thomas insisted his departure had nothing to do with the allegations I had made. He said a man named Rob Braver had offered him the position of branch manager at another securities firm. Chairman Conner had disclosed earlier that Braver was his stockbroker. So now, Chairman Conner was about to hear critical testimony from the person I had alleged constructively terminated me, who, according to Barton's testimony, happened to be good friends with Conner's own stockbroker—someone Conner surely implicitly trusted. Since Braver and Thomas were good friends, it would stand to reason Chairman Conner was likely to find Thomas' testimony credible.

Day got right to the point. "Did you fire Keith Schooley on September 28, 1992?"

"No, I did not," Thomas answered.

"What did you find when you came into your office on the morning of September 28?" Day asked.

"I found a copy of that letter to the board of directors in my chair, not on my desk, it was not presented to me personally," Thomas replied. "It was put in my chair, so when I pulled my chair out, it would be there."

"Did you tell Barry Clark, the week preceding September 28 at any point or anytime prior to September 28, Mr. Schooley was a cancer and you would not let him infect Michael Deline or Mr. Stong, the other two FCs?" Day asked.

"I'm sure I did not say Keith personally was a cancer," Thomas responded. "I knew I had conversations in the office that dealt with negative attitude, negative statements about the firm I had chosen to make a career of and that Keith had chosen to make a career of, and I would do everything I could to keep those attitudes from detrimentally affecting my other brokers."

Day asked Thomas what his reaction was when he read the letter. "I'd have to say I was incensed," Thomas replied.

"Why were you incensed?"

"Well, because I got in this business as a total career change in 1987 at age 41. And I have—knock on wood—to this date, not even a complaint that was called to the office, a written complaint, a letter to any regulatory agencies as a producer or a manager prior to this time. And getting into this industry when I did, it was too late for me to have my career derailed by something, especially something that was not true."

"What did you do?"

"I picked up the phone, I called an attorney, a friend of mine who is still a member of the bar. He is not a practicing attorney. He suggested I go to Keith and tell him that what he had written in there was an obvious lie, and it was known to be a lie. And I didn't feel like I could do that, because I was too mad. So I chose to write it in my memo that I gave to him, and did not want that misconstrued or misinterpreted, so I had Michael Deline come in and witness and listen to and read that statement word for word."

"Now, is it true that you were not a participant in or aware of a cheat sheet conspiracy or scheme inside of Merrill Lynch while you were employed?" Day asked.

"Absolutely."

"And were you aware of any other improper activity regarding the taking of the state insurance continuing education examinations?"

"No."

"So in what manner did you make this delivery of the statement? Were you angry, were you upset, were you demonstrative?"

"I was not demonstrative. I would say it was very controlled anger."

"And what was the response of Mr. Schooley?"

"Not really much response at all, other than requesting a copy of this document."

"Did you intend Mr. Schooley to leave the offices of Merrill Lynch at that time?"

"No."

"And did he, in fact?"

"He did not leave right away, no."

"Did he come to work the following day?"

"Yes, he did." Thomas then explained on that following day he and I had a conversation about making up the training program I missed as a result of my meeting in New York with Mandel, Mihaly, and Dineen. I had already testified I was in the office several hours on September 29, the day after Thomas read his statement, to collect documents in anticipation of a lawsuit from Thomas. When I was on my way out the door at 2:30 P.M. to meet with Stephen Jones, Thomas mentioned the training program, but I had other things on my mind. In view of Thomas' hostile attitude the day before, my only thought as to why he would bring up the training program was because perhaps he was now having second thoughts about his actions toward me.

"Did you speak and had you spoken to any Merrill Lynch attorneys prior to that time regarding the statement that you made to Keith Schooley?" Day asked.

"No," Thomas answered.

"And were you acting in your capacity as the manager of the Merrill Lynch office?" Day asked.

"In writing this?"

"Yes."

"Yes."

"You were telling him, as the manager of the Merrill Lynch office, that you were going to sue him on behalf of Merrill Lynch?"

"No, no, not at all. This, in my opinion, was a personal situation. It was not Merrill Lynch against Keith Schooley. It was me wanting a retraction of a statement I considered damaging to my career."

"And did you think you could work in the same office with Keith Schooley during the pendency of such a claim?"

"I felt like I could."

"Did Barry Mandel attempt to induce you not to sue Keith Schooley for libel?"

"Yes."

"But he was not your personal lawyer. He couldn't make you do that, could he?"

"No, he could not."

"Did you ever sue Mr. Schooley for libel?"

"No."

"Why didn't you?"

"Because at the request of Barry Mandel, from a company stand-point, he wanted to try and work this deal out and not, I guess, pour any more gasoline on the fire."

"So is it your testimony, as you sit here today, that if Mr. Schooley would have returned to work, that you believe you could have worked with him in an environment he could have functioned in?"

"Yes, I do."

"And you believe that because of what?"

"Again, because this was strictly between Keith and I. And I felt I could keep it that way."

Day asked Thomas that if the statement he read to me was personal, why he used Merrill Lynch letterhead for it.

"It was the first piece of paper I could find," Thomas answered.

"Did you know you were not supposed to utilize Merrill Lynch letterhead for personal communication?" Day asked.

"I didn't think about that," Thomas responded. "I picked up that piece of paper and I wrote out, you know, what I needed to say, and I didn't look for a scratch pad or anything else."

Thomas ignored the fact that the first piece of paper he could find to write on was not the same piece of paper he presented to me. What he presented to me had been typed by Feightner.

Thomas continued testifying, claiming that my allegation that he was one of the managers who was either aware of, or participated in, the improper methods of taking the insurance examinations, was a lie. This was why he considered suing me for libel.

However, I believed Thomas had no case. I had evidence he had to be aware of my suspicion about cheat sheets since I had mentioned it in my January 20 letter, which he and Ellis handled as Barton testified. I also assumed Thomas was aware of the fact that the eight FCs who Hall led through the exam on a question-by-question basis were going to have to retake the exam as a result of Meditz' investigation; after all, that had been decided days, if not weeks, before Thomas threatened to sue me.

In Gore's cross-examination, he questioned Thomas about the January 20 letter. "Mr. Thomas, I'm going to refer you to claimant's exhibit 20. Have you ever seen that before?"

Thomas answered he had and Gore asked him when that was.

"I don't think I saw this actual memo until the other day when I was going through some of the documents that I was supposed to examine," Thomas replied.

"So you didn't see it in January of 1992?" Gore asked.

"Not that I recall, no."

"Do you remember when Keith was in New York, I guess it was around maybe September 24 or somewhere in that area?"

"Uh-huh."

"There was a meeting in the Enid office with someone from New York named Paul. Do you recall that?"

"No, I don't."

"When Mr. Schooley sent his letter to the board of directors, did anyone call you and tell you about that letter?"

"I think the way I found out about that, is what I would usually do when I would drive in to the office, I would call the Enid office and/or call the Oklahoma City office, because I still was a producing manager and would call to see if I had any messages. And I think that's when I first learned of this."

"I'm sorry, what day was that?"

"That would have been on Monday morning, the 28th, I guess."

"And I'm sorry, who told you that?"

"It would have to have been either Brent or Quint."

"Okay. And I believe you stated Mr. Schooley put a copy of the board of directors letter of September 17 in your chair; is that right?"

"That's correct."

"Did you see him do that?"

"No."

"Do you remember when Mr. Schooley and Mr. Deline left for New York on or around September 22, 1992?"

"Yes, sir."

Gore, trying again, asked, "Was there not a meeting in your office that day with Quinton Ellis and somebody named Paul from New York?"

"In the Enid office?"

"Yes, sir."

"Not that I recall."

"Okay. Do you recall asking Michael Deline to wait before going to the airport for a few minutes so he would be there when Paul arrived?"

"No."

Still not knowing who Paul was, I could not believe Thomas was not remembering the meeting with him. Thomas had a clear memory of Deline and me going to New York, the circumstances surrounding what happened on September 28 and the day after, as well as other circumstances around that same time—but for some reason he could not remember a meeting with a Paul from New York. This struck me as highly suspicious.

Gore briefly asked Thomas about some of the other allegations I had made against him and then returned to the subject of Thomas' reaction to my letter.

"Barry Clark testified here earlier that on September 24, you stated something along the lines that Mr. Schooley was a cancer and you weren't going to have him in the office infecting Michael and Greg," Gore said. "I know you've already been asked about that. You don't remember it?"

"No, I don't remember saying Keith, as a person, was a cancer," Thomas responded. "His negative attitude was, in my opinion, something that left to run rampant could be cancerous to the attitude of the office and could spread, and I did not want that to happen."

"And Mr. Clark indicated you were extremely angry on that day, on September 24," Gore continued. "Do you remember when you made those remarks?"

"No, I don't. Because I was not extremely angry until I got this memo on the 28th."

"So you weren't referring to that board of directors letter on September 24 to Mr. Clark?"

"No, I was not."

"So Mr. Clark and yours would differ—I mean, that was Mr. Clark's recollection—that was what you were upset about."

"No, it was not."

"What were you upset about?"

"I was not upset at that time. What I understood at that time was, if I remember right, instead of going to PDP, he was now in New York, and he was having to discuss all of his situations with the people in New York. And that's the way, I think, this conversation came up, that went on with Barry, was in regards to that, and all of that stuff that was involved in that letter…I mean, in that…in his meeting."

"All right, sir," Gore said. "In your letter to Keith, I believe you threatened to sue him, is that correct?"

"Yes."

"What were you going to sue him for?"

"Anything I could, preferably libel or defamation of character."

"And at that point, you were definitely mad at him, right?"

"Yes."

"And you don't care for him today, do you?"

"I'd say that's a fair statement."

"Do you hate him?"

"No, I wouldn't say that."

"But you'd just as soon never see him again?"

"That would be fine."

"Have you ever retracted your threat to sue him?"

"No, it's never been addressed."

"You never communicated to him that you weren't going to sue him?"

"No."

"And to your knowledge, Merrill Lynch never did anything like that to him?"

"Never told Keith that I was not going to sue him?"

"Right."

"As far as I know."

"They never had authority to say that, did they?"

"No."

Gore continued, establishing the Enid office was small, both in physical size and in the number of staff. Gore asked Thomas, "Could you work in an office where your boss was suing you?"

"Yes," Thomas replied.

"You could do that?"

"Yes."

"You could function normally with the boss suing you?"

"As long as he was willing to keep it a personal matter that was not addressed daily or antagonistic or whatever."

"Did you ever tell Mr. Schooley that your lawsuit wouldn't be addressed on a daily basis, and we'll keep it personal, and we won't worry about it at work?"

"We never spoke. We haven't spoken to this day."

Later that day, Schmidt would tell Gore and me he noticed Arbitrator Barnes laugh when Thomas testified he could work in an office where his boss was suing him. My attorneys and I, already confident we had a strong constructive discharge case, were encouraged by Barnes' reaction.

Gore continued to press Thomas. "Had you stated to Mr. Schooley that his termination letter was 'for the record'?"

"Yes."

"And did you indicate he's a liar, is that correct?"

"Yes, I did."

"When you said you were going to sue 'you and yours,' were you referring to his wife by 'yours'?"

"Whomever."

"Could you tell me what Mr. Schooley lied about?"

"He knew for a fact I was not a participant in any cheat sheet scheme or even was not in attendance."

"Thank you," Gore said. "That's all I have."

Day wanted to redirect. "Now, you held and did not demonstrate any animosity during…with the one exception of this one incident with this memorandum, which you said you would not hold against him subsequently in working at the office. It was also your testimony that during the course of Mr. Schooley's employment…did you ever otherwise demonstrate any animosity toward him?"

"No."

"Or otherwise create adverse working conditions?"

"No."

Gore wished to recross, so he asked Thomas, "You never communicated to Keith that you weren't going to sue him, did you?"

"No," Thomas answered.

It went back to Day again. "You never had the opportunity ever to retract or otherwise work out some arrangement of working with him?"

"Not at all."

Gore's turn again. "You never wrote him a letter and said, 'By the way, I withdraw that. I'm not going to sue you.' You never did anything like that?"

"No," Thomas replied.

"And you could have communicated that way?" Gore asked.

"It would have been possible," Thomas responded.

Arbitrator Preston then had a couple of questions for Thomas. I would find Thomas' answers remarkably interesting.

"Mr. Thomas, after you delivered the September 28, 1992, memo to Mr. Schooley, from that point to any time thereafter, did anyone with Merrill Lynch or representing Merrill Lynch have any discussions with you concerning the memo?" Preston asked.

"No," Thomas replied. "Other than Barry Mandel saying, what we talked about earlier, about not filing a lawsuit."

Preston then asked, "Did anyone say anything about the fact that the memo was on a piece of Merrill Lynch stationery?"

"No."

Again I was stunned. It made absolutely no sense that Thomas' memo to me, on Merrill Lynch stationery, was his own action but he was not even reprimanded by his immediate superiors or by New York for his aggressive action at what was an incredibly sensitive point in time. I wondered how Thomas could *not* have gotten into trouble.

It would be later, after I learned who Paul was, that I would conclude the only logical reason Thomas did not get into trouble was because he was probably executing the plans of senior management given by Paul in the Enid meeting on September 22, 1992.

I could not believe Thomas had testified he had not learned of my 31-page letter until Monday, September 28, on his drive to the Enid office, and that after he saw a copy of the letter in his chair he simply reacted by grabbing the first piece of paper he could find to write his statement on. In fact, Thomas had said in his statement to me on that Monday afternoon, "It should come as no surprise to you that I have been made aware of what is going on." Indeed, it was hardly plausible my own manager would not learn of the 31-page letter until a week after it had arrived in New York. It sure looked to me like Jack Thomas was lying big time and I assumed the panel would see it too.

As I saw it, both Merrill Lynch and Thomas were covering up the meeting with Paul by supporting two legal documents Merrill Lynch had filed with the NYSE prior to the arbitration hearing—its amended answer and its motion for preliminary hearing to expedite the arbitration process.

Merrill Lynch represented in its amended answer that Thomas learned of my letter to the board on September 28, 1992, and attached to its motion was Thomas' affidavit wherein he represented that he learned of the 31-page letter on or about September 28, 1992. Both representations would be hard to support if Paul flew to Enid, Oklahoma, on September 21, the day my 13 overnight envelopes arrived in New York. I believe Thomas and Merrill Lynch thought it would play better if Thomas first learned of and saw my letter on Monday, September 28, and then just simply *reacted*.

Professor Michael Rustad: A Multiplicity of Smoking Guns

My last witness was Professor Michael Rustad, an expert on punitive damages. Dr. Rustad was well known in the legal community for his work on punitive damages and was considered by many to be the nation's leading authority on the subject. Rustad gave an overview of his legal background including that he had done his thesis on punitive damages at Harvard Law School. Rustad told the panel he had spent most of his academic career doing empirical work on punitive damages.

Rustad said he had been commissioned by the American Bar Association to write a paper on punitive damages. He had written numerous law review articles on the subject and had testified on punitive damages before both branches of Congress—the House of Representatives and the Senate.

Rustad told the panel he had never testified in a case involving a private plaintiff before. I was pleased I had been able to get him to help with my case. I had learned about Rustad from an attorney in Enid. When I called Rustad to discuss my litigation with Merrill Lynch, he was intrigued. He asked me to send him documents that related to my lawsuit. Rustad became even more interested after reviewing the material. He could see I was courageously fighting a giant corporation whose actions and behavior cried out for punishment. Rustad saw the need for punitive damages in my case, and upon learning about my financial circumstances in the aftermath of my termination from Merrill Lynch agreed to provide his testimony for a reduced fee so I could afford him.

Gore asked Rustad, "What is the legal standard for Oklahoma punitive damages?"

"The legal standard is whether the defendant is guilty of conduct evincing wanton or reckless disregard for the rights of another, oppression, fraud, or malice, and that can be either actual or implied," Rustad answered. "You can prove punitive damages by bad motive or the state of mind nucleus, and that's what fraud and malice are about. Or by something more than negligence and less than intentional misconduct, and that's what's meant by wanton or reckless disregard."

"And what are the functions of Oklahoma punitive damages?" Gore asked.

"Well, the functions are set up by statute," Rustad replied. "Punishment and deterrence are the primary...the Siamese twins. The issue is whether the defendant should be punished for the injury, which is either inflicted—can be inflicted on Keith Schooley, but also an injury to the consuming public. For example, if the allegations are true, that if this panel finds there's reasonable support for the allegations that there's been discrepancies in terms of the licensing of insurance brokers, there's a question of whether Merrill Lynch should be punished for deviating from accepted practices. The issue of deterrence...I mean, there's first of all, the general deterrence. Is this the kind of circumstance in which you want to send a message to the entire securities industry? Then there's a specific deterrence. Is this the kind of deterrence that you do not want Merrill Lynch to repeat these actions?

"It has been alleged that information from this hotline leaked back to the Enid office. It has been alleged that Merrill Lynch had blacklisted Keith Schooley, retaliated against him, and ruined his life, and that's a deterrence function. The question is, do you need to send a message that this should not be done again? You need to ensure that Merrill Lynch would not repeat this course of conduct. If it's true there are cheat sheets, that people are actually obtaining cheat sheets, taking this examination, having cheat sheets, or worse, not taking the examination at all, every wrong deserves a punishment. If, in fact, information was leaked from the hotline back to the Enid office and Mr. Jack Thomas behaved differently after receiving this, there has to be some payment for ruining Schooley's life and jeopardizing the consuming public here in Oklahoma. There are licensure laws, and I am familiar with those. I've looked at the licensure laws. Agents have to be licensed.

"Finally, there's one other thing I want to mention," Rustad continued. "Punitive damages play a valuable role in our society. Let me explain what the private attorney general is. It's written about quite frequently in punitive damages. There is a recognition that the public prosecutors can't do all the work. And I did look at the Merrill Lynch literature. Here's a company that holds itself of having not only high ethical standards, but the highest ethical standards. And we have an employee who is there less than a year, and sees lots of activities to deviate from those standards. I mean, this is the kind of case that cries out for having a private attorney general in whistle-blowing. It's not surprising that people see illegal and unethical activities all the time and don't report them. For example, in the Lincoln Savings and Loan, we needed a Keith Schooley. And how is it possible hundreds and hundreds of professionals are doing these accounting sheets, and seeing things and not reporting them. The reason is that people are fearful. And that's why the legal system needs to protect people like Schooley. The idea of blowing the whistle came from England when the bobbies had their whistles. They saw wrongdoing, they reported it, you blew the whistle. Merrill Lynch is asking Keith Schooley to swallow the whistle.

"And I think that is what you have to consider. Even if we disregard what would happen to him, what about the next case? What about the securities industry? I mean, it's difficult to observe all forms of illegal or unethical behavior in these kinds of settings. We're talking about 75-year-old ladies buying life insurance. How can we observe whether [FCs] are properly licensed, if they've taken the test? If they haven't taken the test, they can make decisions that would place consumers at risk. And there's not enough physical resources to cover all these possible kinds of wrongdoing; and only the person on the inside can uncover them."

Rustad went on to explain that the cap on punitive damages can be lifted if there is clear and convincing evidence of conduct evincing wanton or reckless disregard for the rights of another, oppression, fraud, or malice. Gore then asked if my case qualified for the cap to be lifted.

"This is a case where lifting the cap is, if the facts are…the record that I looked at, this is clearly a case," Rustad responded. "There's no question. This is well beyond the ordinary burden. Here we have not only just one smoking gun, but we have a multiplicity of smoking guns that indicate conduct worthy of punishment, conduct you want to deter. There is certainly a strong public policy for refusing to participate in illegal or unethical acts. And what Keith was asked to participate in was this Tour de France contest, which was a sham, it was a masquerade. They were going to use his figures for the whole—and Merrill has already admitted that."

"And have you had an opportunity to look at Merrill Lynch's assets to give you some idea of what a punitive damage award should be?" Gore asked.

"Well, in punitive damage awards, wealth can be taken into account in terms of the wealth of the defendant," Rustad responded. "You have to have an amount which will send a signal to Merrill Lynch's boardroom. What's helpful is to look at the amount of punitive damages in looking at what is the need to punish Merrill Lynch, what is the need to deter Merrill Lynch. Merrill Lynch's sales—I'm getting from their public disclosure statements, 12–30–1994, their net sales were $18.233 billion. That's one basis you could use, the percentage of net sales. You do not want to bankrupt Merrill Lynch, but at the same time you cannot send a pea-shooter up at Godzilla. So the question is taking a look at the wealth of the defendant. It might be a percentage of net sales, it might be a percentage of net income. Net income, for example, in 1994, was $1.02 billion. We're talking about a large Fortune 500 corporation. The question is, what would be the amount that would be needed to get their attention?"

"Would you just give the panel a range of what you think is appropriate?" Gore asked.

"The median award I found, and this is all retaliatory discharges nationwide, was $3.3 million," Rustad answered. "But I'm not sure that's appropriate. I think you have to look at the enormity of the wrong. I think you have to look at the wrong for the cost of society, you have to look at the net worth of Merrill. I looked at some 59 punitive damage awards between 1987 and 1994. It's always calibrated against the wealth. If you look at the award against Shearson or you look at the award against one of the large energy corporations, which was a retaliatory discharge of $80 million—you're talking about a large corporation comparable to Merrill Lynch. And for example, in the American Continental Corporation, like the savings and loan and securities cases, for example, those are powerful, large corporations. They were awarded $410 million. I'm not suggesting there's any one figure that...you have to always link it back to the punishment, the deterrence, and the wealth. But there is a precedent for large awards in this area. One of the reasons why you see a large number of awards in the magnitude of $100 million in this area, I mean, the Pennzoil case, was one of the first big ones, which was also a business contracts case—$3 billion in punitive damages.

"One of the reasons why we see these kinds of large awards is not because juries have gone wild, but punitive damages have to be appropriately calibrated to the wealth of the company. So we're talking about calibration by the size of the enterprise. And you can do that when you find clear and convincing evidence that there's been wrongdoing, which I think there's a substantial case of that."

Gore had no other questions but with figures in the millions and billions flying around, you could bet Day wanted to cross-examine.

"Doctor, do you often render punitive damage opinions on cases that you have not heard?" Day asked.

"As a matter of fact I do," Rustad answered.

"That's fine," Day said.

Rustad wished to elaborate. "Let me answer the question. I'm asked frequently by the news media to comment on both pending cases and cases…I'm often given a lot less than I have looked at in this case. For example, I commented on the Exxon Valdez case to *The National Law Journal*. I have commented to *The Washington Post* when the GMC pickup case came down. I commented on the facts and foundations, size of award in *The New York Times*, in *The Wall Street Journal*."

Day had heard enough. He had no further questions and neither did Gore. Rustad's testimony was critical because what he told the arbitration panel was clear. He, a leading expert in punitive damages, felt that my case presented an occasion where lifting the cap was justified, well beyond the ordinary burden. He outlined there was not just one smoking gun, but a multiplicity of them and they indicated conduct worthy of punishment, conduct the panel and the securities industry would want to deter.

Meditz and Mandel had already testified the wrongdoing I reported had in fact occurred—except of course, the allegation of the widespread use of improper means in taking the insurance exam. However, in light of Hall's testimony and other evidence including the Pictorial 77-page computer printout, I believed the arbitrators had to see through Meditz' and Mandel's testimony—especially since each investigator had essentially interviewed only Sarah Graham in his *thorough* investigation of the insurance cheating. Now, Rustad had established how this conduct should be addressed and I hoped the panel had heard that message loud and clear as well.

Alan Rockler: I'm Getting Confused— This Has Gone On for So Long

Day was ready to call Merrill Lynch's last witness, Alan Rockler, a securities expert from Los Angeles.

Rockler gave a brief overview of his background, including that he began his career in the securities industry in 1953. He started consulting as an expert witness in 1985 and had testified in probably 200 cases.

He also had served as an arbitrator approximately 150 times for the NYSE, NASD, American Arbitration Association, and others.

Day asked Rockler for his opinion regarding Merrill Lynch's position in the industry. "Well, first of all, as you know, the industry is categorized into different groups, and Merrill Lynch is categorized as a large, fully serviced wirehouse," Rockler responded. "In that sense, there are probably six, seven firms that you would compare them with, and Merrill Lynch, as far as I'm concerned, is ranked right at the top, in virtually all categories."

"And you've sat here and you've heard the evidence in this case," Day said. "Do you have an opinion regarding the response that Merrill Lynch made to Mr. Schooley's claims?"

"Yes, I do," Rockler answered.

"And what is that opinion?"

"Again, looking at all the other wirehouses, and I've worked for them, I've worked against them, I've worked with them, I would say Merrill Lynch went way beyond the norm of the industry for what you do in a questionable issue or a complaint or anything of that sort. Their whole investigation process was way up there. The amount of firepower they sent in to investigate this—first, the one group investigating, headed by Mr. Meditz, then the next group came in headed by Mr. Barry Mandel. They certainly looked at every single allegation that was made. They responded to it, they acted upon it. Then when that was all done, they had to react and respond to the regulatory authorities. I saw a whole series of letters that Mr. Mandel had to write to the New York Stock Exchange, the SEC, the NASD, the Oklahoma Insurance Commission, and so on. So they were very actively involved and did everything they were supposed to do, and I don't know what they could have done any more. Certainly, I don't think any other firm would have done what they did."

"Do you have an opinion regarding the gravity or severity of the claims made by Mr. Schooley in this matter?"

"Well, the only item that could have affected the public and the only item that could have been a regulatory item, I think, would have been the insurance 'cheat sheets,' which were never established that there were cheat sheets."

"Do you have an opinion regarding the U-5 that was filed regarding Mr. Schooley?"

"In the firms I've worked for, the U-5s were generally filled out by the registration department in the main office. But the branch manager was the one who took the step of ending the relationship with the account executive or financial consultant. And in my case, as branch manager, I would always notify the registration department as to what to put on the U-5. I don't know how you could possibly put anything on the U-5 except job abandonment, under the facts that I've heard in this case."

Day had no further questions. Schmidt would cross-examine Rockler and rip him apart.

Schmidt quickly established Rockler had not heard all the evidence in my case, as Day implied, but had only come in the day before, missing two whole days of the hearing and only catching about an hour of my testimony.

"Okay," Schmidt said. "So everything you've related is based on what?"

"It's based on documents and letters that I've read, exhibits," Rockler responded. "I mean, I was sent a book of exhibits about this high." He motioned with his hand.

"How much of Mr. Schooley's testimony did you hear that dealt with how he was treated at Merrill Lynch?" Schmidt asked.

"I didn't hear his testimony, as you just asked," Rockler replied. "I wasn't here. I read his letters."

"So you didn't hear Mr. Schooley's side of this case at all?"

"I think I did through his letters. I understand what he was saying."

"Well, I'm just talking about the direct evidence in front of the panel."

"Oh, no, no. I certainly did not."

Schmidt moved on to the subject of my U-5 form. He established with Rockler that instead of listing "job abandonment" as the reason I was no longer with the firm, it would have been possible for Merrill Lynch to put "disagreement with management." This would have had much less of a stigma with other possible employers in the securities industry.

"Do you know if Oklahoma Blue Sky laws require dishonest and unethical practices in the securities business to be addressed?" Schmidt asked.

"I would think so," Rockler answered.

"Did you hear Mr. Bill Hall's testimony yesterday?"

"Yes."

"And did he say there was something over and above cheat sheets going on?"

"I was very confused by that. Because first of all, I was sitting too far away and I couldn't quite hear every word he said."

"Well, don't you believe in your experience as an expert in this industry that it was incumbent upon Mr. Schooley, if he thought cheat sheets or something worse, i.e., testing filled out for agents was going on, it was incumbent upon him to report that, would it not?"

"Sir, I guess it would be if he felt it was. You know, you can take an event or a fact and blow it up into something that it's not or you can make it into something that it is. And I'm not sure that Mr. Schooley ever really understood what happened on this particular day."

I continued to be amazed. It was not me who was confused, as suggested by Rockler, but Rockler himself. That "particular day" Rockler was referring to presumably was the Saturday morning meeting where Hall led eight FCs through the exam on a question-by-question basis. It was separate from the allegation of the use of cheat sheets, or what Hall had testified to concerning the girls filling out the testing requirements for the FCs.

"Okay," Schmidt said. "You said Schooley should not have done anything on the cheat sheet issue because he made something out of nothing?"

"Because he didn't have the facts."

"That's right. So is he supposed to become the investigator or is he supposed to go to Merrill Lynch and ask for the investigation?"

"I think—I may be wrong—I thought Mr. Schooley was acting as an investigator. He was interrogating a lot of people, he was asking a lot of questions all over the place. I think he was doing an investigation."

"Now, at what point in time are you talking about?"

"I'm getting confused. This has gone on for so long."

Schmidt said he had no further questions.

Merrill Lynch's distinguished securities expert—who had testified as an expert witness in about 200 cases and had served as an arbitrator in about 150 cases—was confused. But at least he was right on one thing—this matter had gone on for too long. Little did Rockler, or anybody else, know it still had a long way to go.

Closing Arguments: An Extremely Unusual Case

It was time for closing arguments. Day went first.

"I think the one thing we can all agree on is the extremely unusual nature of the case that we've just been discussing," Day said. "In directly addressing whether we have an actual discharge or not here, I think the evidence has been clear that Keith Schooley was not intended to be and was not, in point of fact, discharged by Merrill Lynch.

"The reaction of Jack Thomas was understandable, it could have been contemplated, it was quite reasonable. The allegations Mr. Schooley made were beyond outrageous, particularly as they related to Mr. Thomas. Mr. Thomas has stated he was directed to and would not pursue his damage claim or his libel claim, his defamation claim." What Day chose to ignore was Thomas' intentions not to pursue the lawsuit were never communicated to me.

"Mr. Schooley was repeatedly asked to come back to work," Day continued. "And I believe it's proper to look at the context of his actions here, and as the testimony has demonstrated them. But if we can remember our elements for a constructive discharge of a whistle-blower, they are: first, that the issues, the violations, which are the subject matter of the complaints, need to be violations of law, regulation, or constitution arising a public policy concern. Second, that the whistle-blower be acting in good faith and not spitefully and not maliciously and not with personal economic gain in mind. But last, that in point of fact, a reasonable man in the same or similar context would have felt he could not remain employed under the circumstances in which he found himself.

"Let's look at the allegations again and the evidence just quickly. The new account contest violations were a use of poor judgment by Mr. Ellis. There was no customer impact by any of these actions, no losses, no economic impact. This is not a public policy issue. It's an internal issue. Merrill Lynch addressed it in its admonition, in its punishment of Mr. Ellis.

"The use of a country club membership list for solicitation by Mr. Barton, I think, almost epitomizes—truly does epitomize—the kind of perspective that Mr. Schooley was approaching his employment in. He was looking for things to complain about. The seminar expenses for the open house, certainly an internal accounting issue—no fraud, no embezzlement, no personal conversion of funds. There's been no evidence, no testimony offered that Mr. Barton took one dime illicitly as a result of that. There's been no testimony and there's no evidence that those funds were not expended in the best interest of Merrill Lynch. And it was more than apt punishment to remove the man from management for 18 months. A public policy issue? Obviously not.

"How about the transfer of assets to Barry Clark? Now, what in the world have we been listening to that for? If there was a promise by and between Merrill Lynch and an individual regarding the transfer of assets, that issue was by and between that individual and Merrill Lynch. It is not an issue that the public at large is concerned about. And it certainly doesn't impact anybody.

"Joe Bazzelle's termination. Try that one. Merrill Lynch terminated the man for soliciting, while on Merrill Lynch premises, on behalf of a lawyer, lawsuits against another New York Stock Exchange firm. Did they have a right to terminate him? Yes.

"MuniYield fund. Mr. Barton was mistaken. Is there a customer complaint? Is there a customer loss? Was there a danger of a customer loss? A public policy issue? No.

"Failure to properly register agents for out-of-state sales. I'm a former securities administrator and I was very active and diligent in enforcing other state agents to pay our state fees whenever an issue came to the floor. Doesn't it strike you as an oddity Mr. Schooley's complaint here arose out of his brother-in-law's accounts and he's turning himself in as a...he's claiming whistle-blower status for the failure to register Mr. Thomas in that state? This is the ultimate technical violation.

"Mr. Schooley made a remark in his 31-page letter to the board. He said, 'I can appreciate isolated instances. I would not condemn isolated instances of error or impropriety. But when they involve a multitude of illegalities, amounting to, involving violations of the laws for which imprisonment might be proper, then I cannot stand it.'

"Show me the imprisonment exposure here. Show me the public policy issue. Show me, in any evidence presented to this panel here today—and you have to admit, you have never seen a case as widely reviewed by an assorted manner of regulatory agencies as have these allegations here. You'll never see it.

"The question kept arising, was anybody talking with him, was anybody communicating with Mr. Schooley about—it's just not severe? It's not hanging offenses you're bringing forward. We'll address them, we'll resolve them, we'll take action. Thank you for bringing them to our attention." When Day said this, I could not help but think about Bazzelle's termination for trying to help his clients and the threat of my immediate termination if I were again to "rebate" $15 to another client.

"There was no fear on the part of Merrill Lynch in any part of this," Day continued. "There was no basis for claiming that they were going to cover up and involve themselves in a national conspiracy because of these claims.

"And did you hear that? A national conspiracy involving the top corporate officers of Merrill Lynch to cover up this. There's only one issue here that could possibly be claimed as a public policy concern, and that is Mr. Schooley's allegation of a cheat sheet.

"And think about the timing of this one. He's in production the first 30 days when he begins consulting with Stephen Jones. And that's when he hears Sarah Graham say, 'I'm going to send you a cheat sheet.' He gets a practice exam answer sheet. And does Mr. Schooley call her back and say, 'Gosh, Sarah, I'm really concerned with what you said. You said "cheat sheet." My gosh, I'm a real honest man and that really upset me and I certainly don't want my employer to be engaged in such a thing'? Did Mr. Schooley do that?

"Within nine months, if you'll notice, and please do note this, in his September 17 letter, the first third of that letter dealt with a nation-wide scheme to violate state insurance laws using cheat sheets. And Mr. Schooley, who knew at the time he wrote the letter, that he never had been provided a cheat sheet, had never seen a cheat sheet, had no basis for making that claim. He wanted Sarah Graham fingerprinted. Fingerprinted?

"I viewed his actions here...and particularly, even Bill Hall at this stage. He gets Mr. Hall on the phone and he tries to entrap him. And this is even after the September 17 letter. He gets no admissions out of Mr. Hall. Mr. Hall had no idea he was being taped, but he absolutely denied the use of cheat sheets or that his actions violated any laws in his continuing education efforts."

I hoped this comment made the arbitrators take note, just as Day had requested them to. Hall absolutely denied the use of cheat sheets? Had he not said, without any prompting from me, cheat sheets were floating around? Day must have been hoping the arbitrators' memories would prove to be just as weak as those of Merrill Lynch's witnesses.

Day continued, saying my allegations were malicious and therefore deprived me of any claim of good faith in bringing them forth. He said saying this was a matter of public policy was a lie and that no evidence or testimony had been presented to suggest otherwise.

Day went on to imply Hall "attacked" Champion only out of a personal dislike for the man and Merrill Lynch. He said my only substantive charge, that of cheating on the insurance exams, was a baseless and malicious allegation in which I named individuals with complete disregard for the possible negative effects it might have on them or their careers.

"What was he about?" Day continued. "What is this man about? What was he doing? The whistle-blower? You can't do that spitefully. You can't do that maliciously. You can't do that for personal gain. If I've ever seen an act—listen, I'm an attorney, not a psychiatrist, and I can't make speculations as to what was in this man's mind. But he was consulting with an attorney from the very first.

"And when the last, but not least, you got to be fired, when Jack reacts. Schooley himself admits four days later on the phone, he keeps entrapping himself. The best you've heard in this case were Keith Schooley's notes demonstrating his attitude in what he was trying to do and his own actions.

"Four days later, he obviously doesn't view himself as being actually discharged, and he doesn't view himself as being constructively discharged. Truthfully, when the man is asked to come back to work, he has the ultimate guardian angel, Bob Dineen, the number four man in the company, call him on Monday morning and said, 'Keith, you got any problem, anybody bugging you, call me. Here's my number.'"

Day continued to spin out the Merrill Lynch line. In the days following the incident with Thomas, it was made perfectly clear, several times over in fact, both Jones and I adamantly felt I had been discharged. There was no confusion about that on our part. I had never "entrapped" myself even once, never mind repeatedly as Day said. I wondered how he could listen to the same words I heard and yet completely ignore or twist them in his arguments.

Day then proceeded to accuse me of being obsessed with my case against Merrill Lynch. He claimed I had no intention of going back to work. Again, Day was ignoring evidence. I had clearly stated I tried to get work in the securities industry and had indeed returned to work in the oil and gas business.

Day concluded, "This obsession needs to stop. You didn't make it, you did not contrive it, you didn't get it together here. Merrill Lynch, for being put through this one more time, ultimately and primarily deserves compensation for its cost incurred here. And we request this panel grant us our fees and costs in this matter for defending it. Thank you."

I was not surprised at Day's closing argument. By now I knew what to expect. Of course, Thomas' reaction would appear understandable and reasonable *if* you believed he had not found out about my naming him in the insurance cheating scandal section of my letter to the board until September 28, which I believed was not true. Of course, my allegation of cheating on the insurance exams would appear malicious and of no public concern *if* you did not believe all the evidence I had brought forth, including Hall's own words, which clearly Day and Merrill Lynch had no problem doing.

I knew I had met Day's three elements for a constructive discharge of a whistle-blower. First, the majority of the allegations *were* violations of law, regulation, or constitution arising a public policy concern. Second, I *was* acting in good faith, not with economic gain in mind. Finally, any reasonable man in a similar situation would have felt that he could *not* remain employed under the circumstances.

Gore now had the floor.

"Merrill Lynch espouses the highest ethical standards in the industry—or that's what they say they live by, or that's what they want everybody to believe," Gore said. "They require their employees to sign a statement that says every employee makes a personal commitment to assert the highest ethical standards and exercise the proper judgment in all aspects of their business dealings. They require you to sign that.

"Mr. Schooley is…and there's been absolutely not a shred of evidence in this hearing anywhere that he's not an honest person. There's not been a shred of evidence in this hearing that he's not ethical, principled, yet Merrill Lynch is doing their best to paint him as a fanatic.

"And maybe he is a little different, shall we say. He's obviously very driven, very motivated in whatever it is he does. He did score in the top 1 percent on his Series 7 examination and he was one of the top 10 producers for his classification out of 400 people after six or eight months. So obviously, he is a motivated person. And whatever it is, I think, that he goes after, he goes after it at 110 percent. I think if the evidence shows anything, that's what it shows.

"If he was a troublemaker and the kind of person who is just going around looking for lawsuits and ways to retire out of a lawsuit, things of that nature, he's worked for several oil companies, been around the oil business, with plenty of problems there. I'm sure somewhere along the road he would have had an employment problem or a lawsuit or something, but he never did. This is the first time he's had a problem.

"He takes his job seriously. He took that oath they required him to sign seriously, a lot more seriously than anybody else we've heard from, I believe. And he did what he thought was right. When he saw something he felt was wrong, he reported it. Does he have to be the investigator? Does he have to be the police department or the FBI? Does he have to go out and get evidence and prove these things are occurring, or if he gets an indication, an independent indication from someone else that there's wrongdoing, had he done his job when he reports it to the proper authorities?

"But what is a whistle-blower anyway? Somebody who reports things that he doesn't believe is proper. The *Guidelines for Business Conduct* includes an obligation to report misconduct. 'Employees should be diligent in questioning situations that they believe violate Merrill Lynch's high ethical standards. Improprieties should be reported to whatever level of management necessary.' That's a quote out of Merrill Lynch's book. 'To report unethical behavior on a confidential basis, the general counsel's office has established a hotline.' Now, it doesn't say, 'We don't want to hear from you if it's not a felony. We don't want to hear from you if somebody isn't going to jail. We don't want to hear from you if somebody isn't going to get terminated. We don't want to hear from you if somebody isn't going to get fined or cited by some regulatory agency.' It says, 'We want you to report unethical behavior at a minimum.' And I'm sure that anything above unethical behavior, they'd like to hear that also, or at least that's what their publication says.

"Unfortunately, they didn't tell him that the hotline may not be confidential, they may leak that back to the boss, that may get back to your manager. The manager who's involved, primarily Quinton Ellis, who's been here the whole time, but never took the stand. And Brent Barton, who you heard from, are the managers we are talking about. And I think it's safe to say neither one of them care too much for Keith Schooley, wish they'd never seen him, wished he'd never been hired, probably lost their position with Merrill Lynch because of him. There's certainly evidence in the record to that effect."

Gore and Schmidt had decided not to call Ellis as a witness, since his wrongdoing and lack of character had already been covered by others' testimony. Furthermore, we believed he would likely have great difficulty in supporting anything I said.

"Keith Schooley simply observed what he felt was wrongdoing and reported it," Gore continued. "It's that simple. When Merrill Lynch came back and said we're investigating it and told him we had finished our investigation, we don't see there's anything wrong and either what you saw didn't happen or it's just not serious, it upset him. He'd gone through a lot of trouble to report these things and that just didn't fly. It's that simple. And Mr. Meditz said, 'Hey, we've done all we're going to do. We're not going to do anything'—that was at the August 13 meeting.

"You know, you've heard from the witnesses, you believe who you want, but I believe he was pressured by them to suck it up and go on down the road like everybody else. You know, 'you didn't see anything, you didn't hear anything, now get out there and sell some stock and keep your mouth shut. Just go back and do your job.' The results of that first investigation—nothing's going to happen to anybody, virtually.

"So Mr. Schooley took it upon himself to write the board because he didn't feel like he had any choice. He had gone as high as he could go around here and nobody was paying any attention to him. He was talking to their investigator from New York. He wasn't going to do anything. I mean, who's left, you know? You got to go up there somewhere, so he did what he felt he had to do, and he followed their guidelines and went to whatever level of management he felt was necessary.

"When he did that, the management hostility toward him escalated, of course. And even the people he met with in New York made snide remarks about his reporting of these things and then [Mihaly] said, 'Yeah, you have certainly reported everything.' And Mr. Meditz, you know, why would he indicate—and he admitted—why would he indicate, 'Gee, I wish you hadn't done that in writing'? He admitted that here today, you know, 'If you had done it verbally, maybe we could sweep it under the rug. When you do it in writing, then we got to do something about it.'

"While Mr. Schooley was in New York, Mr. Barton is saying, 'Well, Keith's a liar and got a small twisted mind,' and Jack Thomas saying, 'He's a cancer in the office and I don't want him infecting Michael and Greg.' Keith finds out about these statements. You know, he figures the hammer is going to fall on him pretty soon. And sure enough when he gets back from New York, as far as Keith's concerned, the hammer falls, and he gets jerked into the office and handed a letter that this is official, this is, 'for the record' on Merrill Lynch stationery. 'I've got a witness, I want you to sign and date it, and I want you to get the hell out of here.'

"Now you can take that, I guess, any way you want, but when the letter is from my boss, he says he's going to sue me and my family—I don't know about you, I've been a defendant in a couple of lawsuits in my life, and when I did it, it was not pleasant. I am a lawyer, but it still is not pleasant. I've been on the witness stand. I've been through the whole bailiwick and I tell you right now, I couldn't work in an office with somebody else suing me, let alone working in an office where the boss is suing me. I don't know how you feel but that is the most outrageous thing I've ever heard.

"Mr. Schooley was so shocked, as a matter of fact, I think, by that whole situation, which I think anybody would be. I would be. I think he did the only thing he could do. He gathered the information that he felt he needed to go talk to a lawyer and take the advice of his lawyer, and that's exactly what he did. He gathered the documents he felt he needed and he went to see Stephen Jones. He took Stephen Jones' advice and from that day forward, Stephen Jones had represented him and advised him, up until the point in time we took this case.

"Mr. Schooley is a man of principle. When Mr. Thomas asked him to retract the things he had said, he refused because he believed there was a valid basis for every one of them. When Mr. Thomas threatened to sue him, he still stood by what he believed to be right. And to this day, of course, Merrill Lynch is saying they are the most outrageous and baseless allegations that have ever been made. They don't like Mr. Schooley. I know Merrill Lynch doesn't like Mr. Schooley; however, the evidence is this...."

At this point, Gore briefly went over my call with Sarah Graham, the Saturday morning meeting Hall conducted, Hall's testimony, the information from Pictorial, and other evidence related to the allegations I had made against Merrill Lynch. Gore asked the panel if Merrill Lynch felt it had done nothing wrong, why had it taken certain actions like requiring those FCs at the Saturday morning meeting to retake the insurance exam, asking Barton to remove the country club list from his computer, making rescission offers for the MuniYield fund and Singapore Air stock, and making Barton and Ellis pay back their Tour de France CMA contest trips?

"And what I do think is outrageous is them putting job abandonment on his U-5 and blacklisting him from ever being able to work in the securities industry again, or making it extremely difficult for him to do that," Gore continued. "Especially, in light of the fact that they didn't follow their own manual in putting that there, and that he was not absent three days without notification. They had all the notification they needed about what was going on and they knew he didn't abandon his job, and they knew they had a manager who threatened to sue him and knew he felt he had been terminated. They knew there was a problem, blamed it all on him. It's all his problem.

"A wrongful discharge on public policy grounds for whistle-blowing exposes wrongdoing by an employer. It's that simple. That's all there is to it. If this isn't one of those, I don't know what is.

"In my view, Merrill Lynch cleaned house in order to minimize the damage with the NASD. If you'll notice, Brent Barton, got rid of him in January of 1994; Quinton Ellis, later in 1994; Leo Roepke retired. All within a four-month period, they get rid of three people, all for other reasons of course. Needless to say, they're not going to cite that this is the reason because that would hurt them in this lawsuit.

"And there was indication they were doing everything they could to minimize the damage this lawsuit might have because they knew it existed. But that's speculation on my part, and of course, Bill Hall, he was fired too. He was just fired a little bit early. They didn't get rid of him in that four-month period right before the NASD investigation when the report came out. But I certainly see them going to them and say, 'We've cleaned house, go light on us.' And they did—letters of caution.

"The results of Mr. Schooley's reporting hopefully would be that insurance agents will be properly tested and licensed. There won't be any misuse of mailing lists. There will be no more falsification of expenses to the detriment of Merrill Lynch stockholders. Securities will be represented properly to the consumers. Agents will be properly registered in foreign states. Internal contests are to be run so no one is harmed. There will be no more sales of unregistered securities.

"Mr. Schooley did a good job for Merrill Lynch. He did something for them they should be thanking him for instead of firing him for. What they should have done was come back and say, 'Mr. Thomas, you're way out of line using our stationery to threaten a lawsuit against that man, that whistle-blower. Sorry, but we're going to have to transfer you to Oklahoma City or something.' And say, 'Mr. Schooley, we cleaned up the office. It's not a hostile environment anymore, you may go back.' They didn't do that. They said, 'Hey, get over there and go to work. I know the boss is suing you, but get over there and go to work, you ought to be able to handle it.' I don't know about you, but I couldn't handle it.

"The wrongful discharge is a violation of public policy, it's a tort. There is authority to award punitive damages. We would request that you do that to deter this activity, otherwise, it will continue. And I think the best evidence of that came from Barry Clark's mouth.

"Because I asked him, I said, 'You know all this stuff. You knew everything Keith was doing, you knew everything that was going on, you saw every bit of it. Barry, why didn't you report this?' And I know Barry is low-key and I know you were here listening. And Barry said, 'I'm sorry, but I just could not afford it. I could not afford to lose my job.' So Barry Clark said it about as well as it can be said. It takes a guy, a little different guy with the guts to do what Mr. Schooley did to ruin your life, end up getting divorced, to take the chance like he did.

"Mr. Clark couldn't do it, most people won't. If Mr. Schooley walks away empty-handed, I think you're telling the world, 'Yeah, you don't report any wrongdoing, go with the flow. If you see something wrong, forget about it, this whistle-blowing stuff is not the thing to do.' Thank you."

At that point, Chairman Conner reminded us we would be informed in writing of the arbitrators' decision. On behalf of the panel, he thanked and commended the parties for their presentations and announced the hearing adjourned.

After more than three years, the war between Merrill Lynch and me was finally over. It had gone the distance, all the way through binding arbitration, which meant, for all intents and purposes, the decision would be final with no right of appeal. I felt good. I knew I had put on an impressive performance which presented all that my attorneys and I had hoped for. I was incredibly relieved. Finally, I had put behind me three years of an intense fight. I had made it through one of the most emotional times in my life. I had experienced four days of adrenaline-pumping, head-to-head confrontation in a conference room with several men and a "company" that hated my guts, and I never backed down.

The only question I had now was how large my award would be—especially given the powerful testimony that Professor Rustad provided concerning punitive damages.

That evening I took Professor Rustad to dinner. We discussed the day's hearing and I was pleased to hear him echo my feelings on how well it had gone. Rustad knew my case well and also believed Merrill Lynch should have to pay for its reprehensible conduct. I thanked Rustad for coming to Oklahoma to testify on my behalf in what was, as I had learned earlier in the day, his first occasion to testify on behalf of a private litigant.

The next day I had lunch with Gore, Schmidt, and several other attorneys with Mahaffey & Gore. Spirits were high. There was no doubt in our minds who won the four-day arbitration hearing. Gore told me in his more than 20 years of litigating, at the end of every trial he had been involved in, there were always things he wished had gone better or things that should have been done or not done. Gore said my arbitration hearing was his first litigation that had been virtually flawless. Since the victory seemed so clear, we all agreed we would stay low-key and not get cocky, out of fear of the traditional jinx, as we waited for the arbitration decision.

Gore and Schmidt told me when they received the written decision they would have their paralegal call me and let me know the decision was on its way via fax. That way I could see the decision with my own eyes just as they would.

As I drove back to Enid, not only did I feel good about how the arbitration hearing had gone but also I felt as though a tremendous load had been lifted from my shoulders. Binding arbitration was "binding." It really *was* over. I truly felt like a new man as I realized my future thoughts would no longer have to include Merrill Lynch. I was more than ready to move on and was emotionally and mentally already doing just that.

I believed Merrill Lynch's biggest fear was not any possible damages it might have to pay me, but rather the exposure senior management would have in a ruling that showed its twice covered-up investigation of the insurance cheating. Given all I had learned, I had my own thoughts as to how events had unfolded in connection with the cheating.

I speculated that perhaps by Hall reporting the cheating in the summer of 1991 to his superiors, word got back to New York about the use of cheat sheets or other improper means in taking the exam, not only by the Oklahoma FCs but also by others in Merrill Lynch offices in Texas. Consequently, I believe local management received word from New York to put a stop to the cheating that could do serious damage to the firm's well-cultivated reputation. This directive by New York resulted in a new approach, at least by some FCs, to taking the exam—the Saturday morning meeting. Pictorial's printout showed the eight FCs who attended the Saturday morning meeting led by Hall received credit for the exam on September 6, 1991.

Then, on November 15, 1991, Graham told me in our phone conversation the FCs were getting the exam behind them by using a cheat sheet. Graham, still in the Dallas San Jacinto office where Champion had been until recently, was likely intending to do what I think she had been doing all along under the supervision of Champion. But I suspected Graham told her new superior, Hall, what she was going to send to me, and Hall told her under no circumstances was she to proceed. Consequently, Graham instead sent an answer key to a practice exam—an exam that was not provided to FCs who were going to take the *Estate Planning Training Course* for state credit, as I would be doing.

Meanwhile, Merrill Lynch was looking to come up with a new system that would replace the Pictorial system that allowed for cheating. From what I knew, the Pictorial exam was not routinely changed to thwart potential cheating by exam takers; supposedly in January 1992, Merrill Lynch started offering a new system by a different provider. Nevertheless, some Merrill Lynch FCs were still taking the Pictorial exam for state credit between January 1 and August 26, 1992, as evidenced by the Pictorial computer printout.

This scenario would explain why Ellis, Thomas, and Barton never questioned me concerning the reference I made in my January 20, 1992, letter about being provided a cheat sheet. It would also explain why Murphy, with worldwide security in the general counsel's office in New York, never bothered to question me as to what I meant by saying, on March 11, 1992, I tended to rock the boat by disagreeing with the use of cheat sheets. Under my scenario, no one needed to ask me any questions about what I meant because local management and personnel in New York would know *exactly* what I was talking about.

Something that particularly intrigued me, *especially* in view of the downside I thought senior management would face if a cover-up was exposed, was that Merrill Lynch had never made a serious offer to settle my case. It had proposed a settlement of $10,000, which was so insignificant it could not even be considered a legitimate offer. However, Merrill Lynch had no problem in settling Barton's and Clark's claims just months earlier.

I knew that most large corporations when facing litigation make a business decision concerning the cost to litigate as well as other potential costs, financial and otherwise, and try to resolve the matter by settlement so as to avoid the downside in a potentially adverse judgment. For some reason though, Merrill Lynch, in my case, did not behave as expected.

I believed I knew why Merrill Lynch behaved so differently. As I saw it, Hammerman's goal was to prevent the exposure of Merrill Lynch's wrongdoing to an outside investigator. Hammerman would claim to the directors that, pursuant to the first investigation, none of my allegations was either serious or justifiable and so did not merit an independent investigator. Making a legitimate settlement, on the other hand, could appear as an admission that something seriously wrong had occurred. This would contradict Hammerman's assertions to the contrary and damage his argument that an outside investigation was not necessary.

On October 16, 1995, I received the eagerly anticipated phone call from a paralegal at Mahaffey & Gore. She informed me the arbitration decision had been received and would be faxed to me shortly. I took some deep breaths. What I was about to see could have a huge effect on my life—either positive or negative. My expectations were high considering how well my attorneys and I felt the arbitration hearing had gone.

Within seconds I heard my upstairs fax machine ring. As the four-page fax was being received, I walked up the stairs and sat at my office desk waiting for the decision page—the third page—to come out. I anxiously scanned the decision to find the damages awarded and quickly saw the amount $2,300,000. I was somewhat pleased, momentarily. I was actually hoping for a considerably larger amount because of Rustad's powerful testimony on the need to punish Merrill Lynch.

I then realized the $2,300,000 I was seeing was simply the amount I had claimed for actual damages when I filed my action against Merrill Lynch. I looked at the next column, which had the heading Award Data. I could not believe my eyes. My award damages were $0. My punitive damages, $0 as well.

CHAPTER 10

Litany of Litigation

I would not go away...

—KS

I stared at the decision for several minutes. My mind and emotions were having a hard time comprehending what my eyes saw. As I sat and reflected, there was no anger, just utter disbelief. If I was the same person I had been just about a year earlier, I surely would have been bouncing off the walls, going ballistic.

Instead, I phoned my family and friends who were anxiously awaiting any news. When I shared the decision with my sister Anne, I said to her, "I don't understand why this happened, but I know there's a reason." My best guess was it was just God's will for things to work out this way. I thought I could deal with a substantial award but maybe He knew better. Perhaps a large sum of money would have messed up all I had built with Him in the last year.

However, my calm was not to be mistaken for acceptance. I knew justice had not been done. I knew the facts and the evidence the arbitrators used to arrive at their unanimous decision. I knew the decision was wrong.

I called Mahaffey & Gore and spoke to Schmidt. He was also dumbfounded by the decision and told me Gore was hot when he saw it. I wanted to know what we could do. Schmidt told me since the decision was the result of binding arbitration, short of proving fraud in the procurement of the decision, there really was not much that could be done.

There was no doubt in my mind I had decisively won the arbitration hearing. Yet, for some reason, the arbitrators still decided in favor of Merrill Lynch. Something was not right.

Specifically, the one thing above everything else that *absolutely* convinced me something was amiss was the fact that the arbitrators had decided the placement of "job abandonment" on my U-5 form was *not* a false statement. There could be no dispute I had a valid basis for believing I had been constructively terminated as a result of Thomas' hostile actions on September 28, 1992, and Jones informed Merrill Lynch of my position within three days of September 28. Nevertheless, the arbitrators decided that I did abandon my job which, according to Merrill Lynch's *Supervisor's Manual,* was *serious* misconduct. I now believed if Merrill Lynch had placed on my U-5 form that I had caused the stock market crash of 1929, the arbitrators would have agreed with that too.

While the decision on "job abandonment" was the telltale clue, it was abundantly clear to me, knowing what I knew, the arbitrators' decision was equally flawed concerning the other important issues. How could the arbitrators not have determined the Enid office was an extraordinarily hostile one for me, one so hostile that it would be unreasonable to have expected me to be able to work in it? Merrill Lynch did not promise me I would be protected from Thomas' threatened lawsuit. Thomas testified he was planning to sue me for anything he could. Barton, second in command of the Oklahoma City Complex at the time, testified he disliked me intensely and there were times he felt he could claim authorship to calling me the world's biggest liar with a twisted mind. Even Mandel, Merrill Lynch's very own assistant general counsel, testified he did not know if he could work in an office where his manager was threatening to sue him.

I could only imagine how Ellis felt about the rookie FC who was in his charge. Ellis, along with Barton, was a primary subject of both my memorandum and 31-page letter. I had minced no words in my meetings with Meditz, Roepke, Mandel, Mihaly, and Dineen that Ellis and Barton should be terminated.

I was calm but certainly not happy. I thought about what I had repeatedly told my athletically competitive son over the years: "You've got to find a way to win." The arbitration was over but I was far from finished.

Professor Rustad had asked me to let him know the outcome of the hearing so I called him with the news. He could not believe it either. In our 20-minute conversation, Rustad told me no fewer than five times he was stunned. He said in his more than 20 years of legal practice he had seen cases where justice was not done but that my case stood out.

I got busy. On October 27, 1995, I faxed 10 different memos to my attorneys that contained information I thought might keep my case against Merrill Lynch alive. Gore and Schmidt reviewed what I sent but they were not confident binding arbitration could be circumvented.

Gore called me on November 1 saying Professional Reporters, which provided the court reporter at the hearing, had informed him Merrill Lynch was having a transcript made of Meditz' and Thomas' testimony. I was intrigued with this development but not sure what to make of it. I intended to have a transcript made of everyone's testimony but because of my financial circumstances I had to wait. However, I learned I could get a copy of the transcript Merrill Lynch was having made of Meditz' and Thomas' testimony for a significantly reduced rate, so I did.

I believed both Meditz and Thomas had lied in their testimony and I was eager to get the transcript so I could go over their words with a fine-tooth comb. The transcript was ready on November 8 so I drove to Oklahoma City to get my copy. That same day, I read the transcript and decided what I needed to do first was to figure out who "Paul" was that Thomas could not remember meeting with on September 22, 1992, in the Enid office.

I remembered that another rookie FC in the Merrill Lynch Enid office in 1992, told me Paul had spent the night at the local Ramada Inn so that is where I headed first.

I went to the front desk and asked the manager if she had records going back to September 1992 that would show who stayed at the motel. She informed me since then, the motel had been sold and that records going back that far would be in the possession of the previous owner, Dafell Inc., a business located in Enid.

I then went to Dafell's office and met with Carol Carpenter, who said she thought they would have records going back to 1992 but she would have to search for them in the file room. Carpenter and I went into the file room and in about 10 minutes, she located the storage box containing the September 1992 records. I told her I needed to see if a person with Merrill Lynch who had the first name Paul had spent the night there on Monday, September 21.

Carpenter flipped through the pages of information until she came to the report for September 21. Twenty-eight guests stayed at the Ramada Inn that night, two of whom had the first name Paul. The first one was Paul Stein and the second one was Paul Pederson. Carpenter told me she knew who Pederson was and he definitely was not with Merrill Lynch. I knew Paul Stein was my only hope in learning who the man from Princeton was who met with Thomas and Ellis on September 22, 1992. At this point I still thought Paul was someone with the firm who evaluated rural offices. However, since neither Thomas nor Merrill Lynch seemed to know anyone by the name of Paul from headquarters, I suspected Paul had been intentionally hidden from me before and during my recently concluded arbitration hearing.

I asked Carpenter if she would make a copy of the September 21 report. I now had to find out if Paul Stein worked for Merrill Lynch, and if so, in what capacity.

As I headed back to my townhouse, I remembered that some of Merrill Lynch's annual reports listed senior management members. Given the relatively few senior management members with Merrill Lynch, I thought it highly unlikely I would find a Paul Stein listed. Upon arriving home, I looked at the 1992 annual report since that was the year Paul visited Enid. As I scanned the alphabetical listing of senior management members, I quickly located those with last names starting with S. It hit me, and I was floored. I was amazed with what I saw. Paul Stein was indeed a member of *senior management*. What was even more amazing was Thomas, and evidently Ellis as demonstrated by the response to my discovery request concerning Paul, claimed they could not remember meeting with such a high-ranking executive.

I wanted to know more. I had to find out what position Paul Stein held with Merrill Lynch so I could try to figure out why he would have met with Thomas and Ellis and why it would have been kept from me. I decided to call Merrill Lynch's world headquarters in New York. The receptionist provided a phone number for Stein at the Princeton corporate campus. I called it and spoke to his secretary. I asked her what Stein's official position was and she informed me he was Merrill Lynch's *director of special market offices*. It blew my mind.

Stein was *the* person in charge of all Merrill Lynch special market offices, which included the Enid office. I had evidence he went to Enid the same day the 13 overnight envelopes of my 31-page letter to the directors arrived in New York. Yet in my arbitration, New York, Thomas, and evidently Ellis had been unable to remember someone by the name of Paul who met with Thomas and Ellis in Enid on September 22, 1992. Not remembering a meeting with such a high-ranking Merrill Lynch senior executive at such an emotionally charged time would be like not remembering a personal visit to the Merrill Lynch Enid office by the president of the United States.

I realized the next day I failed to ask Stein's secretary an important question, although I thought I already likely knew the answer. I called her back and asked her how long Stein had been the director of special market offices and she answered since 1991.

I knew I had once again pulled another one out of the hat. I believed Merrill Lynch's apparent lies about Stein were huge and knew that could be played to my advantage.

It seemed clear to me that as a result of Stein's visit to Enid on September 21 and 22, Thomas was very much aware of my 31-page letter to the board of directors well before September 28, which was the date he testified he learned of it and then *reacted*. I also remembered that Feightner, in overhearing what was being said in the meeting between Paul, Thomas, and Ellis, told my wife at the time I would not have liked what was being said. It was also clear that when Thomas made his cancer comments to Clark on September 24, he already knew about my 31-page letter, notwithstanding his sworn testimony to the contrary. It looked obvious to me that Merrill Lynch's game plan in-

cluded hiding *the truth* of what happened during those days and hours
leading up to Thomas' hostile actions against me.

I discussed my discovery about Stein with Gore and Schmidt and
talked about how Merrill Lynch's failure to disclose his identity had
seriously damaged my case. I saw fraud everywhere and I wanted to
address it. However, much to my surprise, Gore and Schmidt were not
convinced this new information would be enough to overturn the binding arbitration decision. On November 30, after considering the
possibility of appealing or otherwise addressing the arbitration decision, Gore informed me his firm was unwilling to continue as my counsel.
They viewed binding arbitration as binding. I was disappointed. Now
was not the time to be conservative or timid. Now was the time to
scream fraud and get on with the fight.

Just two weeks earlier, Merrill Lynch had been granted a judgment
by the federal court confirming the arbitration decision. The clock was
running and once again, I had no attorney.

As I thought about what attorney could possibly help me, I remembered a meeting I had with Craig Dodd in late 1992 when Stephen
Jones was representing me. Dodd, an Enid attorney, at the time was
renting space in Jones' office. Jones had asked Dodd to take a look at
my case since he had considerable employment law experience. As a
result, I met with Dodd after his review of the materials and he told me
I had a great case. I also had a general awareness then that Dodd was
someone who was not afraid of a fight. So now, in late 1995 with time
running short, I called him.

Dodd and I first spoke on the same day Gore told me his firm
would be unwilling to continue as my counsel. I was not disappointed
in my conversation with Dodd. I could tell he was the kind of attorney
who instinctively looked for a way to win in the face of adversity. While
I knew Dodd had a reputation for being a fighter, I had no idea what he
was really made of. Within minutes, I knew I had the attorney I wanted
and ceased considering other possibilities. Dodd, a savvy and fearless
street fighter, could see fraud everywhere in my case against Merrill
Lynch. The thought of mixing it up with the largest securities firm on
Wall Street and one of the most prominent law firms in Oklahoma did
not intimidate Dodd. His only concern was he had recently decided to

avoid controversial cases, which had been his practice for the previous 10 years or more. He had decided he wanted some nice, quiet days with his wife and family in the years ahead.

However, Dodd saw I was in a bind and knew if he did not help me, it would be unlikely that I would obtain counsel elsewhere given the nature and circumstances of my case. Dodd told me he knew he should not get involved but would anyway. I thanked him.

I was soon impressed with Dodd's legal instincts and ability to strategize ways to win. Later, another Enid attorney who used to be Jones' partner told me Jones thought Dodd had a brilliant legal mind. I knew for someone like Jones, who virtually everyone agreed had a brilliant legal mind of his own, to say that about Dodd said a lot. Not only did Dodd have extensive experience in employment law, but also he was experienced as a trial attorney and appellate attorney. I could not believe my stroke of luck. I was far from being out of bullets.

James Craig Dodd was a decorated Vietnam war veteran. He also had a checkered background. Dodd had his license to practice law in Oklahoma suspended for 90 days in 1994 for violations of the Code of Professional Responsibility. Dodd was now able to practice in Oklahoma state court as well as before the 10th Circuit Court of Appeals but had not reinstated his license in the U.S. District Court of the Western District of Oklahoma, the court that had recently confirmed the arbitration decision to judgment.

Over the years, as Dodd took the lead in a number of controversial situations, he had made some enemies, political and otherwise. Dodd described it best in his own words taken from an August 1996 letter he sent to another Enid attorney who was attempting to destroy him: "I successfully removed the most corrupt judge in Oklahoma County. I also prosecuted the most corrupt governor we have had in office since David Hall. I have also forced from office the Oklahoma Insurance Commissioner, her Deputy Commissioner and her General Counsel.... As a result of these and many other pro bono actions I have undertaken, I have disrupted hundreds of millions of dollars in graft and corruption. As a result of these successful attacks, I have attracted dangerous, powerful, wealthy enemies who are unrestrained by any sense of right or wrong and who work timelessly to rid themselves of me.... My controversial reputation results from the fact that I neither flatter wealth nor cringe before power. To the contrary, I sue the bastards who use their wealth to corrupt public officials and the public officials who use their power to enrich themselves."

Dodd made an unsuccessful but spirited run for the U.S. House of Representatives in 1984, losing to a five-term Democratic incumbent. He also served as general counsel of the Oklahoma Republican Party for several years during the 1980s.

Dodd was unsuccessfully solicited by GOP supporters to run for state attorney general in 1986, the year that Robert Henry, a veteran Democratic state legislator, won the position. There was no love lost between these two men. Ironically, Henry, as a 10th Circuit Court of Appeals judge in 1997, would write the order concerning the case between Merrill Lynch and me regarding the issue of the appropriateness of arbitration.

When Henry was about to resign his position as attorney general in 1991, early in his second term and prior to becoming a judge with the 10th Circuit, he was helping Governor Walters in his search for a successor. Day was a leading candidate for Henry's replacement, although someone else was ultimately selected. Day and three other attorneys in his law firm would represent Merrill Lynch before the 10th Circuit in my appeal. Merrill Lynch and Day seemed to be connected in every direction, but I would not let that stop me.

Dodd quickly immersed himself in the details of my case including reading the four volumes of transcripts of the arbitration hearing that I now had in my possession. After reading the transcripts and looking at the arbitration exhibits, Dodd told me he could not understand how I lost. He said in a civil case you only need the preponderance of evidence and not only did I present clear and convincing evidence, I also presented evidence that was beyond any reasonable doubt.

Dodd, after being briefed by Schmidt about certain aspects of the case, told me he thought a reason my previous lawyers were unwilling to pursue an appeal was because Day's law firm had threatened to seek sanctions against them if I fought the binding arbitration decision. In June 1998, after continuous hard-fought legal battles, Day's firm would attempt the same tactic of intimidation against Dodd and me by threatening to seek sanctions against us unless I dismissed a pending motion and surrendered any right to an appeal of a certain legal proceeding. Dodd and I did not blink.

Judge Alley was the presiding judge over *Keith A. Schooley v. Merrill Lynch, Pierce, Fenner & Smith* and had recently confirmed the arbitration decision to judgment. My first course of action was to appeal that decision to the 10th Circuit Court of Appeals. On December 15, 1995, I filed a notice of appeal in the U.S. District Court of the Western District of Oklahoma. I filed my notice pro se since Dodd had not reinstated his license with that particular federal court.

On December 22, I filed a pro se motion to set aside the judgment with the federal district court. In this action I was attempting to get the judgment thrown out by Alley himself, since I felt I was denied a fair arbitration hearing. In it, I accused Merrill Lynch of committing fraud upon the court and the arbitration panel, which made it impossible for me to present my full case. I cited that fraud had taken place when the firm claimed it had no documents or information concerning a "Paul." I explained that the identity, and more importantly, the title or position Paul had with Merrill Lynch was critically important to my case, especially when it turned out he was the director of special market offices. I said not knowing Paul's identity made it impossible for my lawyers to subpoena him and take his deposition about the meeting he had with Thomas.

On January 2, 1996, Judge Alley threw out my motion to set aside the judgment. The court clerk had noticed that my motion was improperly signed and not in compliance with certain rules. Also, the judge said his court no longer had jurisdiction over the matter. Alley said by filing my notice of appeal to the 10th Circuit any action on his part would interfere with the efficient administration of justice by duplicating efforts.

Dodd told me Alley's order was incorrect because his court did, in fact, have the discretion to hear my motion, notwithstanding the filing of the notice of appeal. Also, the court had the discretion to allow latitude to pro se litigants who inadvertently did not comply with all the court's rules. Dodd informed me Alley's order was a clear signal of what to expect in the future from the judge. Consequently, I did not appeal

Alley's order or file a motion to reconsider. Instead, I chose to let Dodd proceed with the 10th Circuit appeal, which would pertain only to the issue of whether Alley was in error when, in September 1994, he granted Merrill Lynch's motion to compel arbitration and forced me into binding arbitration. It would be later, in a state court action, that I would pursue my claim of fraud concerning Paul.

I had lost on Merrill Lynch's motion to compel arbitration, on the arbitration decision, on Merrill Lynch's application to confirm the arbitration award to judgment, and now on my motion to set aside the judgment. The score was 0 to 4 but it was not even halftime yet.

On January 30, 1996, I became a shareholder of Merrill Lynch by acquiring one share at the price of $57.25. I was far from finished and was preparing for what lay ahead.

On June 26, Dodd filed a brief with the 10th Circuit arguing, among other propositions, that the trial court erred when it concluded NYSE Rule 347 mandated arbitration of my claims against Merrill Lynch. He argued Merrill Lynch did not have a legal right to request arbitration under the rules of the NYSE because such a request directly contravened the employment contract privately negotiated between Merrill Lynch and me, which provided that it was to be construed and governed by the laws of Oklahoma. Since the Oklahoma Uniform Arbitration Act does not apply to employer-employee relations, the employment dispute between Merrill Lynch and me must be resolved at a jury trial.

Merrill Lynch filed its answer to my brief on September 3, 1996, obviously arguing the opposite side of the points Dodd made.

That same month, Dodd told me about some bizarre problems he was having that were originating from Enid. Dodd had many enemies but they were all outside of Enid. He explained that over the years as he took on various government officials, he purposely chose not to get involved in local conflicts in Enid since that was where he and his family lived, and he wanted a peaceful home for his wife and children.

Dodd told me the incidents started in early 1996, as he was getting the record on appeal together for my case. Dodd showed me a letter he had recently written to a locally prominent lawyer who had attempted to get Dodd arrested. The matter concerned an automobile transaction that had taken place between Dodd, his son, and the lawyer's client. The lawyer did not know Dodd but had written him a rude and abrasive letter, made false allegations against him, and tried to have him charged with a crime.

I became suspicious. Dodd explained that before taking my case, Enid had been a peaceful community in which to live and practice law. The lawyer in this incident just happened to be with the same law firm as an attorney with whom Thomas had lunch on August 25, 1992—the day after Ellis had written Thomas at the conclusion of the TGIF contest, instructing him to investigate me. I wondered if this could simply be a coincidence *or* if someone like Day, who had grown up in Pond Creek just 18 miles north of Enid and who I had been told was best buddies with Ellis, had plugged into one of his lawyer friends in Enid in an effort to intimidate Dodd. After all, if I had no attorney, I was history. In addition, the attorney I did have was potentially a nightmare for Day and Merrill Lynch—a fearless attorney with a brilliant legal mind.

On September 22, 1996, Dodd filed my reply to Merrill Lynch's answer. He argued that none of the rules or regulations the firm had mentioned in its answer required the arbitration of any controversy between Merrill Lynch and me. Dodd was confident in his leading argument that the U-4 form I signed when I agreed to employment with Merrill Lynch said I agreed to arbitrate any dispute, claim, or controversy that may arise only if it was required to be arbitrated under the rules, constitutions, or bylaws of the organizations with which I registered. Dodd insisted any prudent analysis would conclude that none of the rules, constitutions, or bylaws of any of the organizations I had registered with, including the NYSE and NASD, required that I arbitrate any dispute or claim. I had high hopes that the 10th Circuit would agree with Dodd's argument and allow me to have my day in court before a jury of my peers.

Dodd continued to tell me about suspicious and bizarre incidents that were happening to him. He told me he had received about five death threats in the last three months. He said he had received death threats before but not for about the last 18 months, until the recent ones. The next day Dodd told me attacks originating from Enid were coming at him from all directions and he was now in a fighting mood. Dodd told me to trust no one, not even him.

On February 5, 1997, the 10th Circuit issued an order confirming the lower court's decision to compel arbitration. The court, by way of footnote, addressed what Dodd thought was my winning argument by saying that in my reply brief I contended that a certain NYSE rule requires the existence of a written agreement to arbitrate in addition to the U-4 form. The court said I did not raise this argument in the district court or in my opening brief, therefore they would not consider it. Dodd told me the court had the discretion to consider this rule argument but elected not to. I was now 0 and 5.

When I received the 10th Circuit's decision I saw that Henry was the judge who had written the order. I could not believe it. I believed there could hardly have been a more potentially unfavorable federal appellate judge in the nation to consider my case. I knew in the real world it was possible for biases to subconsciously influence a person in his decision making, whether they were a result of friendship, politics, or otherwise. Given the circumstances I was aware of, Henry was in a decision-making position where he could use his discretion either way, and here that worked against me.

I also believed my ex-wife did not want me to win my Merrill Lynch case for at least two reasons. First, she had considerable anger toward me as a result of our custody fight and divorce. Second, our divorce settlement agreement limited her share of any Merrill Lynch settlement or award I might receive to $12,500. The last thing my ex-wife would want was for me to win millions of dollars when she could only see $12,500 of it.

I believed my ex-wife's feelings complicated things since Henry was politically close to her father. Furthermore, Henry was good friends with her sister's husband as well. Henry was just too close to those who had interests opposed to mine, as I assumed my ex-wife's father and brother-in-law were 100 percent supportive of her feelings.

On February 24, 1997, Dodd filed a petition for rehearing, arguing that the panel was wrong in refusing to consider the NYSE rule I mentioned in my reply brief. That same day, Dodd filed a suggestion for rehearing en banc saying the appeal should be reheard by all the judges of the 10th Circuit.

On April 1, 1997, the 10th Circuit denied both the petition for rehearing and the suggestion for rehearing en banc. With these two losses I was now 0 and 7.

I still was not finished. On September 29, 1997, I filed a petition in Garfield County, Oklahoma, against Thomas, Ellis, Stein, and Merrill Lynch, Pierce, Fenner & Smith. I alleged, among other things, that between July 1, 1991, and June 29, 1992, I became aware of activities that offended me and that I felt did not meet the ethical standards required of Merrill Lynch employees. I said I followed the pledge I was required to make through the firm's *Guidelines for Business Conduct* when I reported these situations. I described the actions I took and the resulting sequence of events, and alleged that Thomas' "...outrageously insulting, demeaning and hostile letter...reflected a coordinated and unlawful plan developed by Paul Stein." I alleged this plan was designed to "create such a hostile, insulting and embarrassing situation" I would resign my position.

I also alleged Stein's plan "...was an illegal, civil conspiracy" and its purpose was to cover up the firm's wrongdoing and neutralize my ability to make the wrongdoing public, or far worse, bring it to the attention of law enforcement officials or elements within Merrill Lynch that would make sure the wrongdoing was exposed and properly punished.

On November 5, 1997, Merrill Lynch and the other parties I had filed against, filed a notice for removal with the U.S. District Court of the Western District of Oklahoma. The reason was that all the defendants were out-of-state residents at the time I filed my petition.

The case was soon assigned to Judge Alley, not my biggest ally. Dodd and I believed we could not win with him so on November 21, I filed a notice of dismissal with the federal court dismissing my suit against Thomas, Ellis, Stein, and Merrill Lynch.

Next, we decided to sue Day and his law firm, and only them, both Oklahoma defendants, in state court alleging their role in a civil conspiracy to conceal Paul Stein. On November 26, my petition was filed in Garfield County.

Soon after, Dodd asked me if my heart was really in this action. Everything he was doing was making other attorneys extremely upset with him. This did not bother him; however, he did not want to forge ahead unless I really wanted to continue. I told him I was absolutely committed to seeing this through to the end.

On February 4, 1998, my new opponents, Day and his firm, filed four voluminous motions and briefs.

The fur was flying and emotions were intense. I would not go away and my appeals were relentless. At this point, Merrill Lynch decided to go on the offensive. On February 12, Merrill Lynch and others filed a lawsuit against me in the U.S. District Court of the Western District of Oklahoma seeking to shut me down.

On March 16, 1998, I filed a pro se motion to have Merrill Lynch's action against me dismissed. The firm responded on April 7 by filing an objection to my motion to dismiss.

On April 17, a Garfield County district judge ordered that my law-suit against Day and his firm be transferred to Oklahoma County.

On May 11, Day and his firm filed a motion to dismiss my lawsuit against them. On May 29, Dodd filed my response to their motion. About a week later Day and his firm filed a reply to my response.

On June 8, Judge Alley denied my motion to dismiss Merrill Lynch's lawsuit against me. The case would go forward in federal court.

On June 12, Day and his firm were granted their motion to dismiss and my lawsuit against them was thrown out. The court said unless the judgment entered by the federal court that confirmed the arbitration decision was first vacated, no relief could be granted to me in my state court action.

On June 22, Dodd filed a motion asking the court to reconsider throwing out my lawsuit against Day and his firm. In response to this motion, Heggy, sent a letter to Dodd. In the letter Heggy, on behalf of the defendants, proposed they would not seek sanctions, attorney fees, and costs related to the case if I dropped my suit and surrendered any right to appeal.

Dodd wrote back saying the fraud we alleged in regard to Paul Stein was clear and he asked Day's firm to stop trying to scare him off. Dodd told me Heggy's proposal was a contemptible hardball threat. Dodd and I did not accept the offer. As a result, the defendants filed an objection to my motion that attempted to overturn the ruling that dismissed my lawsuit against Day and his firm.

On June 29, 1998, Michael Roberts, the attorney I had now retained for the federal case of Merrill Lynch and others against me, filed my answer to their lawsuit. I had become acquainted with Roberts when he was with Jones' law firm at the time Jones represented me.

Also in June of that year, Ellis became the resident vice president of the Merrill Lynch San Diego office. It appeared to me that Ellis' teamwork and loyalty to his superiors in New York were being rewarded as he now found himself in his best position yet in his almost 27-year career with the firm.

On July 24, the court denied my motion to reconsider dismissing my case against Day and his firm. The count was now a whopping 0 to 10. Despite the dim outlook, I still saw other avenues I could explore and I could never rest until I knew I had done everything possible.

On August 24, Dodd filed a petition with the Supreme Court of the State of Oklahoma appealing the ruling in favor of Day and his firm to dismiss my lawsuit against them. On September 8, Day and his firm filed their response to my petition. The Supreme Court soon assigned the appeal to the Court of Civil Appeals, which meant it would be decided by a three-judge panel.

On November 17, I again filed a lawsuit against Merrill Lynch and the others; however, this time I did it in Oklahoma County as opposed to Garfield County. The action was filed in order to meet a possible statute of limitations deadline so I would not lose my civil conspiracy claim against those defendants.

On February 16, 1999, the Court of Civil Appeals affirmed the order to dismiss my lawsuit against Day and his firm. That made it 0 and 11.

That same month, two unexpected things happened. First, Barton was fired from the securities firm he was employed with for violating firm policy when he borrowed money from a client. Barton was still playing fast and loose.

Second, Judge Alley filed an order in Merrill Lynch's lawsuit against me, removing himself from the case because his wife purchased stock in

Merrill Lynch on November 16, 1998, which he did not know about until February 21, 1999. The federal case was then assigned to Judge Vicki Miles-LaGrange.

Roberts told me he thought the timing of Alley's recusal was curious. It came just weeks after all the briefs had been filed concerning the plaintiffs' motion for summary judgment. Roberts told me Alley could have disclosed he had just learned of his wife's purchase of Merrill Lynch stock to see if either the plaintiffs or I had any objection. The only party who likely would have objected would have been me, but in view of the fact that even a decision in my favor would surely have no impact on the value of Merrill Lynch stock, I would not have been concerned.

I was surprised Judge Alley would so willingly recuse himself in this case. I knew he was a tough, no-nonsense judge who was not afraid to make difficult decisions. He did not even recuse himself when asked to from the Timothy McVeigh case, even though the bombing took place right across the street from the federal courthouse and affected many people Alley worked with. The 10th Circuit Court of Appeals would, in fact, have to remove Alley from the Oklahoma City bombing case.

I also thought that assuming Judge Alley's knowledge that his wife invested in the stock market, he might have informed her when a publicly traded company was a litigant in a case over which he was presiding. Therefore, she would not unwittingly purchase shares of a company which could result in his having to recuse himself.

I knew in November, before his wife purchased the Merrill Lynch stock, Alley was aware of the case. I could not help but wonder if Alley knew of his wife's plans to buy Merrill Lynch stock in November so if he wanted a way to bail out of the case, he could do so.

On March 8, 1999, Dodd filed a petition with the Supreme Court of the State of Oklahoma requesting that it review the recent decision by the Court of Civil Appeals to affirm the order to dismiss my lawsuit against Day and his firm. Everything proceeded as usual with the defendants filing an answer to my petition and then Dodd filing a reply to the answer. Ultimately, the Oklahoma Supreme Court denied my petition. The official count: 0 and 12.

My lawsuit against Day and his firm was dead. So was my lawsuit against Thomas, Ellis, Stein, and Merrill Lynch, Pierce, Fenner & Smith since it too addressed the issue of civil conspiracy the Oklahoma Supreme Court had just dismissed. I never got to argue, in a court of law, the merits or facts concerning Paul Stein that occurred during my arbitration. Those merits and facts were buried under an avalanche of legal arguments.

On August 24, 1999, Judge Miles-LaGrange issued an order in Merrill Lynch's and the others' lawsuit against me saying there were no longer any pending state court cases seeking relief based upon alleged fraud on the tribunal. In light of this fact, the court dismissed the lawsuit.

After my long string of losses this was good news. Merrill Lynch could no longer sue me; however, it looked like I could no longer sue them either. It appeared I had taken the situation as far as it could go in the legal system. However, I was still not finished. I had a few more moves in my playbook. Each morning I woke up and the fight was still in me. Perhaps one day I would wake up and discover it was gone, but until that day, I would continue my quest to see Merrill Lynch live up to its own reputation.

CHAPTER 11

The Final Bid

*There is one place we do not
want to be number one. We do not
want to be number one or even show up
on the bestseller's list.*

—SH

    Exactly seven years after I sent my 31-page letter to each of Merrill Lynch's 13 board members, I decided to, now as a shareholder, send a second letter. This one would be dated September 17, 1999, and would be sent to each of Merrill Lynch's 10 *outside* directors. I decided it was time to tell the outside directors, as representatives of Merrill Lynch's shareholders, they had been deceived by senior management and/or certain inside directors concerning the two internal investigations.

    I first reminded the outside directors it was their statutory duty to manage the corporation in compliance with the law and for the benefit of Merrill Lynch's shareholders. I then introduced myself as a former employee of Merrill Lynch who, pursuant to company policy, reported wrongdoing. As a result of my actions, my superior retaliated against me. Consequently, I pursued my legal rights as a wrongfully terminated employee.

    I told the outside directors they should be aware of some of the testimony that was given at my arbitration hearing in September 1995.

It, along with other information, led me to believe Merrill Lynch had intentionally deceived the outside directors concerning the thoroughness and veracity of both investigations into the wrongdoing I reported. I said I believed they would be "appalled and disturbed to learn of the dissembling 'results' of the investigations, part of which is discussed herein."

I explained that in Meditz' and Mandel's testimony (as well as Mihaly's letter to the Oklahoma Department of Insurance and Mandel's letter to the SEC) each represented that Merrill Lynch's investigations were thorough. Additionally, Mihaly's and Mandel's letters were replete with inaccuracies and misleading statements. Mandel had also testified he advised the directors concerning this matter. I presumed that report contained essentially the same information as his letter to the SEC, which meant that as representatives of Merrill Lynch's shareholders, the outside directors had been misled too.

I wanted to illustrate that deception took place during the internal investigations. I asked the directors to refer to a section of my previous letter to the board I had attached that provided details about the insurance cheating scandal. I then discussed how it was possible that Merrill Lynch never found any evidence to support my allegation of the apparent widespread use of cheat sheets or other improper means concerning the examinations.

I told the directors how the firm's efforts to find and interview individuals possibly connected to the wrongdoing, or just knowledgeable about it, were dismal at best. Some it spoke to were likely asked the wrong questions. Others, many of them pertinent players, were never contacted at all. This included the 300 leads I had provided Merrill Lynch when I listed 15 management and 4 insurance personnel, and referred to 281 FCs from the Texoma District who received credit for the Pictorial examination during the time in question. Fourteen of the 15 members of management listed likewise had received credit for the exam. Hall was also excluded from the investigations, even though Merrill Lynch had his permanent address all along, as evidenced by the ease at which it reached him just before my arbitration hearing. I then provided the directors with details of Hall's testimony to demonstrate for them the critical information he could have contributed to the investigations.

I continued, "It cannot be credibly argued that those parties responsible for Merrill Lynch's two internal investigations, and those parties with oversight thereof, exercised *particular vigilance* (or for that matter, reasonable vigilance) concerning the use of 'cheat sheets' or other methods of cheating as discussed above."

I told the directors it seemed clear to me from the beginning that Merrill Lynch had no desire to uncover the truth concerning the reported wrongdoing. I trusted they would fulfill their legal responsibilities as directors of Merrill Lynch and expose the investigations for the cover-ups they were.

I quoted Hammerman's own words that the cost of letting integrity slip and take second place to revenue "could be fatal."

I concluded with, "The shareholders of Merrill Lynch deserve a senior management that has integrity even when difficult circumstances must be addressed. Anything less is a deception against the shareholders by allowing for an environment that tolerates violative behavior and corruption that ultimately may negatively impact the value of the corporation."

The 10 individual overnight envelopes for the outside directors were delivered to Merrill Lynch's World Financial Center headquarters on September 21 at 10:30 A.M. However, to my surprise, on October 1, I received a message on my answering machine from someone in Merrill Lynch's mailroom. When I returned the phone call I was amazed to learn the envelopes had not been delivered. The employee I spoke to told me the mailroom did not know how to deliver the 10 envelopes. They had been floating around from one office building to another, from the South Tower and North Tower of the World Financial Center to the litigation offices on Broadway, and had just been returned to the mailroom.

Merrill Lynch purportedly did not know how to locate the parties to whom the envelopes were addressed, even though each envelope identified its addressee as an outside director. I believed Hammerman was still in fear that senior management's conduct would be exposed.

I thought Merrill Lynch was bluffing so I decided to send all the letters to one outside director who could then forward them to the other nine outside directors. The outside director who appeared easiest to locate was Aulana Peters, a partner in the law firm Gibson, Dunn & Crutcher. Peters was a former commissioner of the SEC and had been a Merrill Lynch director since 1994. On October 4, 1999, I sent the letters to Peters, explaining that I needed her to forward them to the other outside directors since Merrill Lynch was being uncooperative in doing so.

Months went by. I heard nothing from Peters or any of the other outside directors. I had not even received confirmation that any of the 10 letters arrived at their proper destinations. When a year went by without any word, I decided to try to find out what had happened.

On September 17, 2000, exactly a year to the date I wrote my letter to the outside directors, I wrote another letter, this time to Hammerman.

I told Merrill Lynch's general counsel and vice chairman that it had been a year since I wrote to the outside directors and that I never received a response of any kind from them. I also mentioned what Hammerman himself said in the May/June 1992 issue of Merrill Lynch's *We The People*. "It is wonderful to hear that we are number one in so many business categories. But there is one place we do not want to be number one. We do not want to be number one or even show up on the bestseller's list. Anyone who thinks that integrity is just a word, please read *Burning Down The House: The Fall of E.F. Hutton*. Integrity is not just important in Merrill Lynch, it is vital." I then asked Hammerman to please advise me as to what happened after I sent my letter to the outside directors.

I received a response dated October 11, 2000, from George Schieren, now a senior vice president and general counsel of Merrill Lynch, Pierce, Fenner & Smith. Schieren said my September 17, 1999, letter to the firm's outside directors was carefully reviewed. Additionally, he said Merrill Lynch was satisfied the investigation conducted eight years ago was complete and the appropriate action was taken.

I was not surprised. Even though I had documented that the two investigations of eight years ago were far from being "complete," I knew

Merrill Lynch would never admit to it. To do so would reveal cover-ups and expose those in charge of the investigations and those with oversight of them including Hammerman, the review committee, and ultimately the directors.

CHAPTER 12

Court of Public Opinion

You be the judge.

—KS

It has been an interesting 10 years. One thing I have learned—as have so many others—justice is not always obtained in the courts. There have been plenty of incidents in our judicial system of bribery, undue influence, and other forms of corruption. Who really knows for sure how decisions are made? For some reason, the wealthy and powerful do seem to have a knack for winning far more than their fair share of court-room battles—even if the facts are not on their side.

Although I did not have success in the "courts," I have no doubt I should have. My concerns about securities arbitration are serious. I have absolutely no doubt the arbitrators in my hearing arrived at the wrong decision. Why they did, I can only speculate. Whether the influence was direct or indirect I am not sure, but I believe it was there.

However, there is also the court of public opinion. That is where I now take my case. I have accurately and impartially presented all the relevant facts pertaining to this matter. The record speaks for itself.

I am confident if my career with Merrill Lynch had gone smoothly, both my family and marriage would still be intact today. I am not blaming Merrill Lynch for the destruction of my marriage. Only my ex-wife and I can take responsibility for that. However, I believe if my position with Merrill Lynch had provided the financial stability we thought it would when I joined the firm, instead of leading to nothing but turmoil, I would have had my family.

These days, I am still involved with the oil and gas business. However, my ex-wife's career is much more interesting. Just when I thought I had seen it all, in the fall of 2000 I found out she had accepted a position to work for Merrill Lynch in its Enid office, starting in January 2001. She would be in partnership with her brother who had worked at Merrill Lynch for about three years and was the one who informed her of the opportunity. Interesting timing.

I remembered that about two weeks after Hammerman received my September 17, 2000, letter (wherein I referred to his quote about Merrill Lynch not wanting to show up on the bestseller's list), for the first time my ex-wife, Donna, made a comment to my son about me working on a book. I had never discussed my project with Donna but apparently when she and my son were talking about saving funds for his college education, out of the blue she told him I might not be able to help much since I was so busy with my book. I suspected New York, perhaps through intermediaries, might have talked to Donna's brother to see what he could find out, through her, about any book I might be writing. I told Tyler he was free to tell his mother a book was indeed on its way.

Then I found out about Donna taking a job in the Merrill Lynch Enid office. Was this just a coincidence? I doubted it—not in light of everything else that happened the past 10 years. I was disappointed about Donna's decision, especially because it placed our two children in the middle. One parent is working for Merrill Lynch while the other is trying to expose them.

And then several months later, as though there already had not been enough "coincidences," I was astonished at what I learned. On the morning of May 16, 2001, as I was scanning my *Enid News & Eagle*, a headline grabbed my attention—"Enid's Merrill Lynch to move to OKC." The article told that Merrill Lynch would be moving its Enid and Edmond offices to a new exclusive location in far north Oklahoma City. Edmond, a suburb of Oklahoma City, was only a few miles northeast of where the new office would be located. There was nothing unusual with this move; however, the move from Enid to the new Oklahoma

City office would be almost 80 miles. It appeared to me the Enid office was not "moving" but was closing. There could be no question Merrill Lynch was abandoning any serious efforts to compete for clients in northwest Oklahoma.

I quickly called my ex-wife to see if this development might cause her to move to Oklahoma City. I was concerned about my children, who would be, if she were to move, torn between staying with me in Enid or going with her. I learned she would not have to move. She would commute to the new location in Oklahoma City twice a week and would be provided a small office in Enid where she could meet with clients. However, the large, new office in Enid that Merrill Lynch had just remodeled and moved to in January 2001—to accommodate the seven FCs it then had—was going to be closed.

I was incredulous. There had been a Merrill Lynch office in Enid for 10 years. It also appeared to be a very profitable office. Not only had the firm recently increased the number of FCs in that office, but also it had relocated to a much larger and beautifully designed office suite. Furthermore, the new Enid office was just in the first few months of a five-year lease. Donna said she was really surprised at what had happened, and her brother, with whom she was in partnership, could not believe it either.

I was really curious and had my suspicions. I decided to call the reporter who wrote the article to see what I could find out. He, too, was puzzled at the closing, since it was also his impression the office was very profitable. The reporter had learned the decision to close the Enid office was made in New York. He said he had asked the Merrill Lynch Enid resident manager if the firm was closing offices elsewhere. The resident manager said he was unaware of any other offices closing. I assumed if other offices were being closed as part of a corporate restructuring, the Enid resident manager would have been informed of that.

I believed the closing of the Enid office was no coincidence. I now suspected, since Merrill Lynch knew my book was on the way, the Enid office was shut down for public relations purposes. Obviously, if a storm hit, it would be easier to reassure the firm's clients and the public that not only were all the bad apples gone but so was the Enid office. I believed there was only one problem with this: New York, not Enid, was where changes needed to be made. The Enid office had been cleaned up years earlier. New York, however, in my view, still had dirty hands.

The only two people in this world whose opinions matter most to me, by far, are my children. If I ever had any doubts about whether they supported me or not, on Father's Day 2000 those thoughts were firmly put to rest.

On that special day I received cards from both my daughter and my son, who were 12 and 15, respectively. They gave the cards to me together and I first read Tara's aloud. The printed message said she still remembered being loved was the first thing I taught her. Tara had written in her own hand, "That's for sure." At the bottom of the card she also wrote, "I love you sooooo much! We have so many good times together! I love being with you. You make my life a lot happier!"

It was a very touching card that communicated the relationship she and I truly have—one of lots of love. I knew it came from her heart.

Tyler then handed his card to me and I started reading it aloud also. Part of it read, "When I think of the word STRENGTH I think of you. I think of the strength of your convictions...the ways you stand up for what you believe in. You've taught me that integrity comes from refusing to compromise on what is right and wrong." At this point I became too emotional to continue reading aloud. Tears started flowing from my eyes and I had to read the rest of the card silently to myself.

The rest of the message praised the strength of my love for our family and for God and closed with, "I hope you know just how much you're loved too, Dad...and how wonderful I think you are."

I knew exactly where Tyler was coming from because we had talked for many hours over the years about the Merrill Lynch situation. He knew the pain I had been through and the sacrifices I had made. He told me when he saw this card at the store he knew it was the one he had to give me.

I gave both my children huge hugs and told them how much I loved them and how much I appreciated their support over all these years. I knew they too had made many sacrifices of their own because of my situation. At that moment, I knew no matter what became of the Merrill Lynch situation, I was truly a winner because my own children knew who I was and were behind me all the way.

And what a long way it has been. All these years the fight has been in me. No matter how tired I got, I still felt compelled to continue my journey. Maybe one day I will find that need has disappeared, but I cannot predict that. I will know when that time comes, if it does. That being said, I really do want it all to be over with, but only if it is concluded by things being put right. I believe this book can do the job the courts and regulators did not. If it does not, as long as the spark is in me to keep up the fight and I can find other tactics that might work, I will pursue them.

I believe people are usually savvy enough to know when something is the truth and when it is just spin. However, sometimes we are fooled. Merrill Lynch enjoys a basically unblemished reputation, which I believe is undeserved. I am sure there are a number of upstanding people within the company; however, I am just as sure that some principal members of senior management are not part of this group. I want people to see what I do—that these individuals care most about what is best for the bottom line, not what is ethical.

I ask you to consider the following questions. While you do, remember Merrill Lynch's public campaign that insists it values integrity and never tolerates unethical behavior.

Tell me:

Do you think there was widespread insurance cheating involving a multitude of FCs and members of management?

Do you think senior management covered up widespread insurance cheating? Twice?

Do you think Jack Thomas was unaware of my letter to the board until the day he threatened to sue me and kicked me out of his Enid office?

Do you think everyone had legitimate memory lapses when it came to recalling Paul Stein's visit to the Enid office on September 22, 1992?

Do you think Merrill Lynch's game plan included hiding the truth of what happened during those days and hours leading up to Thomas' hostile actions against me?

Do you think I abandoned my job?

Do you think it was reasonable for Merrill Lynch and the arbitrators to expect me to return to work in a small office where my manager was threatening to sue me?

Do you agree with Professor Michael Rustad that there was a multiplicity of smoking guns that indicated conduct worthy of punishment?

Do you think Merrill Lynch truly believes in the principles of client focus, respect for the individual, responsible citizenship, and integrity?

What would Charlie Merrill think?
You be the judge.

ACKNOWLEDGMENTS

First, I thank my parents for teaching me the difference between right and wrong.

Second, I thank Lynn Smith, Pete Earley, Anne Dempsey, Stephen Jones, Cecil McCurdy, and Mike Roberts for reviewing portions of my manuscript and offering their thoughts and encouragement. A big thanks to Erica Widdup, Sue Collier, and Heather Florence for adding the finishing touches to my book project.

Third, I thank Pastor "C," who told me to go up against the adversary just as David went up against the Philistines; Jamie who instructed me to let the Lord be my defense and the Holy Spirit lead; and Lois who told me I would get back what the enemy has stolen. I pray the world would love as taught by the example at Christ The King church in Enid, Oklahoma.

Last, I thank my sister Anne, who has much wisdom and discernment and who was a constant source of encouragement during these years. And I especially thank my two precious children, Tyler and Tara—who were 7 and 4, respectively, when this ordeal with Merrill Lynch began in 1992, and who are now 17 and 14—for always believing in, supporting, and loving me during some incredibly difficult years.

—Keith Schooley, March 2002

INDEX

Give the Gift of

Merrill Lynch:
The Cost Could Be Fatal

to Your Friends and Colleagues

CHECK YOUR LEADING BOOKSTORE OR ORDER HERE

❑ YES, I want _____ copies of *Merrill Lynch: The Cost Could Be Fatal* at $27.95 each, plus $4.95 shipping per book. (Oklahoma residents add $2.33 sales tax per book; Ohio residents add $1.75 per book.) Canadian orders must be accompanied by a postal money order in U.S. funds.

My check or money order for $_____ is enclosed.

Please charge my ❑ Visa ❑ MasterCard
❑ Discover ❑ American Express

Name_____

Organization _____

Address _____

City/State/Zip _____

Phone_____ E-mail _____

Card # _____

Exp. Date_____ Signature _____

Please make your check payable and return to:

BookMasters, Inc.
P.O. Box 388
Ashland, OH 44805

Call your credit card order to: 1-800-247-6553
— or —
Order online at www.TheCostCouldBeFatal.com
Fax: 419-281-6883   Email: order@bookmaster.com